W9-CEI-871

2-30.16

PRAISE FOR
ANATOMY OF A CALLING

"Every once in awhile a book comes along that feels like that companion you've been longing for to hold your hand on the incredible journey of life. Lissa Rankin has beautifully written *The Anatomy of a Calling* for you to transform your desire to do and be more into knowing, once and for all, your sacred purpose for being here. Enjoy this heartfelt journey as you realize that you are the hero in the story she shares."

—KRISTINE CARLSON,
coauthor to the *Don't Sweat the Small Stuff* books

"I made the mistake of starting *The Anatomy of a Calling* near bedtime. Don't do this unless you are willing to lose a lot of sleep! Lissa's story is absolutely riveting, moving, and so wise. Read this book and be awakened to all that life wants for you."

—JENNIFER LOUDEN,
author of *The Woman's Comfort Book* and *A Year of Daily Joy*

"Lissa Rankin has the courage to confront the difficulties of life and the inadequacies of our medical training. I know that as a doctor receiving information but not a full healer's education leads you to treat the result and not the cause. We do not learn to know ourselves or why we became doctors and chose a specific specialty. So we struggle to understand and know ourselves amidst all the pain and suffering we are exposed to. Lissa's words offer us all a guidebook on how to choose the healing paths when life presents us with its various roadblocks."

—BERNIE SIEGEL, MD,
author of *The Art of Healing* and *A Book of Miracles*

"This book will forever change the way you perceive your own physician and our current healthcare system. Lissa's writing is so intimate and confessional, you feel as if you're walking alongside her in Big Sur as she regales you with her miraculous tale. Best of all, it will show you how to heed your own calling—no matter what it is."

—SARAH BAMFORD SEIDELMANN, MD,
author of *Born to FREAK* and *What the Walrus Knows*

THE
ANATOMY OF
A CALLING

A Doctor's Journey
from the Head to the Heart
and a Prescription for
Finding Your Life's Purpose

LISSA RANKIN, MD

RODALE.

RODALE *wellness*

Live happy. Be healthy. Get inspired.

Sign up today to get exclusive access to our authors, exclusive bonuses,
and the most authoritative, useful, and cutting edge information on health,
wellness, fitness, and living your life to the fullest.

Visit us online at RodaleWellness.com
Join us at RodaleWellness.com/Join

Rodale books may be purchased for business or promotional use or for special sales.
For information, please write to:
Special Markets Department, Rodale Inc., 733 Third Avenue, New York, NY 10017

Printed in the United States of America

Rodale Inc. makes every effort to use acid-free ∞, recycled paper ♻.

Book design by Christina Gaugler

Library of Congress Cataloging-in-Publication Data is on file with the publisher.

ISBN 978-1-62336-574-5 hardcover

Distributed to the trade by Macmillan

2 4 6 8 10 9 7 5 3 1   hardcover

We inspire and enable people to improve their lives and the world around them.
rodalewellness.com

For Matt, who unfailingly said yes
when I asked for permission
to follow my heart.

CONTENTS

INTRODUCTION

You are a hero. I am a hero. We are all, every single one of us, on what mythologist Joseph Campbell calls "a hero's journey," carrying within us a Nelson Mandela or Joan of Arc or Luke Skywalker or Mother Teresa or Helen Keller. We are Bilbo Baggins and Erin Brockovich and Oprah and Harry Potter. Like these classic heroes, we are all little sparks of divinity on a mission to step into our true nature and fulfill the Divine assignment our souls chose here on earth.

But if you're like most of us, you may not yet realize what a hero you really are.

Navigating your own hero's journey is one of the cornerstones of living a meaningful, rich, authentic, wholly healthy life. So what does it mean to be on a hero's journey? Joseph Campbell described it best, first in his book *The Hero with a Thousand Faces,* originally published in 1949, and then in *Joseph Campbell and the Power of Myth,* a famous interview with journalist Bill Moyers that aired on PBS. His teachings were translated into Hollywood gold via Christopher Vogler's *The Writer's Journey,* which uses Campbell's work to teach writers how to create a great screenplay or a bestselling novel. And George Lucas credits Campbell with the inspiration for his character Luke Skywalker in *Star Wars.*

So what is the arc of a hero's journey? You're not necessarily writing a screenplay or a novel, but you're writing the movie of your life, and as the hero of your own journey, it can be helpful to view a map of what lies ahead as you wake up to your purpose.

The hero's journey begins with someone who has no idea she has an inner hero. The hero is just Jane Schmoe in the Ordinary World, doing her Jane Schmoe-ish thing, when suddenly there is a call to adventure. The hero initially refuses the call: "Hell no, I ain't doing that!" But then, with reluctance, the hero accepts the Divine assignment. That's when a magical mentor shows up, someone who will guide the hero, offer protection and reassurance, and share wisdom intended to help the hero navigate what is sure to be a challenging journey ahead.

Next comes the crossing of the first threshold, when the hero steps into adventure, leaving the known world and leaping into the unknown, which signals the hero's final separation from the Ordinary World and marks the hero's willingness to undergo metamorphosis. There's often a rupture of some sort, an unraveling, as the hero goes from caterpillar into cellular debris inside the cocoon. In other words, as Yusuf Islam sings, "To be what you must, you must give up what you are."

Then the initiation begins. No hero gets it right on the first try. The Road of Trials consists of a series of tests and obstacles the hero must overcome, and along the way, the hero meets allies and enemies and begins to learn the rules of a world far different than the Ordinary World. Then the hero comes to the edge of a dangerous place—the headquarters of the enemy or the dark cave of the new world or a scary inner place where the reckoning must happen. And the Ordeal usually follows; it is a fight to the death with the forces of darkness, when the hero is at risk of losing it all. Surviving the Ordeal is a rite of passage, an initiation into the new world that graduates the hero into a wiser, more enlightened state of being.

Having survived the Ordeal, the hero is rewarded. The holy grail is found. Life-changing wisdom is earned. An elixir that will serve as the balm for a wounded culture is won. But the hero isn't out of the woods yet. Once the hero finds the holy grail that promises to change the Ordinary World into the new bliss, it's tempting to hold that knowledge dear, to protect it close to the heart, where nobody can threaten it or challenge it or take it away. But that's not what heroes do. Heroes always find the courage to bring the holy grail back home to the Ordinary World so others can benefit, too.

But before the grail comes home, the hero undergoes one more exam, a last-ditch effort from the forces of fear and darkness to derail the hero from bringing the hard-won reward back to the Ordinary World, where it can become the promised land. This last Ordeal nearly brings the hero down—again. Another near-death experience ensues. But once again—phew!—the hero is resurrected. That's when the hero can finally bring the grail home, once and for all. Dorothy makes it back to Kansas with the knowledge that there's no place like home. Luke Skywalker defeats Darth Vader. Nelson Mandela becomes president and dismantles apartheid. You see the light and can use it to illuminate others.

In *Finding Your Way in a Wild New World,* life coach and bestselling author Martha Beck describes us heroes as "wayfinders" and says we possess a set of characteristics that distinguishes us. Most of us feel a sense of mission involving a major transformation in human experience; a strong sense that whatever that mission is, it's getting closer in time; a compulsion to master certain skills in preparation for this half-understood personal mission; high levels of empathy; an urgent desire to lessen the suffering of humans, animals, and plants; and a loneliness stemming from a sense of difference, despite being generally social. According to Martha Beck, other common characteristics include high levels of creativity; an intense love of animals; a difficult, often abusive or traumatic early life; an intense connection to the natural world; resistance to religion accompanied by a strong sense of the spiritual; high levels of emotional sensitivity accompanied by a predilection for anxiety; a sense of connection with particular cultures, languages, or geographic regions; a gregarious personality contrasting with the need for periods of solitude; a persistent or recurring physical illness; and a tendency to dream about healing others. Martha Beck calls us "The Team," and I can tell already that you are one of us.

Some of these characteristics might be viewed as flaws by those who don't know better, so most of us heroes aren't aware of our capacity for greatness because we can't get past how screwed up and ordinary we are. We assume heroes are supposed to fight battles and overcome obstacles and rescue damsels in distress while still looking dashing as they're saving the world. But heroes start out like everybody else, living ordinary lives in Ordinary Worlds. Like every other hero, we feel frightened, we make mistakes, we break promises, we run away from challenges, we numb ourselves when things get painful, we betray those we love, and we fail to make good on our New Year's resolutions. We ward off uncertainty, resist change, hightail it away from danger, and ignore the signs from the Universe that try to reroute us when we're off course. We yell at our kids. We can be ungrateful, bossy, nagging, lazy, insensitive dolts. We even fart. But that doesn't mean we're any less heroic.

We only discover we are heroes when we get disillusioned enough with the dysfunction of our present circumstances. When we feel sad enough and lost enough and hopeless enough and fatigued by the burden of our victim stories, something deep within us has the opportunity to emerge, something stronger and wiser than we may ever have known existed within us. We all have this heroic spark that never dies, even when we're in our darkest moments. This spark within you is fueled by a pressing sense that there is adventure out there, that your life has purpose, that you're on a quest you may not understand yet, that your very small existence on this very big planet could mean something, that there is more to life than the ordinary, dysfunctional world, and that perhaps all it takes is a cape and a mask and some really cool boots in order to help create what author and speaker Charles Eisenstein calls "the more beautiful world our hearts know is possible."

Right when you might start to question your inner superhero and feel tempted to lose hope that your little blip of an existence on this great, big planet could really make a world-changing difference, you're likely to hear the phone ring. It usually rings very softly at first, perhaps so softly that, like your cell phone with the ringer off, you miss it altogether. But when you fail to pick up, the phone is likely to ring louder. Some Divine force turns the ringer on.

Because heroes are inherently curious, you won't be able to resist picking up the jangling phone, yet when you hear what you're being asked to do on your hero's journey, if you're like the rest of us, you're likely to respond with a rousing "Hell, no!" What you are being called on to do is too scary. The dangers are too risky. Your comfort zone is too secure. It would be so much easier to stay in the Ordinary World, even though the Ordinary World is so . . . well, ordinary. There are so many really, really good reasons to hang up the phone and refuse the call. Nobody would blame you. You're only human. It would be natural to turn your back on something so terrifying.

So like all the other heroes who have ever walked a hero's path, you refuse the call. It's how we heroes play hard to get.

When you turn your back on your calling, you won't necessarily be plagued with snakes or bombs or daggers. Your suffering may not look like Armageddon. It may be much more subtle than that. Your suffering may show up as the malaise that is endemic in our society—a less Technicolor life than the one you hoped to live. You may lose your mojo, and you won't know why. You may feel tired, listless, low on energy, and bankrupt on joy. Your relationships may grow stale or fall apart, your sex life may lose its passion, your professional life may unravel, or you may feel the creative frustration of a song within you that is yet unsung. You may experience a loss so painful that you'll think you won't be able to keep living. But you will. Because you're on a hero's journey. And your inner superhero *will* prevail.

However your calling shows up, you are likely to be humbled into submission until you finally, reluctantly, answer the call. It simply won't go away. Because you are a hero, you will finally agree to your task. Because you must. And when the Universe says, "I have a Divine assignment for you," you will finally say, with a humble, trembling voice, "Okay, Universe. I'm in."

Before I talk more about callings, and, in particular, about my calling, I need to acknowledge the One who is doing the calling because that One is a central character in the story I'm about to share with you. I usually refer to the voice on the other end of the call as "the Universe," "Source," "the Divine," "God," or, when I'm pissed because things aren't going my way, "Dude." Sometimes I call this voice "Sebastian," and he's a purple kangaroo, but I'll get to that part of the story later.

You might prefer "Goddess" or "Jesus" or "Buddha" or "Allah" or "Captain Crunch." Novelist Anne Lamott suggests that we call this Force "Howard," as in "Our Father, who art in heaven, Howard be thy name." She says she called God "Phil" for a long time, after a Mexican bracelet maker promised to imprint "Phil 4:4-7," her favorite scripture, upon her bracelet but never got beyond "Phil" before having to dismantle his booth.

It doesn't matter what you call this loving Presence. If you fancy yourself agnostic or even atheist, you might call it "Love" or your "Highest Self," and I can roll with that because I believe we all have within us a little piece of All That Is. Call it "your soul." Call it "your spirit." Call it "your inner superhero." Call it "Consciousness" or "the Creator." Suffice it to say that, just for convenience, I'll mostly call this loving, creative life force energy "the Universe," and I'll let you filter that through your own belief system.

While these name distinctions that religions like to fuss over are immaterial for the purposes of this story, the idea that there is some Light Force out there that guides and protects us as we navigate the trials, pitfalls, and triumphs of our own hero's journey is an essential part of this story. Finding and fulfilling your calling is a spiritual journey, and the reason you need not fear picking up the phone when your call comes is that you will not be journeying alone. The Universe will be your sidekick.

Even though you'll never be alone, that doesn't mean your journey won't be scary. In fact, fear is part and parcel of a hero's journey because you'll be called to get so far out of your comfort zone that you're likely to wind up asking, "How did I end up here?" Yet somewhere, underneath the abject terror, in brief spurts, you're likely to notice this feeling of grounded calm that reassures you that, no matter how ugly it gets, you'll always land on your feet—because you've been called to do this. And the Universe has your back.

I'm obsessed with a quote that is often attributed (perhaps incorrectly) to Albert Einstein: "The most important decision we make is whether we believe we live in a friendly or hostile universe." Whether Einstein said it or not, I've chosen to believe that we live in a purposeful, even friendly Universe. In fact, I have a raging case of *pronoia*, a word I only learned recently, which is the opposite of paranoia and might be defined as "the belief that everything in the Universe is conspiring to support you." I think we need more heroes afflicted with pronoia at this time in human evolution, because the only way to successfully fulfill your mission is to trust—*really trust*—that you live in a friendly universe. In case you doubt me, let me promise you that it's true. I'll offer concrete proof in the story I'm about to tell you, and I'll invite you to start researching and gathering evidence for yourself, as well.

How do you know if you've found your calling? In case fear doesn't clue you in, there will be other telltale signs. You'll notice that the pieces of the puzzle of your life all start to line up, and you'll realize you've been training for your calling since the moment you were born. Even the gritty things— the challenges, the disappointments, the regrets, the screw-ups—have been prepping you for what you're now being called to do. You'll realize that the divorce, the bankruptcy, the death of a loved one, the failure, the cancer, the rejection—this is the hero's school, your soul's curriculum, teaching you the necessary lessons so you can be who you're being called to be.

You'll also notice magical things starting to happen, things you might write off as coincidences, only they're too perfect, too exactly what you need in that particular moment, too much like miracles to call accidents. The synchronicities will fill you with a sense of wonder, because they're proof positive that you're being guided, that you're not in this alone, that Someone is moving mountains to ensure that your mission is a success.

Your calling doesn't need to be grand. The person who starts the non-profit to feed hungry children in Africa is no more important to the collective vibration of the planet than the open-hearted janitor who melts away everyone's armor at the office with his sincere hugs. The author who gets up on stage to speak about global peace is no more valuable than the stay home parent committed to raising compassionate children who are beacons of love and forgiveness. Your loving influence on just one person could affect history in ways you don't even realize.

Finding and fulfilling your calling is about contributing to the wholeness of the world. All that we do, we do to expand creation, not because you're not enough already or the world isn't enough, but just to see how much we can ascend as a collective. This is our true sacred purpose—not because we have to, but because it is the natural impulse of the wholeness of things.

You will recognize that you are smack dab in the center of your purpose because you will feel this sense of fulfillment and wholeness, but you can also trust that you'll be guided with equal precision when you get off course. Doors you longed to walk through will slam shut. If you take the wrong fork in the road of your hero's journey, your path will be littered with barbed wire and mustard gas and dragons and sharp knives. You will get the hint that you've made a wrong turn, that you've steered yourself off course from your date with destiny, when the journey becomes a relentless struggle. The deal will fall through. The money will run out. The mentor who's been providing the magical gifts won't follow you onto the wrong path. People won't sign up. You'll be rerouted just as magically as you were steered to your calling in the first place.

In order to follow the signs that will guide you on the road map of your hero's journey, you have to learn discernment. When you find yourself struggling to get through an obstacle-ridden forest, it can be hard to tell whether you've actually veered off course or your commitment is just being tested (as every hero's is). Obstacles can be a necessary part of your hero's journey, helping with the growth process and the cultivation and initiation of your inner hero. But they can also be signs that you've made a wrong turn.

How can you tell the difference? The guidepost you can trust is a sense of movement toward ease. I'm not suggesting your hero's journey will always be easy. In fact, I'm guaranteeing that there will be challenges. But if the challenges are mounting, things are getting worse, one hard struggle is piling upon the other, you've probably gotten seduced off course from your true calling, and the Universe is just waiting patiently, twiddling its Divine thumbs because you have free will, but never giving up faith that you will find your way back to your calling, which will always lead you to your own holy grail.

One of the obstacles likely to seduce you off course is the resistance you'll bump up against from all the people in your life who think they know what's best for you—better than you do. When you worry about what "everybody" will think, you're probably only talking about a handful of people whose lives you're not looking to model yours after anyway. You may not even like these people so much. You may be referring to your parents or your pastor or your professor or your great aunt Gertrude who clicks her teeth and smells like Pepto-Bismol. It's likely that fewer than 10 people make up your "everybody," yet those people have a tendency to profoundly influence the decisions you make, and their influence over you can produce roadblocks on your hero's journey.

Your "everybody" may erect obstacles that show up as advice or "this is for your own good" interventions. They'll tell you that you're crazy, that you're being reckless, that you'll wind up broke or dead or all alone if you don't stop doing exactly what you're being guided to do. They'll think they're protecting you. They'll call it love. What they won't realize is that they're just projecting their own fears and limiting beliefs onto you and your brave journey. You don't need anyone else to try to protect you. What you need is those who reinforce your courage.

So you have to create a bubble of faith to protect you from what "everybody" thinks. Being questioned by your "everybody" is such a ubiquitous part of finding and fulfilling your calling that Martha Beck recommends finding yourself a new, inspiring, courage-building "everybody." You might already know some of these people—they might be therapists or pastors or really wise friends. It might be your soulful grandmother who wears muumuus and drinks mushroom tea, or it could be your seven-year-old daughter who seems like the Buddha reincarnated. You'll know the people who qualify to be a part of your new "everybody" if you're confident that they have nothing but your best interests at heart, that they're not motivated by fear, and that they've done enough of their own personal growth work to avoid projecting their stuff onto you (or at least they're aware of when they might be doing that!).

If you know even one living person who meets these criteria, consider yourself blessed. Most people don't. So start filling your "everybody" with wise mentors. They don't have to be alive, or even real. You might choose Jesus. Or Buddha. Or Quan Yin. Or Mother Earth. Or Yoda. You might invite in authors of books you've loved, spiritual teachers like the Dalai Lama, people you've lost but know are still with you in spirit, animal spirits, angels, saints, or spirit guides.

When you're finally ready to pick up the ringing phone of your calling, you'll be well served to meet regularly with your new "everybody" because you will be asked to make a lot of tough choices, and no hero wants to make difficult decisions alone. You can do this by writing in a journal or while meditating. Just close your eyes, pose the questions for which you're seeking answers, and let your new "everybody" guide you.

If you're not convinced that your new "everybody" is guiding you to the right path, notice how the decisions you're making feel in your body. If you're making the right decision, you're likely to feel butterflies in your tummy or an opening in your chest or a lightness in your step or a tingling in your pelvis or a blossoming in your throat. Decisions that veer you off course often feel like nausea; clenching in your belly, chest, or throat; heaviness in your torso; gripping in your temples; or other similarly constricting feelings. Your body speaks its own unique language, but when you're on your hero's journey, it's sure to respond with a rousing "Oh, hell, yes!" when you make the decision your soul is ready to make, even as a part of you still quivers with fear.

A strange but welcome side effect of finding and fulfilling your calling is that your health is likely to improve. Not only does this make sense, but there's also research to back it up. In a 2009 study in *JAMA: The Journal of the American Medical Association*, Tait D. Shanafelt, MD, looked at whether viewing your work as a calling could prevent burnout. He made the case that work is just a job for some people. It's a way to pay the bills—period. For others, it's a career—a way to advance professionally, gain accolades and accomplishments, promote feelings of self-worth, and move up the ladder of success. But sometimes work becomes a calling, filled with meaning, purpose, and even a sense of being on a spiritual mission. For most of us, work contains elements of all three. Some tasks feel like a job. Others feel more like a career. But certain parts of our work touch our hearts and uplift our spirits, the way finding and fulfilling our callings can feel. Dr. Shanafelt found that if you view your work as a calling 40 percent of the time, it prevents burnout.[1] Many other studies, some of them listed in my book *Mind Over Medicine,* demonstrate the link between professional burnout, emotional stress, illness, and even premature death. So saying yes to your calling will leave you feeling connected with your life's purpose, and it's also likely to leave you feeling more vital.

You may notice fewer cravings for unhealthy foods, you'll have more energy for moving your body, aches and pains that used to plague you might disappear, you'll feel less tired, and chronic illnesses may start to get better. You may even experience a spontaneous remission from a seemingly incurable disease.

Take music lover Andy Mackie, for example, whose health improved when he found his calling. At 59 years old, Andy had undergone nine heart surgeries and was taking 15 medications to stay alive. But the medicines left him feeling horrible, so one day he told his doctors he wanted to stop the drugs. They told him he would die within a year if he did. Andy decided if he was dying, he would do something he had always wanted to do. So he took the money he would have spent on his medications and used it to buy 300 harmonicas, and he gave them away to children, complete with harmonica lessons. The following month, he was still alive, so he bought another 300 harmonicas. Thirteen years and 20,000 harmonicas later, Andy finally passed away. Now that's a hero who found his calling!

Another common side effect of saying yes to your hero's journey is that the money tends to flow in as you align with your mission. I'm not suggesting that you won't hit a stomach-churning point where you wind up in debt or bankrupt or staring at an empty bank account. But the Universe tends to reward you with financial security, even abundance, if your call to adventure stems from a pure place. Such abundance may not appear easily, though it certainly can.

Many heroes are often asked to demonstrate blind faith. You'll be tempted to build your safety net before you leap, but often your attempts to do so will be thwarted. You're likely to find that the net doesn't appear until you leap into trust. But it's safe to trust when you're leaping into your calling. When you align with one of the Universe's holy ideas in service to Something Larger than yourself, it's as if unseen forces roll out the red carpet, and suddenly, miracles happen because you said yes, even when you had no evidence that it was safe to do so.

---

1 Shanafelt, T. D., "Enhancing Meaning in Work: A Prescription for Preventing Physician Burnout and Promoting Patient-Centered Care," *JAMA: The Journal of the American Medical Association* 302, no. 12 (2009): 1338–40.

Everything I'm describing here—the whole crazy, wild roller coaster ride of the hero's journey—is exactly what happened to me. The disillusionment with the Ordinary World of modern medicine, the sense that there was something more, the cosmic phone call, the resistance from my "everybody," the reluctant acceptance of the call, the appearance of my magical mentors, the approach to my Innermost Cave (what I called my "narrow place"), the dragons I had to slay, the discovery of the holy grail that would help heal health care, the challenges on the road back, and, ultimately, bringing the holy grail back home, which in my case was the hospital.

Recently, I returned to the bridge over a river among the redwoods in Big Sur, where I first reluctantly accepted my call. Five long, painful years had elapsed since I said to the Universe, "I'm in." Upon my return, having just found the holy grail, I dropped to my knees on the bridge, feeling embattled and bruised and not the least bit heroic, and I whispered through tears of relief and gratitude, "Why didn't you warn me how hard it was going to be?"

The Universe said, "Because you wouldn't have said yes."

But I did. And this is my story. But I want you to understand that even though this book may be about me and my calling, it is really about you and your calling. You may not think you're much of a hero right now. If you're like I was, you may even feel more like a cautionary tale. But that's why I'm telling my story, and you'll see that there were plenty of times when pretty much everyone thought I was more of a warning sign than an inspiration. It really may get darkest just before the new you emerges, but it doesn't have to get as hard as I made it. I tend to be dense, so I learn things the hard way. But if you're equipped with some of the tools I'll be sharing with you, your hero's journey can be more peaceful, easier, and less circuitous than mine.

Because I'll be equipping you with a map of your hero's journey, you will soon learn where you are—whether you're still waiting for the phone to ring or you're crossing the first threshold or you're deep in the darkest moments of the Ordeal or you've just found your own holy grail. The key is to keep the faith that the promised land really does lie ahead, and one day, you too will be kneeling on a bridge, awash in gratitude that the worst is behind you, crying tears of joy with the realization that the Universe really does have your back when you're brave enough to accept your Divine assignment.

Consider me one of your magical mentors. I'll be the Yoda to your Luke Skywalker, the Donkey to your Shrek. As I tell you my story, I'll point out where I was in my hero's journey so you can identify where you are in your own journey. And at the end of each chapter, I'll be sharing what I call a "Hero's Guidepost," to help impart some wisdom and direction that you may need at some point along your journey. I'll also be inviting you to participate in a "Hero's Practice," which will contain exercises meant to expedite your journey. Consider these amulets you will have at your disposal.

So come. Let's journey together. None of us are on this path alone.

CHAPTER 1

THE ORDINARY WORLD

In order for you to understand my hero's journey so I can help you map out yours, let me share with you a snapshot from my Ordinary World. Come back with me to Illinois in the late '90s, when I was a third-year resident at a university in the Midwest, working a 36-hour shift in labor and delivery.

"Doctor Rankin, Room 305—stat!"

I burst from the doctors' lounge as if poised on sprinters' blocks, flinging blankets and barbecue potato chips in my wake. I race through the tiled hallways and slam open the door of the delivery room, where the adjustable hospital bed perches, like a throne, in the center of a pink-walled haven that is as homey and cozy as you can make a hospital room. Lying in the center of the bed, I see my patient, Sarah, straddled in the stirrups, her face scarlet as she grabs her knees and pushes until a tiny blood vessel in her eye bursts. Seeing a swath of bright red hair crowning, I throw on a blue paper gown, don a pair of 6½ sterile gloves, and assume the catcher's mitt stance.

The baby's father is counting, "One . . . two . . . three . . . four . . . five . . . six . . . seven . . . eight . . . nine . . . ten. Okay. Deep breath. And again." Queen's "We Are the Champions" blares from the stereo.

Massaging Sarah's perineum, I stretch the skin to make room for the baby's head just as she pushes it out with one last grunt. When I angle the baby's head down, the front shoulder pops out, and when I pull up in the opposite direction, the baby boy slips out like a greased watermelon. The father bursts into tears, which leaves me misty. (Something about watching big, burly guys cry at births gets me every time.) As I place the baby boy on the towel waiting on his mother's belly, the nurse dries him off and rubs his back. Sarah nuzzles her son's wet hair against her cheek.

While the parents bond, I focus on delivering the placenta. But then I hear the nurse press the call button and order, "Call NICU. Stat!" I deliver the placenta and rush to the incubator, where the nurse is inserting suction tubes into the limp newborn's mouth. The nurse whispers, "Baby's not breathing." He looks a dusky shade of purplish blue.

I rummage around for a stethoscope while the nurse covers the baby's mouth with an oxygen mask. My heart races when I realize I'll have to intubate this baby myself if the team from the neonatal intensive care unit doesn't arrive soon. As a third-year OB/GYN resident, I've only intubated a few babies—and they were all plastic dolls in a controlled setting. I swallow hard, running through the steps in my mind, all the while praying that the NICU team will save this baby—and me.

Sarah yells, "What's happening? Why isn't my baby crying?"

The charge nurse pushes the worried father aside and says, "Stay there. Please."

I can hear Sarah wailing in the background as I'm sorting through the equipment, trying to find just the right tube, with the baby getting bluer by the minute.

I pray, "Please God please God please God," and then just, "Help."

I beg the charge nurse to grab my senior resident, the attending physician, the neonatologist—anyone more senior than me who happens to be standing around labor and delivery right now. The stakes are too high. But the charge nurse whispers back, "Lissa, you're it right now."

I feel a sense of mounting dread. I've never done this before, not on a real baby. What if I screw up?

I'm just about to insert the tiny laryngoscope into the newborn's mouth when the NICU team races in and someone with more experience than me grabs the instrument from my hand. I breathe a huge sigh. I'm off the hook.

Within seconds, the baby is intubated and a respiratory therapist starts bag-ventilating him while the NICU nurse listens to his chest with a stethoscope. The NICU nurse yells, "Call a code."

This is not good. The baby is still blue. My heart sinks.

The NICU attending neonatologist, Dr. Bosco, blasts in moments later. Without a word to Sarah, he puts a line into the freshly cut umbilical cord, injecting drugs; pushes medication down the endotracheal tube; and, finally, compresses the tiny baby's blue chest, performing CPR.

By this point, Sarah and her husband are officially freaking out, and my whole body is quivering with adrenaline. The charge nurse sits with her arm around Sarah, and I'm racing between Sarah and the NICU team, trying to translate. But the NICU team is working silently, and I have no clue what's going on.

Was it me? Did I do something wrong? The baby looked great on the fetal monitor all through labor, and the delivery went smoothly. I second-guess myself, which is what OB/GYNs always do when the baby doesn't come out pink and screaming. I wonder if there's anything I could have done to prevent this baby from being so blue. Had I missed some clue on the fetal monitor? Should I have recommended a C-section? Should I have rushed the delivery with forceps or a vacuum? And the unwelcome thought that always needles its way into the minds of obstetricians when the baby comes out blue: *Will I get sued?*

Finally, Dr. Jackson, the attending OB/GYN in charge of me, flings open the door and bellows, "Will somebody tell me what's going on in here?"

I start debriefing him, but he brushes me aside and starts barking at Dr. Bosco, asking questions in a brusque voice. Dr. Bosco shoos him away. He's fully focused on trying to save the blue baby in front of him. Without a word to any of us, the NICU team pushes the incubator out of the delivery room and runs down the hallway. Dr. Jackson races after them, still barking questions.

The room is suddenly still with only Sarah, her husband, the nurse, and me left. Sarah and her husband are both sobbing, and when I place my hand over Sarah's hand, she withdraws it, as if I just burned her. I feel helpless. All I can do is stand there and be present, which doesn't feel like enough. Doctors don't like to feel helpless. At all. It triggers our greatest fear—that others will finally realize that we're imposters, that we don't know what we're doing, that we can't really help our patients, that everything we do is just a finely orchestrated ruse to cover up the truth that we're not in control of whether or not someone lives or dies.

I feel the sinking sensation in the hollows of my stomach that I always feel when I realize I can't control what happens in the hospital, and just at that moment, when I'm feeling really nauseated, my pager blares a 911 message, which means, "COME NOW." I apologize to Sarah and excuse myself from the room.

I feel the tears starting to come, but I can't indulge them because there's a baby about to be born in Room 309. Doctors become masters at stuffing their emotions. We can't cry when we're grieving or when someone has hurt our feelings or when we're sad. We can't let on when we're scared. The only emotion doctors seem to give themselves permission to express is anger. Doctors tend to yell a lot. But when you're a resident, you're not even allowed to yell much. You can only yell down to your medical students or junior residents. You can't yell up to the attending physicians. Either way, yelling isn't so much my style. I'm more the crying type, but my professors have been criticizing me for years when I cry, so I try to hold it together and not let anyone see when things get to me.

It's not just feelings that doctors suppress. We literally have to suppress our urges—to sleep when we're tired, to eat when we're hungry, to stop retracting in surgery when our shoulders are killing us, even to urinate. Looking at the clock, I see that it's past midnight, and I'm so tired and hungry and dizzy from adrenaline that I have a hard time mustering up the energy I'll need to deliver this next baby, but nobody in this labor room needs to know that I'm scared about what's happening to Sarah's baby or that I really want to go to sleep. Let these nice people think I've been hanging out in a call room, reading a good book, just waiting for this very special moment.

Wiping my eyes and pasting on my smiling game face, I open the door.

The baby's head is halfway out of Olive's vagina, and the nurse is playing quarterback, holding the head in with one hand while the other hand pulls back for instruments in case the baby comes before I don my gloves. I get there just in time and step between Olive's blue-draped legs as a contraction comes and the baby shoots out like a cannonball. I fumble the baby, barely catching him in the crook of my arm. Then I clamp the umbilical cord twice and invite the dad to cut it. He can barely chop through the rubbery cord, but once he does, he looks so proud, like he's just thrown a touchdown. With the baby boy untethered, I nestle him onto the blanket over Olive's breast.

Olive gushes, "Oh, my beautiful boy," and the dad tears up and grins. I start to tear up, too. They really do get me every time. But then I look away so I can keep it together.

While I deliver the placenta and inspect a small tear in Olive's vagina, I say, "Happy birthday, baby. Welcome to the world."

I load up my needle driver with a little 2-0 chromic, and just as I'm about to put the needle into Olive's flesh, my pager goes off. The nurse frees it from my waist and pushes the little green button, revealing a page from down the hall. I'm wanted in Room 301. I sew quickly, have my photo taken with Olive and the baby, and make my exit.

———————

In Room 301, all the way at the very end of the labor floor, as far from the sound of happy screaming babies as possible, lies Eve. The charge nurse put her here as an act of compassion, to spare her from the joyful sounds of healthy childbirth, because Eve's birth will not be one of them. When I enter Room 301, I am struck by the unnatural silence. Labor rooms tend to be noisy, chaotic places, but in Room 301, no fetal heart monitor beeps the reassuring bleep-bleep-bleep of a healthy fetal heartbeat. No stereo plays power-pushing tunes or tinkly new age meditation music. The team of people who usually attend a birth are conspicuously absent. Even the grunts and cries emitted from a woman about to give birth are muted by Eve's heavily dosed epidural and a generous hand with the morphine, all aimed at making her as comfortable as possible for something painful on every level.

Eve was 35 weeks along when she wound up with flulike symptoms, which turned out to be caused by listeriosis, a bacterial infection that killed her almost full-term baby. Eve is now about to give birth to the baby she has already lost. When I first introduced myself to Eve earlier in the day, I sat on the edge of her bed, held her hand, and listened to her tell me about the garden mural she had painted on the nursery wall, the vintage christening dress she had found at an antique store, and the dreams for her future life with this baby that she will never experience.

Now the baby's head is right here, about to be born. I brace myself.

Eve pushes, and suddenly, I am holding a grey, lifeless shell of a baby. With silent reverence, the nurse takes the baby girl from my hands and wraps her gingerly in the hand-knit carnation pink blanket donated by the Ladies Auxiliary for women who have lost their babies. The nurse asks Eve whether she wants to hold her baby. Eve nods. We prop her up in bed, and the nurse hands her the baby she has named Amelia. Eve looks so alone with no family at her bedside. My pager is blessedly quiet for a change, so while the nurse finishes up the paperwork, I curl up next to Eve on the labor bed, with my arms around her and her baby. Eve falls asleep in my arms, still holding Amelia.

"Dr. Rankin to Room 315—stat!" I quietly extricate myself from Eve's embrace and leave the room.

In Room 315 a whole team of nurses are attending to Mallory. One holds the fetal monitor to her belly while another turns her first right, then left. Someone else is holding a fetal scalp electrode out to me, my signal to do the procedure that will let us more accurately monitor the baby's heartbeat, which is down in the sixties—half of what it should be. When I insert the scalp electrode, I tickle the baby's head, trying to stimulate the baby's heartbeat, but nothing happens. It stays in the sixties.

Mallory is only 8 centimeters dilated, so I can't grab a pair of forceps or ask her to push. Instead, I yell, "Open the back," my signal to get the operating room ready. Everyone springs to action. The whole time I'm scratching the baby's head with my finger and helping Mallory change positions in hopes that whatever might be compressing the baby's umbilical cord moves out of the way.

The heartbeat has been down for 4 minutes, but it feels like forever. Then, just as we are about to unplug Mallory from the fetal monitor and race her back to the operating room for a crash C-section, the baby's heart rate goes up. We all slow down and watch every beep of the monitor. I finally exhale. We're out of the woods, at least for now. I allow myself a moment of fatigue, the kind that washes over you like a wave and leaves you fantasizing about feather pillows and flannel bedsheets.

But there's no time for fantasies. I pull out Mallory's chart and start jotting notes, when the overhead pager goes off again. "Dr. Rankin to Room 307." Sometimes I seriously fantasize about disabling the damn overhead pager. And flushing my beeper down the toilet. And walking out of the hospital in my scrubs, ignoring all the demands and expectations. I imagine just walking and walking and maybe eventually winding up on a beach in California where I don't even own a phone.

But right now there's another baby to deliver. I run into Room 307; catch the pink, squealing baby; and hug the tearful, happy mother.

Then I check in with Alice in Room 302. Alice couldn't wait for her 20-week ultrasound, when she would find out the sex of her baby. She desperately wanted a girl, and she got her wish. But the ultrasound also picked up abnormalities, and an amniocentesis confirmed that her baby had a lethal chromosome abnormality, Trisomy 18, a disorder that means the baby would die shortly after birth. Faced with a difficult choice—to carry the baby, knowing she would ultimately lose her, or to terminate the pregnancy—Alice opted to end her pregnancy. Earlier in the day, I had inserted the misoprostol pills that would help her prematurely deliver her fetus.

Alice is now due for another dose.

It kills my mother that I do this. She can't stand that I participate in terminating pregnancies, even the ones that were terminal anyway. She begged me not to become an "abortionist," a word I can barely stomach, even though I guess, technically, I am one. I try not to think about my mother as I slide the pills inside Alice's vagina just as the overhead pager calls me again. I can tell by the panicked tone that it's another emergency.

I sprint down the hall to Room 313, where I find Valerie, covered in her own blood. One nurse adjusts her monitor and another squashes a blood pressure cuff on her arm. A third nurse makes reassuring little "it's okay" noises as she flits about, but it is clearly far from okay. My heart pounds as I watch the blood pour out of Valerie, soaking through the bedsheets, sloshing onto the floor, while another nurse puts in a second IV. The flinty smell of blood permeates the room, an odor I usually associate with happy, healthy childbirth, but now the smell makes me nauseated. The charge nurse runs in with a bag of blood from the blood bank, and we work together to hang it quickly while Valerie screams, "My baby! What's happening to my baby?"

Blood keeps cascading out of her from a placenta that has wrongly implanted, a potentially deadly condition called placenta previa. I'm reminded of why so many women used to die in childbirth. This is all it takes. One little accident of nature, and all of a sudden, a woman's entire blood volume erupts like a tsunami.

I'm terrifyingly aware of the fact that one of two things will happen in this moment. Either the bleeding will stop while Valerie is still alive or it will stop after it's too late. It's one of the cardinal rules of medicine: All bleeding stops, eventually. But it's my job to make sure Valerie and her baby survive this. Which means there's no time to waste. It's time to operate.

I'm about to announce my decision to the team, but just then, the bleeding slows, only the teensiest bit, and I second-guess myself. What if the bleeding is about to stop? Twice before in this pregnancy, Valerie's placenta has bled, requiring blood transfusions, but both times, it eventually stopped by itself. Maybe this is that moment, when everything is about to turn around. I certainly don't want to deliver this baby if it's not absolutely necessary. Valerie is only 29 weeks along, 11 weeks from her due date. Her baby is not fully developed and may have problems with breathing, brain development, vision, and bowel function. The baby might not even survive. I catch myself breathing too loud and too fast. Everyone still stares at me, waiting for me to make the call. I am taking too long, and they are getting nervous.

They expect me to make decisions without hesitation. If I let on that I'm not yet sure what to do, something bad would happen. I'm not quite sure what, but it's been imprinted upon me that the doctor always needs to appear confident, especially in emergency settings. If it's not an emergency, it's fine to "curbside" someone, to stop another doctor in the hallway and ask for advice, or to ask for a formal consultation from another physician who might help you make the right decision. But when there's blood splashing on the floor, everyone expects you to take decisive action.

Just as I'm weighing the pros and cons of an emergency C-section in my mind, Valerie's bleeding picks up, and there is no question now. It's definitely time to operate. I can see the relief in everyone's eyes when I announce, "Open the back." The charge nurse calls my attending, who will meet me in the operating room.

I glance at Valerie and see wide, unblinking brown eyes filled with terror. I grab Valerie's IV-tethered hand with both of mine and look deep into her eyes. For a quiet moment, it is just the two of us. I say, "It's time," and she hears me and knows what we must do. I hear her exhale. Valerie and I have been through this before. She has been prepped for this moment since we knew it could happen without much warning. She nods, giving me her silent blessing. I squeeze her hand, and she squeezes back. Then I let go and start barking drill sergeant orders.

"Call anesthesia—now! Somebody alert the NICU. Type and cross her for four more units and send out a CBC, PT/PTT, and a fibrinogen. Get those IVs wide open. And somebody give me a blood pressure." The nurses scatter, and someone yells out, "80 over 40." I say a quick prayer. Valerie is pouring out blood like a faucet, and my legs feel like Jell-O. But I can't let on. I must be a pillar of strength.

I check the baby monitor and discover, with relief, that the baby still looks okay. The baby's heart rate is a little flat, a little too fast, but nothing that screams imminent danger. While the nurses dash around and the anesthesiologist rushes to Valerie's bedside, I unhook the plugs that tie Valerie's labor bed to the wall, yanking the baby monitor cord out of the machine.

We all run like crazy, one person on each corner of Valerie's bed-on-wheels, with me running parallel, holding Valerie's hand. We dart through the hospital hallways, slamming against the automatic doors as we maneuver Valerie into the always-ready emergency operating room. The operating room is meat-locker frigid, with blue drapes and blue towels folded neatly, ready for action.

Valerie looks up at me, and I say, "Don't worry. Everything's gonna be okay."

I'm not sure I'm telling the truth.

A nurse pours Betadine on Valerie's belly, and I pull on sterile latex gloves without bothering to wash my hands while someone helps me into a blue surgical gown. I grab a scalpel off the Mayo stand, and the anesthesiologist fits an oxygen mask over Valerie's face while injecting medication into her vein. We all hold our breath when he starts to intubate her.

Usually, we avoid putting a pregnant woman to sleep before intubation. I saw a young woman die this way. Pregnant women can be much harder to intubate, and if we can't get the tube in, it's over. But the cost of waiting for spinal anesthesia may be two lives, so we can't waste time. I inhale. But the breathing tube slides right in. As soon as the tube is taped, the anesthesiologist yells, "Go!"

My attending rushes in and, seeing the pool of blood on the floor, gives me the nod, my permission to start cutting while he dons his sterile gown. With one swift swipe of the knife, I slice through skin, subcutaneous fat, tough fascia, filmy Saran Wrap–like peritoneum, all the way down to Valerie's uterus, skipping the careful dissection we do when it's not an emergency.

When not pregnant, the uterus is about the size of a woman's fist. It is dark pink, sort of mauve and shaped like a small, upside-down pear. The consistency is slightly tougher than filet mignon. It is, in fact, made almost entirely of smooth muscle. From the wide part of the uterus, two paler pink fallopian tubes snake their way to the ovaries, ending in the fimbriated ends, which look kind of like a sea anemone or a leafy seadragon, with filmy pink strands floating in fluid. On the other side of the fimbria, not attached but hanging out nearby, lie the two ovaries, which look like lumpy sea scallops. Pearly white and glistening, they are about the size of meatballs in reproductive-age women. Tiny egg follicles sometimes dot the surface.

This is how things would normally look, but when a woman is pregnant, everything gets crazy big. The uterus grows like a butternut squash on steroids.

And the blood vessels! A vessel that is normally the size of a spaghetti noodle can grow to be as big as a garden hose. No kidding. I've seen it.

You usually can't see the blood vessels running through the uterine muscle until you make an incision, but because of Valerie's placenta previa, ribbons of arteries and veins slash across the lower segment of the uterus, right where I need to cut. It isn't going to be pretty, but the baby has to come out, so I slice a clean red gash in the lower, skinnier end of the uterus. Blood gushes, flowing over the side of the operating table and drenching my clogs, which I forgot to cover with blue booties. Using my fingers, I stretch open the incision in the uterus, and the muscle gives way, tearing smoothly.

And there it is. A dark swath of hair. Dr. Bellingham, the high-risk obstetrics specialist who has been called in, dons her gloves just as the baby is coming out. My arm shakes from the effort of the delivery, and Dr. Bellingham pushes on the top of the uterus to help bring the baby's head through the incision. The limp baby girl emerges in a slick, slippery second. Then it's clamp, clamp on the umbilical attachment, and I cut cleanly through the gelatinous cord with sterile scissors. After handing the silent baby to the nurse, I deliver the meaty placenta. Then one, two, three, I'm stitching away with a 0-Vicryl suture, closing the uterine incision in one long, continuous line, as if I'm hemming a skirt.

I listen for reassuring little cries or grunts. Anything. But I hear only the clicking of instruments and the puffs of air the neonatologist squeezes into the limp baby's lungs. I panic. What have I done? Did I wait too long? Could I have saved this precious baby if I had acted 1 minute sooner? My knees feel weak.

The anesthesiologist reports Valerie's blood pressure. It's 70 over 30—*way* too low. I must look pale because Dr. Bellingham gives me one of her looks that says, "Don't worry. I've got this."

I exhale. In that moment, I know that Valerie and her baby will not be dying. Not on my watch.

Dr. Bellingham and I sew and sew, trying to stem the flow of blood. We take turns massaging the boggy uterus with our hands, begging the muscle to contract and close off the wide-open blood vessels. While the anesthesiologist injects Methergine and Hemabate and someone inserts misoprostol into Valerie's rectum to try to make the bleeding stop, I pray, "Please God. Please God."

If the bleeding doesn't stop, the next step will be a hysterectomy, since there's not enough time or blood to mess around. If that happens and this baby doesn't make it, Valerie will never be a mother, and it will be all my fault.

I can't let that happen.

I keep sewing, stitch after indigo-dyed stitch, until the uterus is matted with back-and-forth sutures. The anesthesiologist announces that Valerie's blood pressure is up to 100/70. The bleeding is slowing down. We are winning this battle with nature.

Just then, the neonatologist calls out the good news. "Baby's getting pink."

I peek over and see the rosy baby wiggling her tiny limbs. The NICU team wheels her out of the operating room in a little incubator, and I catch a glimpse of her smooth, veiny, see-through skin and her skinny little chicken body.

Be strong, baby. Be strong.

When I look back at Valerie, I can't believe she's barely bleeding, just a tiny ooze, nothing significant. "Onco dry," we call it, referring to the gynecologic cancer surgeons who tolerate a little more oozing than we obstetricians usually do. I look over at Dr. Bellingham, and she nods. Better to quit while you're ahead.

It's the First Law of Gynecology: "The enemy of good is better."

It's time to close. So I clean out the clots from Valerie's abdomen, check the uterus one more time to make sure it hasn't sprung a new leak, and start sewing the tough fascia back together again. I notice that I am breathing again. We have made it.

Just as I'm about to let myself relax, the overhead pager blares out, "Dr. Rankin to Room 316."

Dr. Bellingham says, "You go. I've got this."

I dash out of the operating room, stripping off my gown and racing into another delivery room, where a woman is already pushing. Moments later, I go through my well-rehearsed motions and deliver another healthy baby.

As I take off my gown and wash my hands, I look at the clock. It's just after 3:00 a.m. I haven't peed in hours, and I have to go. But before I do, I walk into Sarah's room, where I find her crying. She tells me it's not looking good for her son. He has been transferred to the Children's Hospital. The doctors think something is very wrong with his heart.

I feel relief. Phew. It's not something I did wrong. Then I instantly feel guilty for having such a thought. I am the world's most insensitive doctor for feeling relieved that Sarah's baby might have a congenital heart defect. My pager is blessedly silent for a change, and I allow myself the luxury of feeling what I *really* feel, which is sad and scared and overwhelmed and exhausted. I sit on the edge of the bed next to Sarah and reach for her hand. She takes it, and we sit together in silence. I allow myself to make eye contact with her, even though I know it is risky. That's when I always lose it: the eyes, the eyes. They speak novels. I stay with Sarah for a while. We hug and hold each other. I can feel her chest rising and falling as she breathes. We let go of our hug and embrace on the other side, so our hearts are touching.

Then my pager goes off again. They need me in Room 304.

I brace myself.

Elizabeth is in Room 304, and she is about to deliver a dead baby.

As humans, but especially as women, we're not wired to deal with the loss of a baby without emotion. However, as doctors, we're taught to treat situations like this with professional detachment. Yet the feminine heart is sensitive, and as an empath, I could literally feel the physical pain in my heart and the emotional pain in my thoughts as I tuned into my patients. My feelings often lived just below the surface of my professional duties, and without much warning, they might bubble up. This left me feeling hypervigilant, always on the alert for displays of emotion that might burst through, so I was always struggling to tamp down my feelings in the name of professionalism. The pain of loss weigh heavily on my heart, and the serial denial of my human emotions led to a sort of fascism of the soul that left me feeling exhausted and burned out. In such moments, I often fantasized about quitting my job. This was before a Buddhist monk told me that meditation was important because it gives us time to process, "Wow, that happened." As a medical resident, I had never even heard of meditation, and I certainly didn't indulge myself time to digest painful experiences. Like most of my colleagues, I was a busy doctor with responsibilities to fulfill, and I was taught to believe that quiet times of reflection were for lazy people. It's no wonder I often wound up crying and sick through the rare vacations I was afforded. It's as if painful emotions would get stored in a bank vault so I could perform up to the standards of what was expected of me. But then, when I was lying on a beach somewhere, memories would pummel me, unbidden, like rocks in an avalanche.

This night in the hospital was one of those nights when the bank vault of trauma was filling up.

Elizabeth couldn't afford health insurance and she didn't qualify for public aid, so she got no prenatal care. At nearly 40 weeks pregnant, her husband found her passed out on the floor in what turned out to be a diabetic coma. By the time the ambulance brought her to the emergency room, her baby had already died. Elizabeth spent nearly a week in a coma in the intensive care unit before her blood sugar stabilized and she woke up. Then, just as her doctors were about to transfer her from the ICU to the obstetrics ward, Elizabeth started contracting and went into labor.

She'd been in labor and delivery during my whole shift, pushing for almost 4 hours. By the time I arrive, the baby just isn't budging. If her baby was alive, we'd have done a C-section long ago, but because she has already lost the baby, we're trying to avoid subjecting her to the risks (because she's diabetic, surgical wounds tend to heal poorly).

But Elizabeth is exhausted. The baby just isn't coming out this way. It's time to try something else.

Because of her uncontrolled diabetes, I expect that Elizabeth's baby will be big. I also expect that the baby's shoulders might get stuck during delivery. I run my plan by Dr. Jackson, who agrees. Then I grab the Leukhardt-Simpson forceps, which look like two giant salad spoons. I yank so hard that I move the whole labor bed, and, finally, I deliver the baby's head.

But the shoulders just aren't coming. It's what we call a "shoulder dystocia." I try the McRoberts maneuver, where the nurses pull back on the mother's legs to make more room for the baby. I also try suprapubic pressure, where someone jumps on the bed and presses her fists right over the mother's pubic bone to try to dislodge a stuck shoulder; the Woods corkscrew maneuver, where you try turning the baby like a corkscrew to see if one of the shoulders will pop out; cutting a big episiotomy, to make more room; reaching in to try to deliver the baby's posterior arm. I stop short of the controversial Zavanelli maneuver, which requires pushing the head back inside and doing a C-section.

Unlike most shoulder dystocias, this is not an emergency because this baby has already died. Elizabeth's epidural is heavily dosed and she's numb from the waist down, so there's time to wait for Dr. Jackson, who strolls in and takes over because I cannot get this baby out. He reaches in and breaks the baby's arm, and the sound of the breaking bone leaves all of us wincing. But it works. The broken arm comes out, and the rest of the baby follows.

Then, without a word of comfort to Elizabeth, Dr. Jackson turns on his heels and walks out. I want to spit on him. I fantasize about breaking *his* arm and then walking out without even an apology. I feel my face flushing with hate for my teacher. But like so many other feelings I'm having during this unusually difficult labor and delivery shift, I suppress my rage and focus on the task at hand.

I am left holding a 10-pound dead baby with a broken arm.

The nurse wraps the baby boy in another blanket from the Ladies Auxiliary, and as I hand the baby to Elizabeth, I whisper, "Lo siento, señora."

She whispers back, "Gracias."

I don't speak Spanish well enough to say the things I'd like to say, so I just crawl into bed next to her and hug her. The nurse leans over and joins our group hug, and the four of us rock back and forth.

Then it's time to go to Alice's room.

I'm dreading this.

I slap on a pair of gloves without even bothering to gown up, and Alice pushes once. The baby is bright pink, and the skin is so thin you can see the blood vessels right through it. The little eyes are fused, and there's no hair anywhere. The whole baby is about the size of a small Barbie doll with a big head. The baby's little arms and legs wiggle, and you can see her little heart beat through the thin skin of her chest. Another knitted Ladies Auxiliary blanket envelops her, and the nurse lays the baby in Alice's arms. Alice hugs her and nuzzles her cheek. After a brief flurry of activity, the baby's limbs stop moving and her little heart stops beating.

This is the moment when I really lose it. When Alice sees me sobbing, she reaches out to hug me, and I feel guilty that my patient is taking care of me when I should be comforting her. My head hurts, my eyes sting, and every muscle in my body aches and shakes. I haven't had a sip of water for at least 6 hours. I still haven't peed. And aside from some potato chips I grabbed in the doctors' lounge, my last meal was at noon the day before.

I'm really feeling sorry for myself, and then I catch myself. Alice just lost her baby, and I'm whining about being tired? I apologize awkwardly and finally excuse myself so I can head to the sanctuary of the women's locker room to pull myself together and stuff my feelings into the emotional bank vault.

As I walk down the hall, staring at the floor to hide my swollen eyes from my colleagues, the charge nurse stops me. The NICU just called. Sarah's baby, the one who turned blue after birth, just died at the Children's Hospital from a congenital heart defect that couldn't be repaired quickly enough. She needs my help. The neonatologists want to do an autopsy, and someone has to ask for Sarah's permission.

I can't do it. I. Can't. Handle. One. More. Dead. Baby.

The nurse is still talking to me when I begin to walk away from her. I feel myself shutting down, like a dark curtain is falling over me. I keep walking, faster and faster, running toward the women's locker room. Dr. Jackson sees me from down the hall and calls out to me.

But I ignore him.

Dr. Jackson stomps after me, but I make it inside the safety of the women's locker room door before he can catch up to me.

He's banging on the locker room door, screaming at me as I crumple into a heap on the bathroom floor. The door swings open and I look up, expecting to see Dr. Jackson violating the women's locker room. But instead, I see two of the midwives blocking the door from Dr. Jackson.

With a venomous voice, Dr. Jackson spews, "Buck up, Rankin. You'll never amount to anything in this business unless you can stop feeling so damn much."

The midwives push the door closed in Dr. Jackson's face and then drop to their knees beside me. Both of them cradle me, rocking me back and forth on that locker room floor. They caress my hair and stroke my cheeks and wipe my tears with the softest touch. We rock like that for I don't know how long, and nobody says a word until one of them looks me right in the eye and says something I'll never forget for the rest of my life.

In a barely audible whisper, she says, "Lissa, don't ever let them break you."

I've since tried to remember to say that to every medical student and resident I meet.

———

The hardest part of that night for me wasn't that I witnessed four babies die. The biggest challenge was that I didn't feel like I was given permission to experience my own vulnerable humanity and grieve for the loss of fellow human lives. Instead, I was shamed, by my teacher and myself, for my reaction to a uniquely traumatic labor and delivery shift. I was left feeling that my femininity—particularly my empathy, my intuition, and my emotions—was a liability I would have to "cure" if I wanted to become a successful doctor. I didn't realize at the time that these feminine qualities are exactly what a true healer must embody in order to help another human being heal. They're also the traits all of us—men and women alike—need to balance within ourselves if we are to become forces for healing, not only within our professions but also for our culture and the planet.

For many years, the masculine principle led us as a culture to accomplish numerous technological advances in medicine, as well as in many other industries, but the masculine and feminine have become unbalanced. The masculine and the feminine within us possess both light and shadow, and because the Divine Feminine has been suppressed, the Profane Masculine has dominated. Greed, competition, scarcity thinking, and the quest for unlimited growth threaten the fabric of not only medicine but also the culture as a whole. The medicine we all need lies within the essence of the Divine Feminine. As the Dalai Lama famously said at the Vancouver Peace Summit in 2009, "The world will be saved by the Western woman." Taken out of context, this might suggest that men aren't equally capable of being heroes, but I'm sure that's not what the Dalai Lama meant. When both men and women are brave enough to balance the feminine and the masculine within, we really can save the world. Our future lies in embracing our human emotions, our vulnerability, our interconnectedness, our intuition, our inclination to collaborate, our caretaking of Mother Earth, and our desire to love one another with an open heart.

Like me, you might feel like you've been asked to sell out the feminine in service to a world dominated by the shadow side of the masculine. You might feel like it's unsafe to be vulnerable and expose your tender underbelly. But your greatest strength lies within your vulnerability. From this soft spot, empathy emerges, and when we feel empathy, we live from the heart and become a source of healing for others.

It helps to keep our hearts open and remind ourselves to be gentle with one another. You just never know what the people you encounter in everyday life are going through. The woman in front of you in the grocery store line just lost her mother after a 9-year battle with cancer. Your boss just found out his wife is having an affair. The other mother you ran into in the schoolyard just discovered that her daughter has a brain tumor. The barista who has been schlepping espresso to fund her dream just got the news that the book she spent 5 years writing got rejected by yet another publisher. The young boy acting out in the restaurant just found out Daddy is going to Iraq. The woman who cut you off in traffic just filed for divorce from her abusive husband. The waiter who forgot to bring you extra salad dressing just lost his son in a car accident.

As Plato said, "Be kind, for everyone you meet is fighting a hard battle."

Every man and woman on this planet is likely to be holding something heavy in his or her heart right now—some loss, some grief, some disappointment, some wound. Somewhere, a woman just lost a baby in the hospital. Somewhere, a doctor just delivered a dead baby. We're all doing the best we can, and we need one another now more than ever if we're going to be successful on our own hero's journey. If we're brave enough to be vulnerable with each other, it's easier to navigate the Ordinary World, which can be filled with trauma. When we're kind to each other, it gives us the courage to do what we must to strap on our gold belts and our knee-high boots when we're called to take our place on The Team.

HERO'S GUIDEPOST:
Your Vulnerability Is Your Greatest Strength

Others might lead you to believe you need to "buck up" and "armor up." But a hero's greatest strength lies in the willingness to lean into joy, sorrow, anger, and any other emotion that arises as you walk your path. Feeling empathy, compassion, and tenderness for yourself and for those you will meet on your hero's journey is a blessing to be nurtured. Even your imperfections can be your strengths when you're brave enough to allow others to see the truth of who you are. The only gateway to true connection lies in your vulnerability, and without true connection along the hero's path, the mission is destined to fail. If you notice yourself pulling away because you're overwhelmed by the emotion your journey is eliciting, challenge yourself to lean in. Your painful emotions are fingers pointing at everything in need of healing in your life, and when you're brave enough to move through them, they pass like clouds in the sky and leave you feeling lighter. When you experience and express your feelings without judging others or indulging in self-pity, you move through your human challenges with the least resistance, and this strengthens your ability to fulfill your spiritual service. As long as you're not afraid to feel what you feel, you will keep your heart open and bless the world.

HERO'S PRACTICE:
Make Empathy a Practice

Pay attention to the people you meet today and every day. Make it a daily practice to consider that every single one of us is going through something hard right now. As you start to engage your senses while processing your own hard battles, find the empathy that allows you to open your heart to others. Find the feeling of Oneness that connects us all and let your heart blossom open. Try doing an Internet search for "Empathy: The Human Connection to Patient Care" to watch a beautiful heart-opening YouTube video posted by the Cleveland Clinic. Or go to TheAnatomyofaCalling.com to download the free Oneness meditation.

CHAPTER 2

LET LOVE FLOW

I certainly wasn't looking for my calling, but that's pretty typical of callings. You don't choose your calling. Your calling chooses you. The first whisperings of mine arrived when I was 7 years old, living in a black-and-white house with red shutters in Florida.

One day, my parents hired a chimney sweep. Along with all the soot, he discovered four baby squirrels so tiny that they had no fur, and their itty-bitty eyes were still fused shut. The chimney sweep handed the nest full of squirrels to my mother, who transferred them into a shoebox until we could figure out what to do with them.

When I laid eyes on those teensy, hairless infant squirrels, something within me bubbled forth. I felt a leaping joy, a jubilant sense of mission and purpose, a battle cry to action. After a family discussion, Mom, always the pragmatist, suggested that we return the squirrels to their nest and put them back in the fireplace, where the squirrel mommy might find them.

But I was having none of that. Instead, I grabbed Dad's black leather doctor bag and sorted through its contents—a stethoscope, a reflex hammer, an otoscope—hoping to find something that would help me rescue those squirrels. At a loss, I handed the doctor bag over to my physician father, deferring to his expertise. I promised Dad he wouldn't have to doctor the squirrels himself. I would help, if only he'd teach me what to do.

I have to credit Mom and Dad. If anyone rolled eyes at my suggestion, I never noticed. No one instilled in me the fear of rabies or lectured me about the natural order of things or told me I didn't have the chops to doctor those squirrels. Instead, Mom made a nest in the shoebox with polyester fiberfill and Dad carted us off to the veterinarian.

19

The jolly, red-cheeked vet with a hearty laugh taught me how to feed the tiny squirrels warmed dog's milk with an eyedropper, how to keep their body temperatures stable with a heat lamp, and how to wipe their little genitals with a warm cloth to help them pee. At night, I became a baby squirrel wet nurse, waking up with an alarm on a strict schedule to feed them. Each time the alarm blared, I remembered the veterinarian's warning that wild animal babies rarely survive in captivity without their mothers. I'd wake up with a knot in my stomach, worried that one of my babies might have died while I slept. Each time that I awoke to find their bluish pink, transparent-skinned bodies squirming in the polyester fiberfill, I said a prayer of thanks.

Then one night, the alarm beeped, and I rolled over, groggy and filled with an unexplainable dread. Sitting straight up in bed, I leaned over the aquarium, where we had transferred the squirrels from the shoebox. When I reached in, three of them squirmed in response to my touch, but one cold, lifeless baby didn't move. Sitting by myself at 2:00 a.m., I held the cold body of that baby squirrel and moaned. By the end of the week, all four babies had died. I grieved as only a child could mourn, with the deluge of unbridled emotion we learn to temper as we grow older. But as much as losing those squirrels broke my heart, I know now that my calling to be a healer was cemented.

After I buried those babies, word got out in my neighborhood that I'd tried to save a nest of abandoned baby squirrels. A while later, when a baby squirrel fell out of a tree and landed with a thud on the top of a family friend's minivan, she brought the injured squirrel to my doorstep. When I saw the little squirrel, curled in a ball with blood coming out of its mouth, something deep and instinctual was once again triggered within me.

This squirrel, whom I named Romulus based on a fleeting obsession with Roman mythology, was a bit older, with big black eyes that peered back at me and a thin coat of brown fur. When I went to feed him the eyedropper of warmed dog's milk, he held it with miniature paws and drank so fast he kept choking himself. When I saw him slurping away like that, my insides felt like tiny bubbles pop, pop, popping at the hope that this baby squirrel might actually survive, and I would get to keep him.

I repeated the same drill as before: nighttime feedings, heat lamps, and a warm cloth for tiny squirrel genitals. My mother got permission for me to bring him to school during the day in a large tote bag so I could feed him between lessons. Every day, he grew stronger and bigger. When I wasn't in school, Romulus lived on my shoulder, where he would bury underneath my hair and sleep. Between naps, he would tumble like a furry little gymnast. If I put him on the ground and walked away, he would run up to me, climb my pant leg, scurry up to my shoulder, and nestle under my hair.

My adoption of Romulus earned me the nickname bestowed upon me by the local newspaper, which published a photograph of Romulus on my shoulder with the caption "The Squirrel Girl" underneath. I proudly bore that title for more than a decade.

A few months later, Romulus started climbing the curtains, pouncing on strangers, and, eventually, biting everyone but me. Sitting me on her lap, Mom stroked my hair and explained that squirrels aren't meant to live in people's houses, that Romulus wanted to get out and find himself a sweet squirrel girlfriend. She explained that unlike dogs and cats, adolescent male squirrels possess wild longings for freedom, and I would have to release him to his natural squirrely habitat. Holding Romulus close to my heart, I wept with the realization that I would have to let him go.

We planned Romulus's release carefully. Standing at Harry P. Leu Gardens amidst flowering trees and brilliant blooms, I placed Romulus on a tree trunk and cried, "Go!" while shooing him away through blubbering tears. Turning my back to him, I ran away from the tree. Then I felt a tugging at the leg of my jeans. It was Romulus! He climbed up my leg, raced up my chest, and buried himself under my long hair. Part of me rejoiced. I had heard that if you love something, set it free. If it comes back to you, it's really yours. I had set Romulus free and he had come back to me. He wanted me more than he wanted squirrely girlfriends! But Mom and I had talked enough that I knew in my heart I would never get to keep Romulus, that he wasn't really mine to keep, that he belonged to the wild.

So I tried again. I kissed Romulus goodbye, placed him gently on a tree branch, and ran away as fast as I could while he chased after me. I tried to outrun him, but Romulus caught up with me twice. Finally, one of the garden caretakers agreed to hold him until I was out of sight. I watched the caretaker finally let him go onto the lawn from behind the tinted window of the family car. My heart hurt so much I considered never getting another pet. Ever.

But Mom also told me that hearts are meant to get broken, that every time we love someone, we grant them permission to break our hearts. And no matter how much it hurts, we must keep giving those we love permission to break our hearts. Each time I found and had to release a rescued squirrel, a part of me wanted to swear off rescuing them forever. Releasing them hurt too much. But one sight of another wounded or abandoned squirrel would call me to action again. The deep-seated love for the life of another and the overwhelming desire to be of service welled up within me, outweighing my dread of the loss I knew lay ahead.

———————————————

My Squirrel Girl skills came in handy during my medical training, because learning to be a doctor is filled with traumas to the heart. When I was a third-year resident, the trauma team paged labor and delivery to warn us that a woman who was 35 weeks pregnant had been stabbed by her boyfriend and was being Life-Flighted in. My high-risk obstetrics attending and I arrived in the ER, prepared to perform an emergency C-section.

When the helicopter arrived, the paramedics announced that they had just lost the woman's pulse. It was a code blue. The team inserted another large-bore IV and put a tube in her airway, attaching it to an Ambu bag. One medical student pumped away at her chest, while another compressed the Ambu bag to breathe for her. The high-risk OB doctor and I squeezed our way between the trauma surgeons to search for a fetal heartbeat with the ultrasound machine. The stab wound had punctured her skin, right over the middle of her uterus, baring a slash of yellow and crimson. On the ultrasound, the baby's heart was beating, but it was slower than it should have been, a worrisome sign.

The trauma surgeons started the advanced cardiac life support protocol. Little shock, big shock, shock shock shock. It was the mnemonic device we all learned in training: three shocks with the paddles, then epinephrine. Another shock, then lidocaine. Another shock, then bretylium, followed by more shocks. Between shocks, the medical students did CPR, pushing the chest in and out, pumping on the Ambu bag to breathe for the patient, while we all watched the EKG machine to see if the mother's heart responded.

It did. Sinus tachycardia, a fast heartbeat. *Hallelujah.* We were getting somewhere.

The anesthesiologist hung blood, and we raced the patient to the operating room, where the trauma surgeons made an incision all the way from her clavicle to her pubic bone. We found the baby's heart rate on ultrasound. It was dangerously low, at 60 beats per minute.

We yelled, "We're losing the baby" as we rushed to do a crash C-section, cutting into our Jane Doe's uterus to try to save the baby, which would hopefully relieve some of the pressure from the mother's circulatory system, making resuscitation efforts easier. The stab wound narrowly missed the fetus, hitting the placenta instead, which filled the uterine cavity with blood.

It took us only seconds to extract the baby. He was blue and limp when we delivered him. The NICU team converged on the infant as soon as we handed him off. The mother's weak and thready pulse didn't last long. They started the life support protocol again, but this time, her heartbeat wasn't responding.

We were losing her.

The trauma team sawed her sternum open and one started massaging her heart directly. By this time, our patient was starting to hemorrhage from her uterus. When people lose that much blood, they use up all of their clotting factors and start to bleed from every orifice as the result of a condition called DIC (disseminated intravascular coagulopathy). Jane Doe poured out blood as quickly as we pumped it into her veins. Struggling to visualize her anatomy, we performed a hysterectomy and packed her pelvis with gauze pads, hoping to slow the bleeding. While we worked in the pelvis, one of the surgeons continued open cardiac massage and another focused on repairing the severed blood vessels in her neck. She still had no pulse, no blood pressure, and no response on the EKG monitor. The flatlining monitor blared, and, thankfully, someone finally turned down the volume.

The doctor holding the patient's heart pumped away for what seemed like over an hour. Time gets distorted in cases like that. About 12 doctors surrounded her table, and everyone was soaked with blood. It was splashed on our masks, coated on our gowns, and splattered on our hair covers and shoe covers. Blood-soaked laparotomy sponges littered the floor, mixed in with instruments that had fallen off the table and empty plastic packets from sterile equipment that had been quickly opened.

The OR was silent as the lead surgeon pumped away.

The doctor across the table from him finally said, "Call it, George."

But the doctor kept pumping, and the team kept sewing and clamping.

"Call it," he said again, louder. "It's time."

George looked up and made eye contact with the other surgeons. They nodded their agreement, and he finally stopped.

"Time of death, 12:17 a.m."

George stepped back from the table, and no one moved. We stood there for a while, silent, with bowed heads. Then I saw George cry, and when he did, it was like he gave the rest of us permission to break down.

We all just stood there like that. We didn't take off our bloody gloves. Nobody ran off to the next emergency. The silence was reverent. In all of my years of training, I had never witnessed anything like this.

The NICU chief, also crying, looked up from the incubator and said, "We lost the baby."

Next thing I knew, all of us, the entire surgical team—doctors, medical students, nurses, and scrub techs—had congregated on the dirty floor of the OR hallway, leaning against the walls, holding one another. Our pagers were going off, but for those 10 minutes, we ignored our pagers. It was downright holy.

Someone finally helped us take off our bloody gowns and gloves and called the chaplain and the social worker; they both came to the OR in scrubs and took turns talking to each of us. Later, the trauma surgeon confessed that he had never seen the surgical team respond to a trauma case in this way. They lost patients every night. But by some miracle, the sacred had found its way into an operating room, and everyone present was touched by it.

The next day, the story had a tiny headline on a back page of the newspaper. Our patient wasn't rich or white. She was an unwed mother, an uninsured patient from the South Side of Chicago. Her death barely got a mention. In the brief snippet afforded her in the local news, our role was trivialized to one sentence. "Doctors tried to save her, but they failed."

Reflecting back on the woman who had been stabbed, contrasting it to my night of four dead babies, I had an epiphany. Both experiences were painful, but only the night of four dead babies resulted in lasting trauma. Why is that? When I felt like I had to deny my human emotions, I suffered from thoughts like "I'm a bad doctor because I feel too much" or "I'll never amount to anything if I don't buck up" or even "Babies aren't supposed to die." In retrospect, I can see how those thoughts created ongoing suffering long after the event was over.

When I allowed myself to feel my emotions in the company of others who were feeling theirs, such painful thoughts and beliefs didn't take root in my psyche, and healing was hastened. Because loss was given room to become holy and because I didn't feel alone, ongoing suffering was avoided.

Dealing with death never gets easy, and perhaps it's good that we never quite get numb to being on the front lines of life and death. Being a good doctor demands getting your heart broken over and over. We don't talk much about love in medicine. It's sort of a taboo subject. But medicine devoid of love is just technology, and you can't facilitate the healing of another living being with technology alone. To be a good doctor, you have to be a channel for Divine love flowing through you. But how do you do this when it hurts so much to love and lose?

The lesson comes in learning to love without attachment, to open your heart all the way and then let go of grasping at any specific outcome. My squirrels taught me at a young age that it's better to love and lose than to never love at all. In order to be a good healer, you have to give your patients permission to break your heart. The hardest thing you'll ever do is to keep your heart open, to avoid armoring up, to lean into the vulnerability of love, even when you know your heart is at risk.

That's what makes a good doctor, the willingness to open your heart, even when you know that your patient might break it. This is where medicine is at risk of losing its soul. When doctors attach to particular outcomes and things don't go as planned, we get our hearts broken time after time, and the grief isn't given room to become holy. The repetitive loss tempts you to build armor around your heart. When you have to survive such pain, it's natural to just shut down, to wall up your heart, to stop feeling so much. But when you armor up, you lose your ability to feel compassion. And when you've lost the ability to feel, you've lost the ability to heal. That's when you know they've broken you, when you've armored up and stopped granting others permission to break your heart, when love feels too risky and you block its natural flow. But as a hero, you *are* love. Love doesn't need to be defended. It's the strongest thing in the whole wide world.

It's not just doctors who are called to their hero's journey early in life, only to get their hearts broken. Many heroes can remember days of innocence, enthusiasm, and passion for a calling that bubbled up in childhood, only to have the youthful purity of that passion squashed by trauma. The Ordinary World is filled with heartbreak, giving heroes plenty of reasons to armor up: He left you for a woman half your age; she died so young, leaving you with three kids under the age of 5 to raise on your own; he overdosed; she cut you out of her life; he had sex with you right before ending your 20-year relationship; your dog, really more like your child, got cancer, and you had to hold her while she was injected with a drug that made her heart still.

As a hero, the hardest thing you'll ever do is keep your heart open in the face of serial heartbreak. Life is full of traumas to the heart. Pain is inevitable, because love hurts. Love feels risky. Love feels unsafe. Love isn't for the faint of heart. Love takes courage. Every day is a lesson in this most important life class. Every day is a choice to keep your heart open, even when you feel it slamming shut. Every day is an opportunity to practice using the tools you'll learn when you keep your heart open. You'll recognize that it's more important to be kind than to be right. You'll stop judging and start understanding why people do what they do. You'll become an expert in the fine art of forgiveness. You'll start practicing discernment so you can trust when it's safe to bare your soul. You'll know when it's time to love yourself enough to walk away—without a lick of judgment or emotional charge. You'll realize that love is a choice you make every day. You'll choose love—over and over and over—until it feels like breathing and you become the walking embodiment of love incarnate. You'll remember who you really are, and in that moment, you will discover the ultimate safety. You'll let down your guard. You'll radiate love. You'll magnetize love. You'll become One with love, and when you do, miracles will happen.

HERO'S GUIDEPOST:
Keep Your Heart Open—
No Matter What

Practice getting comfortable with the vulnerability of keeping your heart open, even in the face of serial heartbreak. This doesn't mean you can't set boundaries when someone is hurtful or abusive. It doesn't mean you don't have the right to protect yourself from a dangerous or hateful person. By all means, it doesn't mean you can't distance yourself or even end a relationship. You can keep yourself safe from people who have forgotten how to love by loving yourself enough to limit access without closing your heart.

Practice discernment without judgment. Let love be unconditional, but let access be completely conditional. If intimate access to your inner circle, your home, your time, your energy, or your bed lies on a scale from 0 to 10 (10=unlimited access, 0=none), set your dial appropriately. If necessary, dial down access with no judgment and a wide-open heart. The capacity to love with an open heart is every hero's stealth superpower. Closing off your heart is the easy way out. It's an understandable defense mechanism when you've been hurt. It makes sense to erect walls to protect yourself. Nobody would blame you. But you'll only succeed on your hero's journey if you keep the love flowing through you.

HERO'S PRACTICE:
Ask Yourself, "What Would Love Do?"

When you find yourself feeling righteous, angry, frustrated, resentful, judgmental, or overwhelmed with grief, you may feel tempted to close your heart, armor up, judge, and defend. It's only natural, so don't judge yourself. We're all prone to such moments of unconsciousness. But make it a practice to see how quickly you can open your heart again. When you notice your heart closing off, shut your eyes and take a quiet moment to contemplate this question: What would love do?

Sometimes love forgives what feels unforgivable. Sometimes love questions everything from a place of curiosity and humility. Sometimes love sets boundaries. Sometimes love prays for help. Sometimes love opens the heart even further than you ever thought possible. Sometimes love confesses an unspeakable truth. Sometimes love leaves you bare and vulnerable, a turtle without a shell in a briar patch. Sometimes love can be a scalpel, slicing through delusion. Sometimes love leaves. Make this question your meditation. Ask yourself multiple times throughout the day. Become One with love and let it live through you.

CHAPTER 3

Trust Yourself

When the pregnancy test came back positive, I could barely breathe.

Ohmygodohmygodohmygod.

Seven years had passed since my night of four dead babies, and I had become a full-fledged board-certified OB/GYN physician in a busy hospital in California. After delivering thousands of other women's babies, my boyfriend, Matt, and I decided to finally have a baby of our own, so when I was 35 years old, we got married and planned to start a family. I had stopped my birth control pills just before our wedding, expecting it might take at least a year to get pregnant, given my age and the fact that I had been manipulating my period with birth control pills for 10 years so I wouldn't menstruate.

But 2 weeks after our wedding day, I missed my period. I couldn't believe I was pregnant already.

I didn't feel ready to be a mother.

I started hyperventilating when I saw the pregnancy test results.

Who was I to ever be a mother? I was too selfish, too narcissistic, too impatient, too ambitious, not maternal enough. I didn't even know how to talk to kids, much less raise one. I was certain I would never be able to pull off being a mother. I mean, come on. No kid was ever going to buy that I was a mother. Kids can *tell*. They can smell fear like animals. If I became a mother, I was certain my own child would see right through me. I'd screw everything up, and the poor bastard would grow up and need therapy. What if I raised a psycho killer?

I tried to make myself breathe.

Since I was on call for the weekend, Matt had gone out of town. I called his cell from the hospital.

"What's wrong, sweetie?" he asked. "Is it your dad?"

I started to cry. "Yes," I lied, "it's Dad."

Right after our wedding, Dad had been diagnosed with prostate cancer. They caught it early, and his doctors reassured us that everything would be just fine, but Dad had gone under the knife in Ohio earlier that morning.

My lie was partly true. The surgery hadn't gone as planned. The tumor was bigger than they expected, and Dad lost a dangerous amount of blood and needed a transfusion. It was touch and go for a while, but he was doing better after getting the blood. I wished I had been able to be with him during the surgery, but I had been scheduled to be on call months in advance, and I couldn't find someone to switch calls with me on such short notice. Somebody had to carry the pager.

Matt heard me sniffle and asked, "Are you crying?"

I said I was, and Matt said, "I'm coming right home."

I got slammed with patients at the hospital that night. After delivering nine babies and doing two emergency surgeries, I nearly crawled through the front door the following morning. Matt was there, waiting to embrace me. That's when I showed him my pregnancy test. He looked as shell-shocked as I felt.

Six months later, I was 24 weeks pregnant with a little girl when the phone rang. I'll never forget the moment. It was one of those moments where every detail of the Ordinary World imprints upon your memory. Just like the day I drove to the hospital to do an early-morning surgery and heard the radio DJ say, "There it goes! The second tower, crumbling to the ground. Both towers of the World Trade Center are gone. Oh, my God. We're under attack."

When I picked up the phone, I was sitting on a beige Italian sofa in my house in San Diego, wrapped under a red merino wool blanket. The air had the first coolness of fall, and my 16-year-old dog Ariel was curled up next to me, resting her head on my belly. I was drinking a steaming cup of Hana Nirvana herbal tea, trying to ignore my aching back by reading *People* magazine.

When I answered the phone, Mom was sobbing. She couldn't speak. She just blubbered and stuttered while I felt my blood pressure rise and my heart race. Finally, taking breaths between each word, Mom told me the news.

"Daddy . . . has . . . a . . . brain . . . tumor."

Mom had called me earlier in the day with concerning news about Dad. They had been at our family vacation home in the North Georgia mountains when Dad started making up nonsense words.

I asked her to put Dad on the phone, and when I asked if he was okay, Dad said Mom was taking him to the "travel one llama center."

What?

Searching my memory banks for my neurology rotation, I remembered Wernicke's aphasia, a type of disordered speech that happens when the brain is damaged, usually from a stroke. People with Wernicke's aphasia can understand and interpret language, but they speak in disorganized or invented words.

Dad said it again, "Travel one llama center."

Trying to interpret, I said, "Dad, do you need to go to a Level I Trauma Center?"

That was it. He put Mom back on the phone. Although Dad had multiple sclerosis, MS shouldn't cause Wernicke's aphasia. I suspected he was having a stroke. I told Mom to get him to a good hospital in Atlanta stat.

When the emergency room doctor ordered a CT scan, Dad—the radiologist—read it himself. He was not having a stroke. Instead, he had an enormous brain tumor in his temporal lobe.

I sprang into doctor mode. My father had a brain tumor. But from what? He had recovered well from his prostate cancer surgery, and a follow-up PSA (prostate-specific antigen) test was normal, indicating that he appeared to be cured. Had Dad's cancer come back so quickly? But that didn't make any sense. Prostate cancer doesn't usually metastasize to the brain. Was this a new, unrelated tumor? I raced through a differential diagnosis, a plan for next steps, an assessment of the risk.

It wasn't until hours later that I got out of doctor mode and absorbed that this was *my* father. I broke down in Matt's arms, with Ariel snuggled up to me and my baby doing somersaults inside.

After a bunch of tests, they discovered that he also had tumors in his liver and studded throughout his body. They did a liver biopsy to determine the cell type, and a couple weeks later, the results of Dad's biopsy came in.

I was expecting the call this time.

When I picked up the phone, Dad said, "Hi, honey." There was something in his voice. I steeled myself.

Dad said, "I have metastatic melanoma."

Just like that. Blah blah blah. *I have metastatic melanoma.* I couldn't speak.

Metastatic melanoma is about as bad as it gets. Like pancreatic cancer, it's swift, merciless, and nearly always a death sentence. Ironically, Dad did his medical school term paper on metastatic melanoma, so like me, he knew that almost no one survived it.

Before we hung up, Dad said, "I love you, honey."

I said, "I love you, too."

Dad said, "I love how we always say that."

We always did. When I'd call home from college, Mom and I would talk, but Dad would be on the line, just listening until it was time to say "I love you" at the end.

Everyone loved Dad. He was the ham-radio-operating, Cessna-flying, camp-counseling, Spanish-speaking white guy who had grown up in Cuba to missionary parents. Because Dad was diagnosed with multiple sclerosis in his thirties, he spent most of his adult life first walking with a cane and then converting to an electric wheelchair. But Dad wasn't a complainer. He accepted his disability without anger or resistance, and his cheerful attitude in the face of his illness inspired many.

Memories of my dad preoccupied me as I started a 36-hour call shift at the hospital. I saw that there were already four women in labor, and I knew it was going to be a long night. My pager started beeping from the minute I turned it on.

"Hi, Dr. Rankin. It's Sadie in triage. We've got a patient here, Marisol. She's a woman in her midthirties at 39 weeks with gestational diabetes. She's ruptured, not contracting. Baby looks good. Blood sugar is 103."

"Okay. Send her up," I said, sighing.

"Labor and delivery is packed. They don't have any rooms. Is it okay if we keep her down here for a while?" Sadie asked.

"Sure," I agreed. "No problem."

Sadie called me back about 20 minutes later. "Can you come down here? We're having a hard time getting the baby to stay on the monitor. Heart rate is in the 120s, but we just can't get a steady tracing. I've got the scanner all ready for you."

I took the stairs to the second floor and introduced myself to Marisol while Sadie translated.

Looking at the monitor, I saw the fetal heart tracing jump around the paper. Some parts traced for 10 minutes at a time and the heartbeat looked normal, but other parts didn't trace at all. Looking at Marisol, I noticed that the baby's heart monitor was placed higher up on her abdomen than usual.

Sadie saw me looking. "Baby's still high," she said. "Must not have dropped yet." This wasn't uncommon when the water bag broke and the mother wasn't in labor yet.

"Are we sure the baby's not breech?" I asked. I held the fetal monitor and slid it across her abdomen, hunting for a strong heartbeat. But I couldn't find it. This was odd. Usually, finding the baby's heartbeat at full term was easy.

I slid the fetal monitor up under Marisol's breasts, and suddenly, I heard it. "Beep beep beep beep." Phew. The monitor traced smoothly, just like it had earlier.

But something wasn't quite right. The baby's heartbeat was slower than usual, not by much but a little bit. On a hunch, I grabbed Marisol's wrist and checked her pulse. Uh oh.

"Sadie," I took a long breath. "This is Marisol's heartbeat, not the baby's."

Usually, it's easy to tell the difference between the mother's heart rate and the baby's. The mother's heart rate will be in the seventies or eighties and the baby's will be between 120 and 160. But Marisol's heartbeat was 110, close to what you might expect for the baby. I got that stomach-in-my-throat, roller-coaster feeling. Where was the baby's heartbeat?

My own heart started to pound. Without saying a word, I grabbed the ultrasound machine and placed the probe on Marisol's pregnant abdomen. I looked at the fetus. It was head first, not breech. And then I saw it. The four-chambered heart view. The heart was just lying there, dead still.

Sadie saw it, too, and said, "Oh, no."

The father of the baby said, "Oh no, por que? Baby no good?"

Back when I was a resident, I'd usually get emotional and cry when I told a woman her baby had died. But after hundreds of experiences giving would-be parents the tragic news about miscarriages, congenital anomalies, and stillbirths, I had learned to stuff my own feelings so I could deliver bad news without tears.

I looked at the father of the baby as Sadie translated. "I'm having trouble seeing your baby's heartbeat. I'm looking at the heart on the ultrasound, and it's not moving. I'm afraid that the baby has died. I'm so sorry."

The father said, "Baby heart okay. Boom boom. I hear."

"No, I don't think so," I said. "I think the monitor was listening to Marisol's own heartbeat."

"No," he said. "Baby heart. Boom. Boom. Boom." He pointed to the monitor. "I hear it."

I looked at Marisol, who didn't appear to understand what I was trying to explain. "When did you last feel the baby move?"

"Tuesday," she said. That was 6 days earlier.

In the exam room next to us, I caught a glimpse of one of the high-risk obstetricians. I asked him if he would consult on the patient and repeat my ultrasound. He came right over and quickly confirmed the fetal death. I relayed the news to the parents and moved on.

As the years went by, I felt increasingly uneasy with the woman I had become. *San Diego Magazine* named me one of its top doctors, and patients sent me love letters every day. Yes, I had excellent surgical skills and kept up to date on all the latest medical literature. I was reputed to have an excellent bedside manner.

But when I thought back to the compassionate, authentic Squirrel Girl, it felt so hard to reconnect with her. What had become of me? I had felt so sure about my calling to be a healer back when I was a child. But as I stood there with swollen pregnancy ankles of my own, giving orders to induce Marisol's labor so she could deliver her dead baby, I felt so out of touch with my calling that I questioned whether I had gotten it all wrong. Maybe I was supposed to be a teacher or a lawyer. I could barely remember why I ever signed up to do this. Why couldn't I have gotten a nine-to-five desk job that might give me better maternity leave and allow me to sleep in on weekends? I fantasized about walking out of the hospital, getting in my convertible, and driving across the border into Mexico. But instead, I spent that night delivering Marisol's baby, along with seven more.

The next morning, jittery with caffeine and weak from low blood sugar, sleep deprivation, and grief over the news about my father, I walked across the street from the hospital to my office, where I was scheduled to see patients all day.

"Dr. Rankin, wait," said my first patient Alexis, just as I finished up her annual exam and was about to leave the room to see my next patient. "Can I just show you my calendar before you go?" From her oversize bag, she pulled out an Anne Geddes calendar filled with photos of babies curled up inside giant flowers.

I sighed loud enough so she could hear. I was already an hour behind schedule. But I nodded.

"See these dates?" She pointed to days marked in red ink. "These are when I get my period." Then she pointed to the days marked with black circles.

"See these? My boyfriend started putting those on there. Those are the days I picked fights with him. He's been telling me I have PMS for ages, but I didn't believe him until he showed me 3 months' worth of this."

It was the classic PMS calendar.

"Dr. Rankin, you have to help me. I'm afraid my boyfriend is going to break up with me if I don't take care of this. I'm such a bitch to him sometimes. I can't go on like this."

With one hand on the door, I looked at my watch. I knew what Alexis needed. If I were a good doctor, I'd sit down with her for another 30 minutes so I could explain how diet and exercise could help her avoid PMS triggers. I'd ask her whether her body was trying to communicate something to her through her PMS symptoms. Was she happy in her relationship with this boyfriend? Was she feeling fulfilled at work? How was she dealing with the loss of her mother, who had died a year earlier?

If I were a good doctor, I would have taken the time to explain the risks and benefits of taking birth control pills versus antidepressants. I would have pulled out handouts and answered any questions she might have had. But instead, glancing at the clock, I pulled out my prescription pad and handed her a script while trying to ignore the sick feeling in my stomach.

In the beginning, when I was fresh out of residency, I was expected to see 25 patients per day, and because I was given so little time to spend with my patients, I often ended up way behind schedule. I couldn't bear to skip over what I knew was good medicine, so I wound up frustrating the nurses and my patients when I took too long and kept people waiting. By the time I had been practicing for 8 years, I was expected to see 40 patients a day. Many of them were double-booked in 15-minute slots, which meant that I only had 7½ minutes with each patient. Every visit was a rush job as I tried to pack in connecting with the patient, performing a physical exam as well as any procedures, ordering lab tests, filling out any medical records paperwork, writing prescriptions, educating, and answering questions. I tried to stuff all these important tasks into increasingly brief windows of time. Yet I felt like I was in a lose-lose situation. If I kept my patients waiting too long, they got understandably angry and frustrated. If I rushed through everything in order to stay on time, patients felt slighted.

I wound up feeling helpless, much like the rats in the "learned helplessness" study by Madelon Visintainer, PhD. In this study, rats were injected with a cancer known to reliably kill them 50 percent of the time if they were left alone. These rats were broken into three groups. The first group was given a mild escapable shock, which the rats could learn to avoid. The second group was given a mild inescapable shock, which they couldn't avoid. The third group was not shocked at all. The only difference between the three groups of rats was their psychological experiences based on the presence or absence of non-life-threatening shocks. Curiously, the rats given escapable shocks had the best outcomes—a 70 percent survival rate, compared to 27 percent survival in the rats that learned helplessness and an expected 50 percent survival in the unshocked rats.[1] This study demonstrated not only the higher death risk of an attitude of helplessness but also a survival advantage, even over those who were never shocked, for those who learn to respond to life's shocks with empowerment.

After 12 years of medical education and 8 years of medical practice, I had become like a listless, helpless, sick rat, at the mercy of shock after shock. Because I was still stuck in my victim story, believing I had no control over a medical system that had betrayed me, I didn't realize that the shocks to my system were actually escapable. No one was holding a gun to my head, making me go to work every day. I was choosing to participate in a system that asked me to violate my ethics, because I was afraid to threaten my security, question the system, and take inspired action. Like so many heroes stuck in the Ordinary World, I had no idea how much power I actually had.

Because I felt helpless, at the mercy of the system, my job satisfaction nearly evaporated. Connecting intimately with my patients was the most satisfying part of my job. As doctors, we're blessed to have a front-row seat on life. I had the privilege of being the first person a new baby looks at.

---

1 Visintainer, M. A., J. R. Volpicelli, and M. Seligman, "Tumor Rejection in Rats after Inescapable and Escapable Shock," *Science* 216, no. 4544 (April 1982): 437–39.

Patients trusted me with their secrets and vulnerabilities. You have to be worthy of such a VIP seat, and I didn't feel worthy anymore. Every day, I felt like I was selling my soul for a paycheck rather than fulfilling my calling to be a healer. Every night, as I fell asleep, I found myself burdened with a heavy question. "Is this as good as it gets?"

One letter from my patient Fiona changed everything.

I received the letter in my box at the office after a long night of delivering babies, when I had almost no reserves left. In her letter, Fiona explained that after she and her husband fought for the gazillionth time about the fact that they hadn't had sex in over a year, he threatened to leave her if she didn't go see a gynecologist to figure out what was wrong. Because my schedule was so packed, she waited 2 months to see me, praying I might have some magical solution that would save her marriage. I had taken care of her a few years back, and her recollection of me was that I was approachable, tender, funny, compassionate, and honest. She felt she could trust me.

In her letter, Fiona explained that on the morning of her appointment, she showered, trimmed her pubic hair, and spritzed on her favorite perfume. She donned her laciest lingerie and wore her favorite dress. When she arrived at my office, she stood in line behind four other people signing in at the front desk and took her seat with the other 20 women in the waiting room. She waited for over an hour, and long past her appointment time, my medical assistant finally put her in a chilly room, where she was ordered to undress and left alone wearing nothing more than a paper gown for 20 minutes. By that time, feeling cold and uncomfortably vulnerable, she started to cry.

Apparently, as she described in her letter, I didn't acknowledge the tears or even apologize for the wait when I finally came in. Fiona wrote that I looked tired. My hair was up in a ponytail, my eyes were puffy and weary, and I wasn't wearing any makeup. I wore my white coat over my wrinkled green surgical scrubs, stretched over my pregnant belly.

She wrote that I made small talk with her as I filled out some papers and got ready to perform her annual exam, but when I asked her if she was having any problems, Fiona hesitated. I stood with my back to her, not making eye contact. Because I was so distracted, she didn't feel safe sharing with me the uncomfortable story of her failing sex life. So she decided to keep her mouth shut. I performed her Pap smear, refilled her prescriptions, and left her alone in the room, kicking herself.

When Fiona got home, she took off her finest dress and put away her lacy lingerie. It took her months to get brave enough to make an appointment with another doctor, but she had found a good one, who didn't accept managed care insurance plans and no longer practiced obstetrics, so the doctor had been able to spend a whole hour with her. Her doctor was helping her improve her hormone balance and getting her off antidepressants, and she and her husband were in therapy together.

She wrote that she didn't intend to judge me or shame me. She was raised to believe that you treat doctors with respect and don't question their advice or their behavior. But she was so hurt by the encounter, so disappointed in my actions, that she felt like she wanted me to know, just in case it helped other patients. She wished me well and congratulated me on my pregnancy and expressed compassion for how busy she knew I was. She signed it, "I believe you're still in there. Love, Fiona."

I wept when I read Fiona's letter. The worst part was that I didn't even remember the encounter, and I couldn't conjure up an image of her face. Fiona was just another faceless, nameless number on the medical assembly line of my practice.

What was happening to me? How had I let myself get so busy that I failed to notice that a patient of mine had been crying? I was called to medicine to be a healer. I was the Squirrel Girl, after all. But what kind of healer leaves a crying, naked woman with a health concern feeling the way Fiona did? When had I stopped caring?

When I called Fiona at home to apologize after reading her letter, she thanked me for the phone call. She told me not to worry or feel badly. I felt unspeakably ashamed.

When I was done with work, still stinging from Fiona's letter and the grueling night shift I had just finished, I stopped by the grocery store. The only thing that was keeping me from my well-deserved bed was a pimply teenager who couldn't seem to get my groceries scanned. I stood there for what felt like an hour, spent, hungry, and disappointed in myself. The kid's face was flushed and his brow was starting to sweat, and I could see him looking helplessly at the other clerks, who were all scanning and swiping with ease.

Then I heard myself say something I still can't believe came out of me.

"If I did my job the way you did your job, there would be dead people everywhere."

Really. I actually said that.

On my way home from the grocery store, a squirrel darted out in front of my car, and I felt my car thump over it. I thought about stopping, checking on the squirrel to see if there was any way I could save it. But I just kept driving, anesthetized and depleted, without even looking back in my rearview mirror.

I couldn't sleep that night, in spite of my exhaustion. I kept tossing from side to side like a tuna, my back hurting, feeling my baby kick my ribs. I thought about my father's cancer. I thought about letting down Fiona and being mean to that poor kid. And the squirrel. *The squirrel.* Something felt squashed in my chest, like a vice was clenching my heart. Tears would have felt welcome. They would have reminded me I was still alive. But they never came. I felt an uprising of pain, but like a shaken Coke bottle with the top still on, the pain had nowhere to go.

It was the first time I had ever thought about suicide.

Just when I started thinking about how I would prefer to die if I killed myself, my baby kicked me, and I remembered that if I killed myself, I'd be killing my little girl, too.

Oh, my God. I couldn't even manage to kill myself.

I felt a tornado of fury funnel up in me. I looked around for something to break—a plate or a vase maybe. But just as I was spinning in circles, finding nothing, I heard a voice.

A gentle, loving whisper said, "Darling, they're about to break you. You have to quit your job."

The moments that followed bathed me with what I can only describe as a flood of unconditional love unlike anything I had ever experienced, a waterfall of grace rushing over me and through me, filling my heart and body and mind with hope and peace. I felt my whole nervous system relax. My mind became silent and I felt myself pop outside of my body until I was no longer Lissa; I was the burst-open Consciousness witnessing Lissa in her pain with unbridled love, compassion, and tenderness. In that moment, the very idea that life could be painful felt almost absurd. Looking down on myself, I saw myself laughing out loud like a crazy person. Perhaps this is what it looked like to lose your mind, but if that's what it felt like to become insane, I didn't have any desire to return to the pain of sanity. I felt weightless, untethered, as if I could be everywhere at once and also nowhere at all, at home in the vast expanse of nothingness that felt, instead of empty, uncommonly full. The idea of suicide suddenly felt ludicrous.

I felt as if I was ballooning all the way out of my body, growing bigger than the bed my body was still lying on, expanding bigger than the bedroom, bigger than the house, bigger than even San Diego itself, as if I was exploding into the atmosphere and beyond, becoming starlight itself, pure weightless, timeless joy and aliveness, glancing back at the earth with unspeakable awe.

Wow. This is awesome—

But then, as quickly as I had popped into this ecstatic state of Consciousness, I flipped out of it. Jolted back into my body, I felt accosted by another voice, a cruel, judging voice that said, "What are you talking about? You can't quit your job! You're about to have a baby. You have a mortgage. Plus, you spent 12 years sacrificing everything so you could be a doctor. You'd be stupid and reckless if you left your job. And what would everybody think? Doctors don't just quit their jobs, especially when they have medical school debt and responsibilities. Not to mention that your dying father would be so disappointed in you. Don't be silly. You have a great job. You have a terrific husband. You live in a gorgeous house. You should suck it up and be grateful for what you have. Now go back to sleep and stop being an idiot."

But the tender, nurturing voice was insistent. "You don't have to do it now, sweetheart. But the time is coming for you to quit your job, so get ready. And don't worry. Everything will be okay, and you will not be alone."

The mean voice piped up, "Don't listen to that nonsense!"

The loving voice said, "Your father is a 59-year-old doctor who will die in 3 months. That could be you. If you found out you only had 3 months to live, would you be living the life you're living now?"

My answer was a resounding, "Hell, no!"

But how could I quit my job? Matt wasn't working outside the house, and I had promised to pay the bills for both of us. I'd have to sell my house. And how could I possibly afford the $120,000 malpractice tail I'd have to pay for the privilege of quitting my job? How would we afford a place in San Diego? We'd have to move. Quitting my job would require a total life overhaul. It was too much to even consider.

The gentle voice said, "You don't have to do anything yet. Just make peace with the truth." I could feel the warmth of that voice surrounding me like a hug. My pulse slowed down. My breathing deepened. I felt invisible arms holding me as I curled up in bed, and the next thing I remember, the sun was rising over San Diego Bay the next morning.

I didn't feel the least bit heroic that night. I was still a hero mired in my victim story in the Ordinary World. But what I didn't know at the time was that my hero's journey began that night with the appearance of the loving, gentle voice speaking the truth I had been unwilling to admit to myself. I had no idea what I was being called to do. I thought medicine was my calling, but my gut instincts, the chronic sick feeling in my stomach, my health issues, Fiona's letter—they all felt like signs from the Universe that something wasn't right. I was being called to do something else, but when I picked up that jangling phone, the message wasn't clear at all.

Maybe you're still slogging through the Ordinary World like I was, reassuring yourself that things could be so much worse and that you should just feel grateful for what you have. You may still be blind to even the possibility that your life could be so much more. You may not realize how you'll one day look back at this time in your life and recognize how relatively dysfunctional, dull, and joy-deficient your Ordinary World was compared to how you'll feel when you find the courage to say yes to your hero's journey. But one day, when you reflect back, you'll understand that it was all a necessary and natural part of the journey, just like it is for every hero. You'll understand that it was all happening in perfect timing and that you were exactly where you were supposed to be until the moment when you were ready to pick up the phone.

If you've heard a voice warning you that change is afoot, you probably can't see what lies ahead yet, but you have a strong sense that there's something more and that the time for you to embark upon your new adventure is coming soon. This is the first step of your hero's journey. The phone rings, but there's no Charlie on the other end of the phone detailing the mission his angels will fulfill. You may hear a voice like I did—or you may get your first message as a vision, a dream, an inner knowing, or a gut feeling—that tells you only your first step, and you may not like what that message has to say. But the message touches your heart with its tenderness and compassion, as if you are a beloved child of the Universe. You *just know* that this message is here to help. Even though the message sounds crazy, you sense you can trust it. This message, which comes from what I call your "Inner Pilot

Light," is delivered by that ever-radiant, gentle, loving, 100 percent authentic spark that lies at your core. I liken it to the pilot light on a stove, the steadfast flame within that may grow dim but never goes out. Call it your essential self, your Divine spark, your Christ consciousness, your Buddha nature, your higher self, your soul, your wise self, your intuition, or your inner healer. The minute sperm met egg (and maybe even before then), this part of you ignited, and it's been glowing ever since. Though it might get shrouded by trauma, limiting beliefs, depression, anxiety, or a doubting intellectual mind, this inner wisdom never leaves you; it is always quietly but steadfastly holding you with unconditional acceptance, no matter how dark life gets.

Your Inner Pilot Light is the essence of who you really are, underneath who your parents taught you to be or how society influenced you. It's the part that may yearn to wear purple peasant skirts, dance to Lady Gaga, ignore the phone when it's judgmental Uncle George, laugh in the middle of church, and burp loudly at the Junior League luncheon. Your Inner Pilot Light isn't always well behaved, because this is the essential part of you that lies deeper than your socialized self. It may be a bit of a wild stallion, hard to tame and difficult to control, or it may be calm, quiet, and deeply contemplative. But regardless of its unique temperament, your Inner Pilot Light always radiates pure Divine love, not only for others but also for the rest of you. This is not icky-sticky love, the kind that asks you to sacrifice yourself in order to gain acceptance or avoid rejection. It's a pure love, bathing you in kindness and helping you reconnect to the strength and softness of the heart.

When you first start hearing this voice, you may worry that your Inner Pilot Light will get you in trouble. After all, if you listen to it, you might wind up doing something crazy, like leaving that job that asks you to betray your integrity. Or you may wind up loving yourself so much that, without a lick of judgment, you leave your unfaithful husband. Your Inner Pilot Light might instruct you to dance on bar tops, play the accordion, write a tell-all memoir, or liquidate your retirement account so you can renovate a villa in the south of France. You may find yourself feeding orphans in Africa or becoming a voice for the voiceless or lobbying to save the rainforests in Ecuador. You might even risk everything for a love that makes no sense to anyone, including yourself.

Your fear voices are likely to argue with the voice of this call to adventure, the one that whispers crazy things like "I have to quit my job" or "I have to leave my marriage" or "I have to go to art school" or "I have to buy this horse ranch" or "I have to join the circus" or "I have to sell all my belongings, move to India, and live in an ashram." The fear voice can be vicious. It can be so loud you barely hear the other voice, the one that feels like truth. But somehow, when you dig down deep and quiet the voice of your fear, you'll feel an inner rightness that can't be denied, even if it sounds crazy to your mind. You may worry that your Inner Pilot Light can't be trusted, that listening to your Inner Pilot Light will be unsafe. But you'd be sorely mistaken, because this is where your ultimate safety lies.

I wasn't sure I could trust that little voice the night it told me I would have to leave my job as a doctor. I would have thought it was the voice of my inner crazy person had it not been accompanied by an experience of such profound infinite love. The voice sounded insane to my mind, yet it rang with the unmistakable truth you will learn to recognize when you start listening to this inner voice. You might hear a similar voice right now, a quiet loving voice that says, "You know what you need to do." You might deny it at first, and that's okay. You may not yet understand what the voice is saying. But trust me, you will know what you must do when the time is right. Until then, just focus on making peace with the truth of what that voice is saying. Just be with whatever emotions come up when you think about acting on that crazy thought. There's no need to rush the process. As bestselling author and medical school professor Rachel Naomi Remen, MD, says, "You can't force a rosebud to blossom by hitting it with a hammer." The first step is simply to be with what is true for you—without judgment.

When you're trying to decide whether to pick up the phone when it rings, Martha Beck suggests asking yourself this question: Does it feel like "shackles on" or "shackles off"? A true calling will always smack of freedom.

So I ask you. Is your phone ringing? Does it feel like freedom? Are you ready to pick up yet?

HERO'S GUIDEPOST:
Let Your Inner Pilot Light
Guide Your Decisions

Inside your mind, you'll hear many voices. The voice of your ego—your Small Self—comes in many disguises. I call it the "Small Self" because it's like a child. It *is* small and can't be trusted to make healthy, discerning, spiritually mature decisions, but it's not something that needs your judgment; it needs your compassion. Your Small Self is the voice that starts shouting when fear is running the show, and it makes it hard to interpret the guidance of your Inner Pilot Light, which tends to whisper. Your Small Self doesn't need to be criticized or denied. It needs your Inner Pilot Light to love and care for it, like an adult would tend and nurture a young, scared child. Any unhealed traumas from your past feed your Small Self, and fear causes this loud, frightened part of your psyche to imagine the worst. As a result, your Small Self tends to chatter away 24/7, filling your mind with anxiety, criticism, judgment, and limiting beliefs. This inner child doesn't trust that you—the adult, the Inner Pilot Light—are taking care of it, protecting it from harm.

There's nothing wrong with this part of you; it's simply a hurt, young, scared, overprotective part of you that can't be trusted to make your decisions. The good news is that your Inner Pilot Light is always available to reparent your Small Self by loving, comforting, and reassuring it. Once you know that both voices exist, you can notice the two of them hashing it out in your mind. Just pay attention and witness both. If you can avoid merging with the identity of your Small Self, you can allow your Inner Pilot Light to take the wheel, and this tends to ramp up your courage.

HERO'S PRACTICE:

Be the Witness

To cultivate a relationship with your Inner Pilot Light, practice becoming the Consciousness that witnesses the dialogues in your mind. Try this exercise the next time your Small Self has a meltdown.

1. When you find your Small Self chattering away with stories of fear, judgment, criticism, anger, frustration, resentment, grief, or shame, make it a practice to become the Consciousness that witnesses the hurt, scared, sad, or angry aspect of your Small Self.

2. If you start to feel an emotional disturbance, name the feeling and notice it. Give your Small Self permission to feel what it feels. Imagine angel wings of love wrapping around this small, scared child within you. Reassure this inner child that you are an adult now and will take

care of it. (Don't deny what your Small Self feels! The "spiritual bypass" doesn't work, so feel what you feel without judging yourself.)

3. Recognize that although your emotions are real and valid, *you are not what you feel*. It's easy to mistakenly identify with those emotions as *who you are*. But what if instead of *being* the emotion, you are simply the soul who is *with* that emotion? What if, instead of saying "I am sad," you shift to "I am *with* sad"? What if, instead of being a sad person, you are the expanse of Consciousness witnessing the part of you that feels sad? Step back and witness the part of you that is disturbed by this feeling. You are not this feeling. You are the soul who is witnessing this feeling. Close your eyes and give yourself as much time as you need to fully witness the emotional disturbance of your Small Self. Let your Inner Pilot Light love, comfort, and hold the small child within you that is suffering.

4. If you need additional help, download the Inner Child Meditation at TheAnatomyofaCalling.com.

CHAPTER 4

THE PERFECT STORM

A few weeks later, our home phone rang late at night. I panicked. Dad!

He was talking so fast I could barely understand him. His speech had been fine since the doctors started him on steroids to reduce the inflammation from the tumor, but that night he was so excited I couldn't follow him. I told him to slow down, and he took a breath and started over.

Dad woke up at 2:23 a.m. and saw the clock radio shining bluish light on his eye medication for his glaucoma. And then it hit him. What a fool he had been for ordering 4 months' worth of this ridiculously expensive eye medication when he knew he wouldn't live long enough to use it all. He felt stupid and foolish and realized with a punch in the gut that his time had come. Game over.

Then he heard a voice. Not a voice from within, like the one I'd heard, but a voice in the room, loud and comforting. The voice said, "David, you are healed."

Dad told me, "The thing is, Lissa, I just know it's true. I'm healed." His voice cracked like a teenage boy.

I so wanted to believe in Dad's miracle. Who's to say an angel couldn't visit my dying father when he was having a dark night of the soul? And who am I to say it would be impossible for my father to be healed from metastatic melanoma?

But the doctors had been so certain. His cancer was incurable. He could try whole-brain radiation to reduce the swelling. It might buy him a couple of months. But that wouldn't even touch the tumors in his liver or belly.

I wanted to believe Dad. I wanted to sigh with relief that God had handpicked Dad to be the one and only patient I'd ever met who would survive metastatic melanoma. But I just didn't believe it. So I faked it.

Before we hung up, Dad said, "I love you, honey."

I said, "I love you, too."

And then, as he so often did, he said, "I love the way we say goodbye."

After that, Dad told his story to anyone who would listen—people at church and on his ham radios, doctors and patients at the hospital. His face lit up when he repeated the story, and people mostly nodded and smiled in a gently condescending sort of way, as if listening to a child who's talking about his imaginary horse Buffalo who can fly, speak French, and grant magic wishes.

A few weeks later, Dad finished his whole-brain radiation and went in for his postradiation MRI. The tumor had doubled in size.

Dad didn't break down in tears. He didn't get angry. He didn't curse whoever lied to him when he was told that he was healed. He simply never mentioned that voice again.

It was around this time that I asked Dad if he was scared of dying.

Dad said, "I'm not scared. I'm joyful."

Dad promised me he'd wait until my baby was born so he could meet his granddaughter and make sure I was okay. We made arrangements to get Dad to California for the C-section birth. We planned to perform an amniocentesis to make sure my baby's lungs were mature, and we scheduled the C-section for 2 weeks before my due date.

I worked right up until the day before my C-section, and when that day arrived, I showed up at my hospital as a patient for the first time. When my doctor said, "Incision," I felt a rush of terror, realizing that I was about to get cut open for the first time in my life. I could see it all in my mind's eye, all the details of what would happen to me when my doctor sliced my skin with the scalpel, but the actual surgery was a fuzzy blur. Before I knew it, I was a mother.

At first, when I looked at my own child for the first time, she looked like any one of the thousands of pink-cheeked, sweet-faced, blue-and-pink-striped-hat-wearing infants that have been coming and going in my life since medical school. Siena could have been anybody's baby, and I felt awkward and shy, as if I *should* know her but didn't, like I was waking up, naked in my bed, next to some drunken one-night stand. But then I looked closer and noticed the double folds under her eyes, the expansive forehead, the tiny little ears, and the long, delicate fingers and toes, and I realized I was gazing at a mini-Matt.

My parents arrived later that afternoon. Dad, with his radiation-bald head and steroid-puffed face, looked nothing like the father I remembered, but I was so relieved to see him that I didn't care. Dad held Siena and gazed at her with an unnatural sort of detachment. That view of my dying father holding my newborn daughter is imprinted in my memory like a tattoo.

Dad looked exhausted, as I expected he would after such a long cross-country trip, so when he asked, "Can I go now?" I said, "Sure, Daddy."

For the next 24 hours, I puked my guts out until there was nothing left to vomit. Although I'm ridiculously sensitive to narcotics, someone had put morphine in my spinal anesthesia, and it set me off. I wound up so dehydrated from throwing up that I stopped making any urine, a dangerous sign postsurgery. The nurse let my IV run dry until I pointed it out, and when, 12 hours later, I was still not making enough urine, my doctor wrote an order in my chart, "Dr. Rankin may manage her own IV fluids."

So there I was, writing my own orders, ordering myself high doses of IV fluids and prescribing Zofran to try to control my vomiting. In the midst of all of this, someone unhooked my hospital gown and held my baby to my breast. The red-faced, dark-haired baby latched on, sucking away like she had always known what to do, but I felt a complete disconnect. Who was this strange creature?

The next few days ran together. I insisted on going home only 24 hours after my C-section, and we all huddled into the little beach house our family had rented for Dad, with a view of the bay and a hospital bed the hospice nurses had brought in. Dad seemed happy enough, though he was getting more and more tired.

One night, when Siena was about a week old, Dad asked my cousin Becca and me to sit down. Mom and my aunt Linda were already there, with red, puffy faces. They told me Dad had something to ask me.

I nodded.

Dad's face looked blank when he asked, "Lissa, can I go now?"

I didn't understand what he meant.

Dad explained. He had not wanted to worry us, but gradually he had lost his ability to see well. He could no longer read the pages of his beloved books, and his brain couldn't quite follow the plots anyway. He couldn't really see the television, and he couldn't really understand what we were all talking about. His days had become a sensory deprivation tank that droned on and on. He had asked for a clock beside his bed, which he used to tick away the minutes, wondering which one might be his last. He tossed and turned at night, wide-awake in spite of the sleeping pills. He stared at the blackness outside the beach house window, but he saw only nothingness, even when the sun finally came up and his family surrounded him to help him make his morning move from the bed to the lounge chair.

I thought Dad was completely content with the bustle of life around him at that beach house. But he had been sparing us. Now he described the agony of waiting and the desire he felt to move on to whatever was next. He was ready. He had waited, but it was time, and he wanted me to give him permission to die.

Mom didn't tell me until much later that Dad had been asking the same question back in the hospital, but she made him promise to wait. She told him he couldn't die on Siena's birthday, so he promised to hold off.

The reality of what Dad was asking me ripped into me like another incision, cutting through the story I had told myself, that Dad would be around for at least another 6 months. The incision on my belly hadn't even healed from my C-section. I couldn't bear both wounds at once.

I begged Dad not to go. I wasn't ready yet to navigate the world without Dad holding the ground steady beneath me.

But Dad just looked at me with cold, empty eyes as I grabbed his arm and pleaded with him. My brother, Chris, and sister, Keli, would be arriving the next day. "Don't you want to see your children before you go, Dad? Aren't you excited to see them?"

Dad was quiet for a moment. Then he said, simply, "No."

That's when I realized that Dad had already left—and I had missed it. I made the mistake of believing I had more time, more days of lounging on the beach reminiscing about how I would sit on his shoulders and run my 5-year-old fingers through his buzz cut, how he was Big Acorn and I was Little Squirrel in our Indian Princess tribe, and how I would sit in the dark next to him while he read x-rays at the hospital. I was just trying to survive those dizzying first postpartum days, to heal from my surgery, to make it through the first attempts at breastfeeding. I thought we'd have time to remember the tears Dad shed at my wedding as he pointed to the same balcony where he spent his honeymoon night with my mother. I thought we would laugh about how he had built a swing for my child years before I ever got pregnant, how much he loved my tomato soup, how much I adored still sitting on his lap, even as a grown-up.

I had no idea that the father I adored had slipped away without anyone noticing.

I had no choice. So I gave Dad my blessing. He planned to quit taking his steroids, the ones that kept his brain from swelling. He would also stop eating or drinking. He agreed to wait for Chris and Keli to arrive so he could say goodbye. Then he would leave us, he said, and go be with God.

When I got home that night, I felt cracked wide open, with my grief weighing on me, and I wrote Siena a letter.

Stop it. Stop staring at me, like you can see inside me, peel me like a tangerine, dismantle my muscles one by one, crack open my rib cage and see my quivering, shy heart. Stop gazing at me with those opalescent eyes and your x-ray vision. You're only 1 week old. But oh, little one, you've had to go through so much already. Meeting your sick papa for the first time. Absorbing your nana's tears. Sleeping bare skin to bare skin against your daddy's chest, nourished by a sort of paternal nursing. And me, then there's me, so broken and humbled and grief-stricken, driven to my knees with the certainty that I have no clue how to be a mother. I will never be the mother my mother was to me, and you can tell, looking through me with your wise guru gaze.

There's so much I want to share with you, experiences I want to kindle, treasures I wish to savor, but I don't even know where to start. My heart is so heavy. Papa will be gone soon, and you'll have lost the best teacher you might have known. From a dying man who says, "I'm not scared, I'm joyful," you could have learned how to honor love, how to cherish beauty, how to respect peace, but I have nothing to give. To those who profess to not knowing how to talk to children, they always say, "Wait until they're yours." But you are mine; I can tell from the matching eyes and the olive skin and the fragile tree-limb fingers. Yet, I still don't know what to say. And you know it. You laugh inside, chuckling, thinking, "Oh Mom, give it up. Stop pretending. Just be you."

Oh, precious, you came into my life in a typhoon of emotion, swirling around you in rivulets of pain and joy that ebb and flow like the moon-driven tides. You should be crying. You should beg for milk and cuddles and a clean diaper when you need it, but instead you are frighteningly quiet. I wonder if something might be wrong with you. But I know, deep down, there is nothing wrong with you. You ask nothing of me because you know I have nothing to give right now. You will ask later, cry when you need me, laugh when you're happy, throw yourself to the floor when you're a teen-ager, drama-queen style. For now, you will just be, floating in the remnants of the eternal pool from which you came, while you gaze at the world you've known before, while you unfold me and gift me your love.

When you were born, I kissed your cheek and said, "Welcome, baby. I have so much to teach you," but what I should have said is "Namaste, teacher."

With Chris and Keli finally with us, Dad announced that he was ready for his final meal. When I walked in for Dad's last supper, he glared at me and said, "What does a dying man have to do to get some spicy chicken wings around here?"

The rest of my family laughed. Apparently, he had been demanding chicken wings from every unsuspecting person who walked in the room. Someone had gone to the grocery store to buy Dad some chicken wings, but they were fried and tasteless.

Finally, someone asked, "David, where can we get the spicy chicken wings you like?"

Dad grinned and said, "Go where the booby ladies are." It was the most animated we had seen him in days.

We all looked at each other, puzzled, until someone piped up, "Hooters! He's talking about Hooters!"

When Matt finally arrived with a gigantic platter of steaming, dripping, greasy chicken wings, smothered in spicy buffalo wing sauce, Dad sighed, "Ahhhh—now that's what I'm talking about."

Sure enough, those chicken wings were the last thing Dad ever ate. And after finishing them, Dad said to me, "I love you."

I said, "I love you, too."

My father leaned over to hug me and said, "I love the way we say goodbye."

Chris managed to snag a couple of chicken wings before Dad finished off the last of them. Shortly afterward, my previously healthy 33-year-old brother, who had just arrived in California less than an hour before eating the wings, wound up in my hospital's emergency room with severe abdominal pain and jaundice.

Initially, I thought Chris must have been having some sort of gallbladder attack, but as soon as the doctors in the ER took one look at the deep yellow color of his skin under the harsh fluorescent lights, they knew something was terribly, terribly wrong. It turned out that Chris was in full-blown liver failure as a rare side effect of the common antibiotic Zithromax, which he was taking for a sinus infection.

I was so overwhelmed by this turn of events that I couldn't even bring myself to go to the hospital to see my brother until the next day. I called the ER myself to speak to the doctors, and then I called one of my partners to ask if she could go care for him in my stead.

Back at the beach house, Dad quietly refused the water bottles brought to him and turned down the ice cream Mom offered him for dessert. He threw away all of his pills, kissed Mom goodnight, curled up, and went to sleep.

The following morning, Dad didn't wake up. We assumed he was just tired, catching up from the endless, tedious nights of insomnia. We were grateful he could finally rest. But by afternoon, when he was still asleep, we started to worry. We tried to wake him up, first gently, then shaking him violently, but Dad didn't respond. I scratched the bottom of his foot with my sharp fingernail, the way I was taught to do on my neurology rotation back in medical school. His big toe stuck up—an abnormal Babinski response—but he didn't wake up. I opened his eyes with my fingertips. But no one was home.

Dad was in a coma.

The "I love yous" we'd shared the night before were the last words Dad ever spoke to me. We just never know when our words to each other will be our last. There can never be enough "I love yous."

I forced myself to go to the hospital that day and spoke to my colleagues about Chris. The news wasn't good. Chris's liver was no longer performing its regular tasks. He couldn't eat at all, and even a little needle stick made him bleed excessively. The injury was so profound that he might need a liver transplant. It was possible he wouldn't make it.

By this point, I was numb.

Since my whole family was together, we had invited Matt's family to come to San Diego so we could baptize Siena while Dad was still with us. The beachfront ceremony was scheduled for that night. Dad's brother, my uncle Larry, a minister, was flying in to perform the ceremony. Since Dad had slipped into a coma, we decided to conduct the ceremony at his bedside rather than on the beach. But Larry's flight was delayed by bad weather, so the family had gathered at the beach house, waiting for the baptism to begin.

Chris was still in the hospital, and I was sitting on the front porch of the beach house, nursing Siena, dressed in her baptism gown, when my sister came running out onto the patio and looked at me with giant eyes.

All she said was, "That sound! That sound!"

I didn't realize until afterward that the sound was my father's last raspy exhale. When I ran into Dad's room holding Keli's hand, I found my mother lying on top of my father's body, weeping. The first thing she said was, "David, I love the way you died."

I was the doctor who called the official time of death.

It wasn't until that moment that I realized that the voice Dad heard in the darkness, the one that told him he was healed, had been correct. Dad had been healed, even though he wasn't cured. There is a difference. I hadn't known it until that moment.

We had been dreading the end, expecting dementia, seizures, headaches, and vomiting. The doctors had prepared us for the worst. But none of that happened. Dad had lived with a large brain tumor and an abdomen riddled with cancer, but he never once experienced pain. He had gradually lost his eyesight, but short of that, Dad hadn't suffered. He ate with gusto until that last spicy chicken wing, without once vomiting or feeling the slightest nausea. He breathed without struggling, spoke without slurring his speech, and stayed awake and alert until the end. He didn't have one single seizure, and then, when he decided it was time to go, Dad ate his last meal, said his good-byes, went to sleep, and simply stopped breathing.

It was a miracle, really, the way he died. Why didn't he have a whole host of neurologic deficits? Why didn't he start making up words again, the way he did in the beginning? His whole brain was shifted to one side on his last MRI, and yet, he was pretty much the same old Dad. How had I not realized that Dad had, in fact, been healed?

If you look it up in the dictionary, to be cured is to be free of disease, but to be healed means to become whole. My father might not have been cured, but he had definitely died whole. I had misunderstood the difference. I think most doctors do.

It took my brother almost a year to fully recover from his liver failure. The events that befell my family were even more traumatic for him than for me. He had to face his own recovery, and he had also missed being at the bedside with the rest of us when Dad died.

In the wake of our grief, when I was still only 2 weeks postpartum, I also lost my beloved 16-year-old dog Ariel, a bichon frise who had been my 21st birthday present. Because of my grueling medical education, Ariel had become the family dog, shunted between my parents' house and mine, depending on my schedule at the hospital. So it seemed fitting that she died right after Dad did. Ariel and Dad always shared a special connection. I was always on the move, rarely staying put in one place for long, but Dad's disability from multiple sclerosis taught him how to sit still, so Ariel discovered that his lap was the best place to hang out. They became best buds. That Ariel died within days of Dad's death reminded me of the song Mom used to sing to us when we were young.

"My grandfather's clock was too large for the shelf, so it stood 90 years on the floor. It was taller by half than the old man himself, though it weighed not a pennyweight more. It was bought on the morn of the day that he was born and was always his treasure and pride. But it stopped short, never to go again, when the old man died."

Perhaps Ariel was like that grandfather clock. When the old man died, she decided it was her time, too.

I call those 2 weeks my "Perfect Storm," a time that bookmarked my life into two parts—life before my Perfect Storm and life after. Things were never the same again. I was no longer able to feel comforted by the illusion of certainty that had been my lifetime companion. After my Perfect Storm,

I realized that the only thing certain in life is uncertainty and that selling my soul for an artificial sense of security was no longer an option.

During this time, everything I knew as "Lissa" began to dissolve. It was a fracture. A rupture. A time of disintegration that Martha Beck describes as the caterpillar in the cocoon. Caterpillars don't just sprout wings to become butterflies. First, they become bug soup, an amorphous mass of undifferentiated cells that long to become a butterfly but aren't quite there yet.

My Perfect Storm thrust me into what author Charles Eisenstein describes as "the space between stories," a state psychologists call "the liminal space." In *The More Beautiful World Our Hearts Know Is Possible*, Eisenstein writes:

> "The old world falls apart but the new has not yet emerged. Everything that once seemed permanent and real is revealed as a kind of hallucination. You don't know what to think, what to do; you don't know what anything means anymore. The life trajectory you had plotted out seems absurd, and you can't imagine another one. Everything is uncertain. Your time frame shrinks from years to this month, this week, today, maybe even this present moment. Without the mirage of order that once seemed to protect you and filter reality, you feel naked and vulnerable, but also a kind of freedom. Possibilities that didn't even exist in the old story lie before you, even if you have no idea how to get there. The challenge in our culture is to allow yourself to be in that space, to trust that the next story will emerge when the time in between has ended, and that you will recognize it."

If you've just experienced your own Perfect Storm through a career change, divorce, the loss of a loved one, illness, bankruptcy, or any other event that disrupts your sense of certainty, you're probably in that space between stories, and you're likely to feel disoriented, scared, and confused, just like I did. A Perfect Storm is often the rupture that launches a hero onto the journey. When you're bug soup, you're likely to melt down, numb out, avoid your emotions, and cling to some new "certainty"—like a rebound romance or another job that isn't the best fit. But these avoidance strategies only delay your evolution.

Your most important job when you're going through a Perfect Storm is to allow yourself to grieve and receive support from the right people. You'll cycle through the phases of grief, feeling denial, anger, sadness, and acceptance, and when you feel them, the key is to just roll with the roller coaster of your emotions without getting stuck in your victim story. As you allow your feelings to pass through you like waves, you'll discover that your resistance to these emotions—and the behaviors we engage in as we try to avoid these emotions—creates more suffering than the emotions themselves. The right people can hold you through the roller coaster of your emotions, ground you, and love you, allowing you to simply feel and experience your emotions without fixing you, trying to hasten your grief, or judging you.

As Martha Beck says in her book *Finding Your Own North Star,* "Dissolving isn't something you do; it's something that happens to you. The closest you'll come to controlling it is relaxing and trusting the process." This is easier to do in the company of compassionate loved ones who can just be present with your process without judging you or trying to fix you.

Becoming bug soup requires letting go of everything you thought you knew about yourself. It's a dissolving of the ego, a letting go of your identity, a sloughing off of what can't come with you on your hero's journey.

Some heroes may be able to allow the necessary dissolving without the trauma of a Perfect Storm. But I was too dense. I needed the hurricane of my Perfect Storm in order to wake up. Perhaps you also needed something to wake you up from the anesthesia of your Ordinary World, but surviving a Perfect Storm isn't a necessary part of the hero's journey initiation. Perhaps you chose to embark upon your journey not as a reaction to trauma or loss but because you were simply ready. Either way, however you get there, at some point, the call to adventure becomes urgent. It's as if your soul, long imprisoned, finally becomes free. And an unleashed soul no longer has much tolerance for being in prison.

Eisenstein writes in *The More Beautiful World Our Hearts Know Is Possible:*

"If you are in the sacred space between stories, allow yourself to be there. It is frightening to lose the old structures of security, but you will find that even as you might lose things that were unthinkable to lose, you will be okay. There is a kind of grace that protects us in the space between stories. It is not that you won't lose your marriage, your money, your job, or your health. In fact, it is very likely that you will lose one of these things. It is that you will discover that even having lost that, you are still okay. You will find yourself in closer contact to something much more precious, something that fires cannot burn and thieves cannot steal, something that no one can take and cannot be lost. We might lose sight of it sometimes, but it is always there waiting for us. This is the resting place we return to when the old story falls apart. Clear of its fog, we can now receive a true vision of the next world, the next story, the next phase of life. From the marriage of this vision and this emptiness, a great power is born."

The space between stories invites us to empty ourselves in order to make room for the possibility of what might be coming. Even in the pit of my despair, I recognized the potency of this call to emptiness from other periods of my life when I had been drawn to the space between stories. Back when I was a senior at Duke University, I took a class called Leadership in Action, which we fondly called "group therapy." There were eight of us taught by two unconventional and popular professors. For our assignment one day, they took us to Toys"R"Us and instructed us to buy a toy that "spoke to us," which we brought back to the classroom to write about. At the time, I had just been accepted into several medical schools, my college sweetheart had just proposed to me, and I saw my life all mapped out—becoming a doctor, the 2½ kids, a house on the lake. Sure, it seemed lovely. But I was 21 years old and it all just looked so . . . certain.

The toy I chose was a plain red plastic box labeled "The Anything Box." A little sticker inside the empty box read, "You can put anything in here." That's what I felt like I wanted. An empty box. I was so tempted to just toss out everything in my life to open up room for possibility, for space, for mystery, for change. I didn't know it then, but I was in that space between stories, and I craved spaciousness in order to open myself into what wanted to be born through me. But I was too scared to begin my hero's journey back then. It took 15 more years, until the night I wanted to die, when the little voice told me it was time to radically change my life.

Shortly after that night, on a mystical trip to Big Sur, I saw a wrought iron box in a shop. I bought it as a talisman, a reminder that I still had an Anything Box and that I could put anything in there, or take out anything that no longer served me.

I went back to the hospital, but I brought my new Anything Box with me. I put it front and center on my desk as a reminder of what I came to know as true—that I would one day quit my job. It wasn't until years later that I actually saw what was in that box for the first time. I had never looked inside when I bought it. I assumed that, like the red plastic box from my college days, it was empty.

But one day the lid fell off, and I found a wrought iron heart lying on a bed of straw inside the box. I laughed out loud, realizing that when you're in the space between stories, the space, while ripe with possibility, is not empty. It's filled with love.

HERO'S GUIDEPOST:
Allow Yourself to Rest in the Space between Stories

Our culture tends to rush us through this space of uncertainty. We get impatient with ourselves and bully ourselves into doing something, while others try to hurry us along. But this space between, when one story is ending and another has not yet begun, is best not rushed. If we rush ourselves into certainty before we're ready, we're likely to veer off course on our journey. Sometimes the best strategy when you're between stories is to just stop. Pause. Take a breather. Wait and pay attention to that quiet loving voice that will guide you when you're ready to take the next step. Stop deluding yourself, because the jig is up. You're busted, *and this is a very good thing*. Make peace with what's true for you, even if the truth feels wildly uncomfortable. Trust that the grace that holds us when we're between stories will protect and even comfort you. Don't be surprised if you're the unwitting recipient of small miracles that remind you that you are not alone. Hold yourself gently, with great compassion. Everything is going to be okay.

HERO'S PRACTICE:
Indulge in Radical Acts of Self-Care

When you're in the space between stories, take a breath before you make any big decisions or leap into action. Instead, make this a time to practice radical acts of self-care. What comforts you? A hug from your best friend? A snuggle with your pup? A feather blanket? A massage? Meditation? Aromatherapy candles? A mug of tea or a glass of green juice? A walk in nature?

Watching an uplifting movie? A personal retreat? Rubbing lotion into your skin? A private dance party with your favorite songs? Making love with your partner? Engaging in an art project? Reading an inspiring book? Lighting incense or spritzing yourself with essential oils? Writing in a journal? Consider what calms your nervous system and comforts your soul, and then give yourself permission to prioritize such activities. When you're in the space between stories, such things are essential. Just think of it as medicine for your soul. For comfort and relaxation of your nervous system when you're in the space between stories, download the free The Space between Stories guided meditation I recorded for you at TheAnatomyofaCalling.com.

CHAPTER 5

Taking the Leap

As OB/GYN physicians, we insist that our patients take 8 weeks of postpartum leave after a C-section. Yet I was back at the hospital only 3 days after my father's funeral, just a few weeks after I had given birth to Siena. I was on call but hiding out in a call room, having lied about seeing a patient in the emergency room so I could lug my breast pump behind a closed door. I hooked myself up to the pump with its humiliating yellow suckers clamped to my breasts as it made that EEE-OWWW sound I hated, the one that made me feel like a farm animal. I was so busy that it had been 6 hours since I last pumped, even though I was supposed to do it every 2 or 3 hours.

My 34 B breasts were engorged to a double D size, feeling like heavy water balloons attached to a running faucet and about to pop. The pump sucked on my aching breasts, but no milk was coming out. I prayed for letdown, but, alas, nothing. I knew how breastfeeding worked. I taught my patients about this all the time. Letdown doesn't happen when you're stressed. So when you're on call in a hospital and stressed not only about work but also about not being stressed so that you'll finally letdown, you're doomed.

I forced myself to close my eyes and take a deep breath. I knew I wouldn't be granted much quiet time, so when I finally felt the electric rush running through my nipples, the one that signals letdown, I let out an audible sigh. The milk finally started spraying into the two bottles attached to the octopus suckers.

Of course, that's right when my pager went off.

I hadn't quite developed the mommy skill of holding both bottles with one hand to free up the other for the telephone, so when I let go of the yellow sucker to check my pager, it popped off and suddenly my boobs were projectile-squirting milk all over the call room bed and the walls and my green scrubs as I dialed the phone.

The nurse answered the phone in a panicked voice and said, "Didn't you hear the overhead page? Come quick—we've got a cord prolapse in 312!"

Uh oh. A cord prolapse—when the umbilical cord falls through the dilated cervix and gets compressed so the baby gets no bloodflow—can be quickly fatal for the baby.

I tossed the suction cups and the hoses clogged with milk and the little yellow-topped plastic bottles with only a few drops of milk onto the milk-soaked comforter cover, and I blasted out of the call room, my breasts still squirting. I found the charge nurse crouching at the bottom of the bed between the patient's straddled legs. She was pushing the baby's head up into the uterus in order to relieve the pressure on the umbilical cord so the baby might get some bloodflow. I could see the muscles quivering in her forearm as she pushed the baby's head up as hard as she could, fighting the strength of the mother's contractions. Everyone was racing around the room, preparing the mother for an emergency C-section.

In the OR, someone poured Betadine straight from the bottle while someone else threw sterile paper drapes over the hasty prep job. The scrub tech slammed instruments onto the OR table without counting or checking them, meaning that after the surgery was over, we'd have to X-ray the patient's abdomen to make sure we didn't leave in any sponges or instruments.

My breasts still squirted and ached, and the nurse between my patient's legs was still squatting underneath me as I leaned in with a sharp blade and surgically delivered the limp baby. The pediatricians hovered beside us, ready to resuscitate.

While I watched them try to resuscitate the baby, I suddenly had a vision of myself as if I was watching the scene from above. There I was, a grieving doctor with a newborn and a fresh scar on her belly and a brother still in the hospital, with two giant wet spots on the front of her scrubs, covered with a blood-soaked surgical gown, holding a bleeding uterus in her hands. Watching myself from this observer position, I had a sudden realization that my life had become utter madness. Surely only a crazy person would be operating in such a state.

But there I was, feeling victimized and helpless and full of self-pity. I hadn't even had a chance to put the breast pads back in my bra, so my wet clothes left me shivering in the frigid operating room. As the pediatricians resuscitated the baby, the infant started to cry, and the minute the baby cried, my breasts just letdown more. Suddenly, I was a cow on a farm, and you could have collected a gallon from me without even trying. Hot tears ran down my face and wet my mask, and the physician assisting me in the surgery noticed the wet stains on my surgical gown and nodded, her eyes flashing a compassionate look of understanding. Like me, she was a doctor who was also a mother. Maybe she didn't get to stay home with her baby either.

That night was just one of many nights in the hospital that gave me the courage to formalize an escape plan. I started searching for a new job, maybe one that allowed me to work fewer hours, someplace quieter than San Diego, maybe further north in California, where I could be closer to my beloved Big Sur. When I found a job in Monterey that agreed to let me work only 3 days per week, I jumped at it. I would take a huge pay cut. It was a much less prestigious job. I would be a salaried employee rather than a partner. But I would be better off than where I was.

I figured my departure would be no surprise for the partners in my practice. I had been asking to work fewer hours and see fewer patients for years. They knew I was unhappy, so I figured they might have anticipated that I would leave one day. But they were shocked when I told them the news.

I was supposed to leave my job in September. Matt, Siena, and I were up in the mountains on a summery Sunday at our vacation home in the quaint gold rush–era town of Julian. Some friends from San Diego were driving up for the day to spend the afternoon with us. I had just put Siena down for a nap and was simmering tomatoes on the stove, preparing heirloom tomato soup to go with the steaks we would throw on the shiny, red Weber kettle grill. Matt was up the hill building some of the wood panels I painted on for my business as a busy professional artist.

For years, I had painted as part of my personal medicine. I had always been the creative type. In college, I was premed, but I majored in English and focused on creative writing. In medical school, I took the required science classes by day and attended continuing education classes in art at night. Medicine was my hemorrhage, but art was my transfusion. So I often spent weekends in Julian filling myself up with painting. Matt had also started painting with the same medium I used—encaustic painting, pigmented beeswax applied to wood panel.

All of a sudden, I heard a sound I'll never forget, a cry like an animal, arising from up in the art studio, and then I heard Matt scream, "I'm so fucked! I'M SO FUCKED!"

My stomach hiccupped into my throat as I ran outside just in time to see Matt holding his gloved left hand in his right as he stumbled down the dirt path. We met on the wooden porch, where he held out his left hand, which was covered with a dirty, leathery work glove. The first two fingers of the glove were cut clean off, and inside of them were Matt's index and middle fingers, severed all the way down to the knuckle, hanging from the glove by a shred of fabric. Shards of bone stuck out like broken icicles surrounded by meaty, shredded skin, and fiber. Blood soaked the glove, and a trail of it marked Matt's hasty journey down the path and onto the porch. Underneath us, a puddle grew as we gaped at Matt's hand. Matt was calm and pale. I was trembling with adrenaline.

My doctor self flew into emergency mode. Matt had just cut two fingers off his hand with a table saw, and we were in the boonies, at least an hour from the closest country hospital. I had to be in control. I had to get him to *my* hospital—but what if he passed out in my car on the windy road, miles from any help? What if he hemorrhaged? And what about Siena, who was sound asleep in her playpen? What should I do with her?

I called 911. I knew they would never find the remote, private sanctuary where we were, up a nearly impassable dirt road that required a four-wheel drive. I'd have to drive Matt down to the main road, where the ambulance could find us. The woman on the phone said, "Don't move him. Stay right there."

But it was too late. I sprung into motion, gathering up Siena from her playpen, rushing around, looking for the car keys. I wrapped Matt's whole hand, glove and all, in a towel. I helped him into the passenger seat of our SUV, and then I strapped Siena into the car seat, whispering, "Pray for Daddy, baby."

With shaking hands, I drove the car down the windy, rocky grade, over the bridge, and up the hill to the main part of town. Minutes later, sirens blared and first one, then two, then five emergency vehicles pulled up and blocked the road to passing traffic. The local fire chief, the sheriff, and the paramedics rushed to the scene. Siena screamed in the back seat until the jovial fire chief climbed in and started to tickle her. Someone unwrapped

Matt's hand, and the next thing I knew, a paramedic was inserting a large-bore IV and pushing 10 milligrams of morphine into Matt's vein.

They were about to whisk him off to the local hospital, and that's when I started shouting orders. There was no way in hell I was going to let those paramedics take my husband to some hospital where they would sew over the bloody nubs of his knuckles and send him home with some Vicodin. Oh, no. No way. They insisted they'd have to take him to the closest hospital, not the hospital where I worked, which was an hour and a half away. But I told them that if they didn't send him to my hospital, where I knew I could rally the best care for him, that I would yank him out of that ambulance with my own two hands and drive him to my hospital myself.

The whole team of men inspected me. I saw myself through their eyes. I was at least 10 years younger than the youngest of them, and from all outward appearances, I was more cheerleader than doctor. They could have easily dismissed me, but I was embracing my inner Mama Bear at the moment, and somehow those big men had the wherewithal not to get in my way. The burly firemen and paramedics agreed to deliver Matt to my hospital back in Southern California. So I sent Matt off with them, along with instructions to keep the morphine flowing, while I tried to track down a microsurgeon and someone to watch Siena.

Before they raced off with sirens blaring, I climbed into the back of the ambulance with Matt and laid my head on his chest. I so wanted to go with Matt, to be the wife instead of the doctor, to cry on his shoulder and let him cry on mine, to hold his good hand in the back of the ambulance. But someone had to take charge.

I asked Matt if he was in pain, and he said, "Honestly, I can't feel a thing." I realized I felt the same way. I felt nothing. My life was unraveling, one thread at a time, and I felt absolutely nothing.

While Matt was in the operating room, I went home and finished the tomato soup I had been cooking. As I pressed the tomatoes through a sieve, I looked at my own fingers and thought of Matt's. He had the most beautiful hands I'd ever seen on a man—slim, long fingers with carefully trimmed, beautifully shaped fingernails, the hands of an artist. Those hands had caressed every inch of my body and played it like a cello. They built wooden masterpieces upon which I painted. They created his art and held Siena. Beautiful yet masculine hands, and I loved them. Matt had admitted that they were his one vanity.

They didn't look the same after he came out of surgery. With yellow pins jutting out from the tips of his replanted fingertips, his nails crusted with Betadine and blood, they looked so . . . surgical. But they were there. When I saw Matt in the recovery room, he handed me his wedding ring. The doctor had tried to cut it off, but Matt had saved it, much to his own discomfort. I wore it on a necklace and held it close to my heart.

Matt's accident forced me to postpone leaving my job. He needed rehab, and we couldn't change insurance in the middle of his treatment for a preexisting condition that was going to require follow-up surgery. Plus, his surgeon felt that it was important for him to stick around for a while during the touch-and-go time when we would wait to see if the finger replants would take.

I felt defeated. Having finally mustered up the courage to quit my job, I was ready to go. Being a lame-duck doctor who was seeing newly pregnant patients made my already difficult job almost intolerable. But I did what I had learned to do so well: Buck up, shelve my emotions, and carry on.

Siena was about a year old when we finally got around to moving to the Monterey peninsula, where I discovered that my new job wasn't quite what I thought it would be. The patients I served were mostly Mexican migrant workers who picked vegetables on commercial farms. They didn't speak English, and my bosses didn't offer me a translator, even though my Spanish wasn't good. When I asked for someone who could help me communicate effectively, I was told that there was no need to talk to my patients, that we knew what was best for them. I was shocked.

My bosses frequently induced labor in pregnant women for reasons I interpreted as unnecessary. Many of these women were having their fourth or fifth baby, and nobody had ever induced their labor in Mexico, so they were understandably confused about being scheduled for elective inductions. But the doctors weren't calling them elective inductions. They were telling the women that the babies were too big or too small or that the babies didn't look good on the fetal monitor. But when I looked at the ultrasound reports, the babies were normal size. And when I reviewed the fetal monitor strips, the babies looked fine. So once I finally had a translator who could help me communicate, I started canceling unnecessary inductions when the patients weren't giving their informed consent.

My bosses were not happy with me. I was told that if I wanted to keep my job, I would need to start complying with "the way we do things around here."

One day, without even running it by me, one of my bosses scheduled me to perform a C-section on a woman pregnant with twins; the babies would be premature if we delivered them so early. With no indication for the C-section and the chance that the premature babies would wind up in the intensive care unit, I questioned the reason for the procedure. Nobody had even performed an amniocentesis to make sure the babies' lungs were mature. I spoke to the head of neonatology, and he agreed that the surgery was a bad idea. He called my boss to try to gather more information, but my boss refused to take his call or mine.

With no apparent indication for the surgery, the neonatology chief breathing down my neck, and a gut feeling that the babies could wind up really sick if I followed my boss's orders, I cancelled the surgery. When my boss got wind of what I had done, she told me she would fire me if I didn't obey her orders.

I gave my notice that day, and when I did, some long dormant part of my soul celebrated. I could feel the bubbling up in my chest of something I recognized but had been suppressing. It wasn't until years later that I realized I was feeling the rush of truth that signals alignment with your own integrity, a feeling that smacks of freedom.

Doctors who abide by the terms of the current medical system often feel like they're selling their souls to some degree. Doctors are called to the lineage of healing, which is as old as our species, much as priests are called to the priesthood. Being a doctor is a calling, and it expects us to serve the calling impeccably. But then we enter into a system that has been usurped by businesspeople who seem to care more about money than patient care. Our ethics demand that we spend time with our patients, that we open our hearts to them, that we tell them the truth, that we put them ahead of bottom lines or the influence of pharmaceutical companies or the fear of malpractice attorneys or the power of politicians. Yet we violate our own ethics when we fail to be present for our patients because we are spending so much time filling out paperwork or entering data into a computer. The doctor-patient relationship is sacred, but our current system has made it challenging for physicians to abide by these values, so doctors wind up in constant internal conflict. We wind up selling out, at least in part, in order to stay within the system. But it's a bad trade. We gain security, but we compromise our souls.

I'm grateful for the doctor who forced me to make a choice on that summer day in 2007. My boss turned out to be one of life's great teachers by requiring me to make an obvious decision between doing what I knew was right and doing what would keep me feeling safe. Until that point, I had been able to get by with choosing what was safe without compromising too much. But in that one defining moment, my soul began the journey of taking back the driver's seat of my life; I had stood up for my own soul and regained my own power, even though it meant losing the stability of my job. I didn't realize it then, but I was also taking a stand for the whole lineage of my profession and reclaiming it.

It was simultaneously the most terrifying and easiest decision of my life. I'm grateful it was made so clear. If I could have rationalized a less compromising way to stay, I might have. These days, one of the most common questions people ask me is, "How did you find the courage to quit your job?" But at the time, my decision didn't feel the least bit courageous. It really didn't even feel like a choice. Courage would be required later, when I decided not to replace one hospital job with another, but at the time, the decision seemed obvious. There was no way I was going to risk the health of two innocent babies just to keep a job.

Thirty days after submitting my resignation notice, I woke up on a Monday morning with nowhere to go for the first time in my entire life. I found myself standing on the back deck of our rental house. I had no plan. No job. No money. No calling. I was bug soup.

Matt wasn't working outside of the home. We had an 18-month-old baby. We had just signed a 1-year lease for a house we could no longer afford.

Now what?

Fortunately, when I told Matt I had just quit my job, he held me in his arms and said, "It's about time." I cried with relief. We talked about our options, and because neither of us knew what to do, we decided to just rest for a little while until we were clear on our next steps. I was comforted not only by Matt's support but also by a strong sense that although things hadn't turned out the way I hoped, things were somehow, strangely, turning out just as they were meant to.

I thought back to the little voice I had heard the night I thought about killing myself, the voice that had warned me that I would soon quit my job. Without any real evidence, I started to feel something I had never really felt before my Perfect Storm. I felt like I was being guided, like every little thing was a sign from the Universe, even the things I judged as negative. Even though it was unknown and terrifying, the way I left my job felt quite purposeful.

I had always believed in some sort of God, but it had always been a tenable faith, an academic faith almost. My faith lived in my mind, not in my heart. After I left my job in medicine, I started experiencing what felt like a more personal relationship with some sort of Universal Intelligence. This new kind of faith didn't emerge overnight. It grew as a seed that had been planted in my heart that night the voice told me I would one day quit my job, and it was fertilized with each sign from the Universe that guided me toward what felt like an unknown but increasingly urgent plan. I sensed that the plan didn't require me to follow it. I knew I had free will and would continue to have the opportunity to make choices. But increasingly, I sensed that I was being asked to participate in something much larger than myself, and my willingness to participate would involve not only myself but also many others.

You might be feeling the same way right now.

Maybe you're facing a big decision yourself, one that's calling you to embark upon your hero's journey. If so, yours might not be as clear as mine was. The choice might be fuzzier. You might feel confused and frightened. When the call to adventure comes, you'll be asked to step bravely into the unknown, and, usually, there are no guarantees.

So how do you know when it's time to answer the call to adventure and take a leap of faith? You'll know it's time to leap when the pain of staying put exceeds your fear of the unknown. Many people spend years standing at the edge of the cliff, peering over into the abyss, debating whether or not to leap. Then, all of a sudden, the answer is obvious, and they pick up the call. The leap is inevitable. If you're on the fence and the answer is uncertain, it's perfectly okay to stay put. You can trust that you will know when the space between stories is over. Your next inspired steps will call you forth, the way I was called to walk away from medicine.

Remember that you will not be navigating your hero's journey alone.

Like me, you will be guided, if only you pay attention. You may not recognize the guidance at first, and if you do, you might write it off as mere coincidence. The guidance is right there, just waiting for you to pay attention, once you have the eyes to see and the ears to hear.

When you're first learning to interpret the signs, this guidance may show up in subtle ways, like a thought or an idea that feels a little crazy. You might read something that feels like it was meant just for you, something that reinforces a crazy idea. Three people might give you the same book within a month. You might have a dream full of strangely specific instructions. You might have a premonition or an inner knowing about something on the horizon. Or if you're dense like me, you might get thwacked upside the head by the proverbial two-by-four because you're not sensitive enough to the subtle signs.

That's how guidance tends to show up. If you don't pay attention to the first whisperings of guidance, then the signs from the Universe tend to get more obvious. You may get physical symptoms because you're not listening to the whispers. Things may start happening to shove you out of your comfort zone. Someone dies and it rocks your world. You get fired. You lose a beloved pet. A business idea fails. At this juncture, you can't help noticing that things aren't going well, and eventually you'll find yourself falling to your knees, broken open.

These kinds of things may signal that you're out of alignment with your hero's journey. You've strayed off course, and you may not have even noticed. These signs are wake-up calls intended to help you get back on course. They're like a Cosmic No, signaling you to change directions, to find realignment with your truth. Though they may be painful, such signs can be a blessing.

But the signs from the Universe aren't always painful. Sometimes they're quite magical. You're worried about how to fund a dream, and then an unexpected check arrives in the mail. You finally start adoption proceedings and then wind up pregnant. You let go of searching for your soul mate and then meet the love of your life at the DMV. You're trying to make a difficult decision, and after asking the Universe for help, a license plate gives you just the answer you needed in a way that feels like more than coincidence. My friend (and well-known personal growth author and artist) SARK walks onto the streets of San Francisco and says, "Miracle, find me now!" Once, five $100 bills literally flew into her hands.

These are the kinds of things that tend to happen when you're receiving and interpreting clear guidance. But what if you don't like the instructions you're being given? You'll often be given a lot of leeway when you first become aware of something you're being called to do. You'll likely be given a sort of grace period (like I was when the voice of my Inner Pilot Light told me I would one day quit my job), a Divine time-out, during which you have the opportunity to make peace with what is being asked of you. It's as if the Universe gives you a break and understands why you're not doing what you know you must, so there are no immediate consequences to failing to heed the guidance. The Universe understands that you're only human and you need time to make peace with what you must do.

Then one day, the grace period is over, and what you're being called to do becomes urgent. The signs from the Universe start coming fast and furious. The Universe is not going to let you off the hook any longer. At this point, you still have a choice. You have free will. But if you don't act on what is being asked of you once your grace period is over, things may start being reorganized for you, and you may feel like you no longer have a choice. It's not that your free will is being taken from you; it's that your soul is grabbing the wheel from your Small Self and orchestrating your life in order to facilitate your hero's journey. So don't resist! Just let go and trust that it's all purposeful, even if it feels terrifying in the moment.

When your grace period is over, you may get fired from that job you've known you were supposed to quit. The relationship you've been thinking about ending will end without your choice. Your life will start realigning in order to make this thing that must happen inevitable, until you're laughing or crying at how obvious it is that you're *just not listening* to what you're being guided to do.

That's when you'll be tempted to do one of two things. Either you'll turn your back, seeking comfort in what can never comfort you—dysfunctional relationships, Ben & Jerry's ice cream, booze, drugs, too much work, gambling, casual sex, or some other favorite vice. Or you'll quit numbing, stop running away, and finally face up to what you must do: *surrender.* If you're like most of us, you'll probably opt for door number 1, because letting go when you're terrified is almost impossibly hard, especially when you have no evidence that it's safe to release your vice grip on life. But somewhere inside, if you listen up, you'll hear that quiet voice of your Inner Pilot Light that says, "Everything is okay." You'll feel the butterflies, that roller coaster feeling in your belly, and you'll strap on your seatbelt because you know that things are about to start moving at warp speed and the road won't always be smooth.

If you've received guidance that your space between stories is over but you haven't acted on what you're being asked to do, it's time to take a close look at where you might be self-sabotaging. What resistance is showing up? How are you ignoring the guidance that pushes you to do what you must? Are you in denial about what's true for yourself? Are you compromising the integrity of your soul?

If you're in this phase of your journey, chances are good that you already know what you're being called to do, that on some cosmic level, you've already made a choice, but you're avoiding doing what you know you must. As psychologist and author Harriet Lerner says in her book *The Dance of Fear*, "It is not fear that stops you from doing the brave and true thing in your daily life. Rather, the problem is avoidance. You want to feel comfortable, so you avoid doing or saying the thing that will evoke fear and other difficult emotions. Avoidance will make you feel less vulnerable in the short run, but it will never make you less afraid." If you stay in denial, avoiding what you must do, waiting until you don't feel afraid, you'll never fulfill this mission you're on. The fear is inevitable as long as you're seeking security and comfort. But when you open yourself to the mystery and make peace with uncertainty, you'll find within you the courage you need in order to leap.

HERO'S GUIDEPOST:
When the Pain of Staying Put Exceeds the Fear of the Unknown, Leap

Most heroes spend a lot of time refusing the call before they finally answer it, and that's perfectly okay. Readiness is crucial, and we're all on our own paths, journeying at our own speeds. You are valuable and worthy and perfect, wherever you are on your hero's journey. If you've heard the call and are still refusing it, don't beat yourself up. It's natural to resist taking scary leaps of faith. Be gentle and loving with yourself while you resist. But know that there will come a time when resisting the call creates more suffering than leaping. You will feel an impossible pull to answer the call, which may be met with an equally forceful draw to hang up the phone. You will know it's time to begin your journey when you *must* answer the call. When that time comes, cave early. Don't delay what must happen. Close your eyes. Trust the unknown. Open yourself to receiving support. Leap into the mystery.

HERO'S PRACTICE:

Make Peace with Uncertainty

Try this exercise from my book *The Fear Cure*. Like strengthening your biceps, changing your relationship with uncertainty requires exercise. Try a bench press for your uncertainty muscles. Push the limits of your comfort zone with activities loaded with built-in uncertainty.

Rejection Therapy. Do you fear the uncertainty of facing possible rejection? Set yourself up to get rejected. Entrepreneur and professional "fearbuster" Jia Jiang was afraid of rejection, so he challenged himself with 100 Days of Rejection, during which he asked for things he expected a no for. Put yourself in situations where you expect to get turned down. Notice that even when rejection happens, you can handle it.

Get Lost. Afraid of the uncertainty of an unplanned road trip? Challenge yourself to get in your car and just keep turning left. I once went on a first date with a guy who did this. We wound up eating frozen lemonade at a Little League baseball game among strangers before having to stop at a gas station to ask for directions back to where we came from. Be willing to experiment. Get adventurous. See where you end up.

Open Yourself to Failure. Afraid of not knowing whether or not you'll succeed? Put yourself in situations where your success is uncertain. Take a class to learn an obscure skill you've never tried. Be willing to put yourself out there and fail. Discover that you're not good at everything, *and that this is okay.* Laugh at your failures. Celebrate how brave you were for trying. Think about how much fun you will have if you go bowling when you don't know how to bowl. Imagine someone roller-skating for the first time. We don't expect children to be good at something the first time they do it, but somehow we expect this of ourselves. Try not to take yourself so seriously. Be willing to fail miserably—or not so miserably! Rather than fixating on mastery, learn to relish the excitement of trying something new.

If you're facing an uncertain situation and finding yourself fearful, download the Uncertainty Meditation at TheAnatomyofaCalling.com.

CHAPTER 6

Trust the Signs

I n the wake of my resignation, my overriding emotion was unadulterated panic. What had I just done? What had possessed me to do something so rash? Why was I not searching for another job? How was I going to support my family? The anxious chatter was a cacophony of fear, dominating the treble clef of my life. But somewhere in the bass line, a new song began to write itself, a song that began in Big Sur.

My spiritual love affair with Big Sur began on my wedding day at the posh, serene Post Ranch Inn in 2005. We had decided to get married in a private ceremony officiated by my best friend, Katsy, and attended by her husband, Dan. Because it would be a small, unorthodox wedding, we had most of the day to ourselves to prepare for our sunset ceremony. On the day of our wedding, I was browsing through the resort's list of activities: yoga, group meditation, a tour of the property, *shamanic journey*.

Now that sounded interesting! Without any idea what a shamanic journey actually was, I suggested to Matt that we try it. I thought it would make for a good story. I was not the woo-woo new age–type at all. But it was my wedding day, and I was happy, and I was feeling a little—I don't know—unusually willing to explore outside of my comfort zone. A shamanic journey to kick off our marriage? Why not?

Matt and I showed up in the yurt in the middle of a meadow expecting to encounter a long-bearded Incan decked out in a tribal robe, maybe smoking a peace pipe. Instead, we found the shaman—a handsome Kiefer Sutherland look-alike—sitting cross-legged in blue jeans.

Ten of us crowded into the yurt, forming a circle, and the shaman began chanting to the four winds, invoking the spirits of nature. Inhaling a floral

75

essence from a bottle, he exhaled misty puffs of fragrance to the north, east, south, and west before asking us to lie on our backs on padded mats. We closed our eyes and listened while he beat a drum like a collective heartbeat.

Begin by drawing your attention to your sixth chakra, your third eye, right between your eyebrows, deep inside, where your intuition lies. Now focus on your fourth chakra, the heart chakra, where you'll find your compassion and love. Now allow yourself to flow through your bloodstream, down to the tips of your fingers and toes, and then down into your mat, through the pebbles and grass and rocky Big Sur terrain, all the way down to the earth's core. Here, in the molten earth, we will walk through four chambers. Now we are here, at the first chamber, where you will meet yourself at a time in your life when you were your most joyful.

In my mind's eye, I saw the Squirrel Girl, the healer, long before medical school and residency did a number on me. The shaman instructed me to take hold of this Lissa's hand.

Now, holding hands with your joyful self, walk with me into the second chamber. Recall a time in your past when you were broken. How has that brokenness changed you? Have you created patterns in your current life as a result of this time of brokenness? What contracts have you made with yourself that no longer serve you?

I thought about the night of four dead babies and all the other times in my medical training when I was shamed for expressing my emotions. I thought of all the people who had died in my family, not only my father but also the other relatives whose funerals I had not been able to attend because I had been too busy at work. I thought of all the times I had sold out my feminine self to get ahead in a man's world. I felt the pain of all the people I had disappointed because I had made my career my priority. And the pain I had suppressed all of those years so I could "Buck up, Rankin" flooded over me, and next thing I knew, I was weeping.

Now I'd like to invite you to release those contracts that no longer serve you. Let them go to the four winds. Release them. You don't need them anymore.

I imagined knives and sandpaper and razor blades flying out of my body into the four winds.

Now we're entering the third chamber. Here, I'd like you to envision the passion in your life that helps you return to the joyful state of your past self.

Visions of being in the art studio, painting without thinking, flooded me. Amorphous egg shapes, interlaced with swirling lines of color and geometry and spontaneity, in cobalt yellow and cadmium red and Payne's grey. Splashes of wax flying around the art studio, permission to be messy, irrational, and creative with a freedom I never felt in the operating room, where I was expected to be organized, structured, restrained, and perfect. A feeling of gratitude rushed over me. How lucky that I had been given this gift of my art.

Now I want you to allow yourself to be filled with this passion that returns you to your joyful being. Let it flow into you. Take it in, and hold it there while we approach the fourth chamber. Here, you will receive a gift. Imagine an object, the first one that comes to mind. This will be your gift.

I saw a stethoscope with a pink paintbrush embellishing the stethoscope's diaphragm.

Now I'd like you to reflect on this gift. Why was it given to you? What does it mean? How might this gift help you resolve the conflict in your life that separates you from your joyful self? How might it return you to your purest state of being?

When the shaman asked us to consider the meaning of the gift we had given ourselves, I thought of the stethoscope with the pink paintbrush on it. Was I supposed to paint my patients? Was I supposed to teach my patients to paint? Was I supposed to practice medicine on artists?

I had no idea what my gift meant. But the shaman told us not to worry about it, that the meaning of our gift would make itself known to us when we were ready.

Now I'd like you to rise up, from deep within the earth's core, up through the layers of rock and soil, through the grass and the California poppies and the lupine, through the floor and up into your mat and back into your body. From your fingertips and toes, into your bloodstream, back to your heart chakra. Rest here for a moment. Feel the peace.

The drumbeat slowed, and the shaman once again blew the misty fragrance to the four winds.

Now draw your attention to your third eye, right between your eyebrows. Live there for a moment. Now take with you your gift, and when you're ready, open your eyes.

Our shamanic journey was complete.

When I opened my eyes, they were bloodshot and puffy from tears. I felt like someone had just flipped me upside down, changed the axis of my earth, and unwound me. What had just happened? Blearily, I looked at my soon-to-be husband, who said, "What a great nap."

Looking back, I realize that the shamanic journey helped launch my hero's journey. Of course it happened in Big Sur. Big Sur had become a sort of catalyst for my spiritual growth, a container for possibility. Perhaps that's why the wrong job moved me so close to Big Sur, so she would be there to catch me when I fell.

After moving to Monterey, I spent a lot of time in Big Sur, and these visits helped lift the veil that had darkened my perception for almost 20 years. I saw glimpses of a Technicolor world I had almost forgotten. How brilliant nature was to mix the bright cobalt purple of lupine on the hillside with the cadmium yellow of mustard grass and the Indian yellow of California poppies! How genius that the mother sea otters became life rafts for their babies so both could nap. How curious that the fog crept from the Pacific over the cliffs of Big Sur, perched like a cat, waiting to pounce. How majestic were the redwoods, where I could climb inside, lean my back against this wooden cradle, and wrap myself in a tree hug from Mama Earth herself.

I found a secret spot hidden away from the tourists at Julia Pfeiffer Burns State Park, where a waterfall splashed onto the sand and ebbed into the tide, and I spent hours on that tucked-away rock, dangling my legs over the sea, listening to whispers from within that I didn't yet know how to interpret. I was not only beginning to regularly hear the voice of my Inner Pilot Light but also beginning to feel my body after over a decade under anesthesia. For years, I had ignored hunger pains, the foggy fatigue that signaled my need for sleep, the pain in my arms and shoulders as I retracted for hours during a 6-hour surgery. As a doctor, numbing my body's signals was adaptive. Over time, I became dissociated enough so that I could deny the needs of my body in service to the needs of my patients.

But Big Sur was changing me. As the anesthesia wore off, my body began to ache all over. I could barely hike because my left hip was killing me and my neck was so stiff. Although it was an expense I couldn't afford, I tried to heal myself with massages. I practiced yoga. After realizing I had been holding my breath for two decades, I tried to teach myself how to breathe again, watching my baby daughter's rising and falling belly.

The more I consciously inhabited my body, the louder my Inner Pilot Light whispered. Every time I drove past the Esalen Institute on Highway 1, a persistent little voice said, "You're supposed to come to Esalen. You're supposed to meet someone here."

I had no idea what Esalen was. It didn't look like much—an unassuming wooden sign, a driveway down the hill, a carefully monitored guardhouse that kept curious people like me from poking around. So I finally searched for it online. Esalen seemed like a new age hippie retreat center with workshops like the Neurodharma of Love or Discovering Your Soul Mandala or Tantra for Homosexual Couples or the Bioenergetics of Emotional Healing.

My first thought was, "This is where crazy people go!" I was not about to start wearing muumuus and talking about auras and rubbing crystals.

I did not grow up crunchy. During the sixties, my parents were Methodists who hung out with navy doctors and church ladies and pilots. My childhood was a happy blur of going to summer camps in North Carolina, eating Pop Rocks on the deck of our mountain cabin, and wearing red-and-white, elephant-adorned clothing handsewn by my mother so my little brother, Mom, and I could all match. I religiously attended Sunday school, sang solos in the children's choir, and earned awards in marksmanship. I not only knew how to hold a rifle but could also nail that bull's-eye, time after time. When I registered to vote at the age of 18, I registered Republican. I didn't know anyone who didn't.

One of the only "alternative" people I knew growing up was my beloved aunt Trudy, a psychologist who wore tie-dyed scarves, talked about "holding space," went on meditation retreats in Santa Fe, practiced Jungian sandplay therapy, drank mushroom tea, and believed there were crystals in your feet that needed to get broken up with something she called reflexology. Aunt Trudy was my favorite aunt, and I was always drawn to her curiosity for the mystical and her reverence for mystery. It felt like she held a key to a gateway of magic. But my father made fun of her, and because I adored my father so much, I felt conflicted about where my loyalty should lie.

Dad loved his brother's wife, and they had a good-humored but adversarial relationship. He teased her in a dismissive, sometimes condescending way that suggested that only quacks and ignorant people believed in such crap, always delivering his little digs with his signature grin. But when Dad was diagnosed with multiple sclerosis, it was Aunt Trudy who showed up, bearing herbs and books and alternative medicine recommendations. When Dad was diagnosed with a brain tumor, it was Aunt Trudy who called me, conspiratorially, to try to enlist me to launch an intervention on his behalf so we could get him treated with a macrobiotic diet, herbs, and a whole host of other holistic health remedies she thought might help. I was hesitant but figured it couldn't hurt. We knew it would be a tough sell. The minute Aunt

Trudy mentioned a macrobiotic diet, Dad ordered a double cheeseburger, spicy chicken wings, and an ice cream sundae. And that was that.

As a physician, Dad typified the conventional medical establishment. He made fun of any medical modality that didn't fit neatly into his black leather medical bag. He considered the holistic health movement nonsense, and after 12 years of my own indoctrination into the medical establishment, so did I. During my medical training, any alternative medicine practice, mind-body medicine notion, faith healing, medical intuitive, or energy medicine rumblings were met with derision and scorn by my professors, my fellow students, and most of the people in my family. If I expressed any curiosity in such woo-woo notions as a medical student or resident, the people in the intellectually elite circles I inhabited rolled their eyes at me. I didn't want to be red-flagged as a quack.

So when the increasingly persistent voice of my Inner Pilot Light told me I was supposed to go to Esalen, I could just hear Dad laughing at me from wherever he was. But the guidance was so clear. I couldn't ignore it anymore, so I flipped through the Esalen workshop catalog. By this point, it had been 9 months since I had officially left medicine, and I had written *I Don't Do Men,* a book about my life as a doctor. So when I saw a workshop with Nancy Aronie titled "Writing from the Heart," I signed up. After all, how scary could a writing workshop be?

When I arrived at Esalen, the grounds were beautiful—a lush green lawn overlooking the ocean, dotted with Adirondack chairs; a pool with a view; and an immense garden sprouting a rainbow of kale, multicolored Swiss chard, zucchini, strawberries, and sunflowers, presided over by a red statue of a dancing goddess. The Esalen dining hall was fragrant with the heady yeast scent of freshly baked bread and the cardamom spice of chai tea. I served myself some tea, slathered peanut butter on a slice of bread, and took a breath.

The long-haired woman at the front desk suggested I settle in with a trip to the natural hot springs baths, perched on a cliff above the Pacific. I love hot tubs, and it was a perfectly sunny but chilly 55-degree spring morning, so I took her advice.

What the long-haired woman failed to warn me about was that the people bathing in these sulfur springs were naked. Men and women, all walking around in their birthday suits without towels, spotlighted in the bright sunlight.

Now, I'm not a prude. I mean, I'm a gynecologist. I've spent my whole life around naked people. But that was clinical. This was Esalen.

The only one in a bathing suit, I felt all the raised eyebrows judging me. Trying to avert my eyes, I slipped into the only bath that didn't have a naked man in it. The view of the ocean distracted me enough to relax a bit. I was falling into a sea trance when a brown-eyed, tattooed woman with enormous breasts and pierced nipples paddled over to me and asked, "So, what brings you to Esalen?"

I tried to look directly into her eyes. I said, "I'm supposed to meet someone here."

After asking me a few questions, she said, "I think you're supposed to meet Rachel Naomi Remen." She recommended I read Dr. Remen's book *Kitchen Table Wisdom*.

The next person I met told me I was supposed to meet Rachel Carlton Abrams. Then another told me I was supposed to meet Martha Beck. I hadn't heard of any of these people, but I made a mental note of their names.

Within an hour of arriving at the baths, I had succumbed to peer pressure and shed my bathing suit, feeling slightly foolish to slink into the dressing room and back to the mineral springs. Soon enough I found myself in conversation with an older gentleman with curly gray hair who introduced himself as Wulf, from Germany. He was wearing a gold necklace bearing the medical caduceus, the same insignia with the staff and snake that was embossed on the medical school ring my father never took off. I asked Wulf if he was a doctor, and he laughed and nodded. He explained that he always forgot that Americans associate this symbol with medicine.

He told me he wore the necklace not to brand himself as a doctor (which he was, by training) but because of the golden Rod of Asclepius from Greek mythology, which he interpreted as a sort of totem after he almost lost a patient. According to Greek mythology, Asclepius was so skilled as a physician that he was reputed to have brought patients back from the dead. For this, he was punished and placed in the heavens as the constellation Ophiuchus, meaning "serpent-bearer." Wulf figured that as long as he wore the necklace, he would never abuse the power of his position and would retain his humility and his power as a true healer.

A part of me cringed when he said the word "healer," but another part of me lit up. As the Squirrel Girl, I once made the mistake of referring to myself as a healer during my medical training, and my professors instantly scoffed at me. In most hospitals, that word was never used. In fact, a group of nurses once told me that shortly after they had gone to a seminar on healing touch and started practicing on patients in the recovery room, a sign appeared in that room, hung there by the hospital administrators: "There will be no healing in this recovery room."

I was so charmed by Wulf that I almost forgot that we were two strangers sitting next to each other naked in a hot spring. He told me how, growing up, he wanted to be a sculptor, but his father had given him two choices: medical school or law school. He trained as a plastic surgeon, and for many years, he practiced his singular form of art—sculpting noses and breasts and faces—before attending a conference in California. On the way from Los Angeles to San Francisco, his car broke down, right in front of Esalen. With no car mechanic anywhere nearby, the guard at the gate into Esalen agreed to let him stay overnight. He ended up staying for a whole year. By the time he returned to Germany, everything had changed. A part of him would no longer allow himself to practice plastic surgery.

Instead, he trained with his grandmother, a traditional healer, who taught him herbal medicine and how to treat a patient's body *and* soul. He began interviewing people about their lives and dreams on film. He'd then edit down the footage to create a small clip of each individual expressing his or her deepest desires. He called himself a "video life coach."

When I told him I was an OB/GYN, he said, "Me too. I birth dreams."

In addition to the two Rachels, Martha Beck, and Wulf, I can now count seven more essential people who came into my life as a result of that week at Esalen, notably Joy, one of the participants in the writing workshop. She was one of the few people in the workshop not already in a healing profession. Almost all the others were alternative medicine practitioners, intuitives, and transformational coaches.

All the critical, skeptical voices showed up, tempting me to dismiss these healing arts. But as I got to know the workshop participants, both through their writing and during long talks over meals, I felt chastened. These people didn't seem like money-hungry quacks with no interest in evidence-based medicine. They seemed like they really cared about their patients. And unlike any of the doctors I'd met, they genuinely loved their work and seemed happy. My curiosity was piqued.

The people I met after heeding the voice that told me I would meet someone at Esalen became my first bits of evidence that the voice instructing me to do crazy things might, in fact, be trustworthy.

The night before my last day at Esalen, the students from my workshop gathered together for dinner. Someone opened a bottle of wine, and when we quickly drank our way through the first bottle, the two men offered to go into town to buy more. As soon as the men were gone, the women gathered around me, excited to have private access to a gynecologist. After 5 days of tears and laughter and the vulnerable secrets we had shared in our writing, we felt like giddy girlfriends at summer camp. Everyone took turns telling stories. One woman described how a fly crawling up her thigh gave her the first orgasm of her young Catholic life. Another shared the trauma of her abortion. Someone else divulged the story of her sexual molestation. Some of these stories had never before been spoken aloud.

After an hour of such stories, the men were still gone, and one woman asked me if she could speak with me privately. We secluded ourselves in the corner of the dining hall, and I held both of her hands in mine while I answered her questions. When I finished answering them, she wiped her tears and kissed my cheek. Another woman took her place in the corner. Then another followed. I felt like Lucy from *Peanuts*, setting up shop: "The Doctor Is In—Five Cents."

The men finally arrived, but we were already high on the Red Tent and didn't need the merlot. By the end of that night, I felt light as air, floating from the dining hall to my bed. I felt a plunk in my belly when I realized the last 9 months had been filled with relief to be free of the medical establishment. But they had also been filled with a longing I didn't realize existed until that moment. That's when I had an epiphany. *You can quit your job, but you can't quit your calling.*

I didn't miss the pressure of surgery and all the fear that fueled the need for perfection in the operating room. I didn't miss being expected to see 40 patients per day or being rushed through rounds in the hospital in the morning. I didn't miss my pager going off all the time. I didn't miss the sleepless nights and the sacrifice of my self-care.

But I missed the sense of connection with women in need of healing, this feeling of communing with our universal feminine experiences. I missed being allowed to feel and express my emotions and bond as a result of the shared vulnerability. What we had just done—our feminine gathering—this was the medicine of the Squirrel Girl. In that moment, I missed medicine so much that my heart ached and my breasts felt strangely heavy, like I was still nursing.

On my very last day at Esalen, my new friend Suzanne, an energy healer, told me I needed to go visit the energy vortex down by the river. I tried to keep an open mind. She described this vortex as a portal where high-vibration energy concentrates and magical things can happen. I had no clue what she was talking about, so I asked her to elaborate. Suzanne told me to think of the earth as a living organism, just like the human body. She said that just like the body has meridians that move energy (they didn't teach us *that* in medical school), the earth also has its own energetic circulatory system. And there are places on earth where more than one of these energy capillaries come together into what she called "lay lines." Where these lay lines intersect, there is an increased amount of palpable energy, like in sacred spots such as Sedona or Stonehenge.

I wasn't completely buying it, but I was curious. So I crossed through the garden, cruised down the hill, and passed the meditation hut, where I opened the gate that took me off Esalen property into the Ventana Wilderness. I walked the mulchy path along the river as it flowed out to the Pacific. Towering redwoods surrounded the path on both sides of the river, and I felt instantly small and insignificant among them, but in a comforting way, as if I was being held in the arms of Mother Earth. A cool fog moved among the tree branches, undulating and alive, chilling me to the core. I reached the bridge Suzanne had described.

Suzanne had warned me to pay attention to some odd physical landmarks that would mark the spot. Several of the stalwart redwoods in the energy vortex spiraled up to the sky, as if a sculptor had chiseled them into wooden corkscrews. The spiraling redwoods framed the wooden bridge on all sides, as if forming a circle of hovering mothers around the flowing water. Certain that I had found the right spot, I stood in the middle of the bridge, holding the metal railing with my hands, which were curled up inside my sweatshirt sleeves in an attempt to keep my fingers warm.

I stood there for at least 20 minutes, overcome with a profound stillness. Riveted to the spot, I was lost in an inexplicable feeling of Oneness with nature. I was the redwoods and the redwoods were me. There was no separation, no feeling of division between me, the mountains, the river, the ocean, and the trees. The feeling was similar but different than the ecstatic feeling I had experienced the night I thought about killing myself. I felt like I was merging with Mother Earth herself, and the overriding emotion was one of peace.

That's the state I was resting in when I noticed a sensation in my hands. The railing of the bridge, which I held with both hands still inside my thick sweatshirt sleeves, was pulsing. It was an unmistakable rhythmic pulse.

My mind clicked in, and I tried to explain it away. There must have been some power lines nearby. Or maybe there was some underground pipeline coursing beneath the bridge. But the pulse grew stronger the longer I stood there. I looked at the second hand on my watch and counted the pulse. It was 72 beats per minute. I checked my own pulse. It was the same—72 beats per minute.

The doctor in me thought that there was probably some physiological explanation. It must have been a blood vessel in my hand pounding against the metal, like when you can hear your pulse in your ears. Maybe my blood pressure, which had been surprisingly low since I quit my job, had spiked up after my hike into the woods. Surely there was a logical explanation that had nothing to do with some mystical energy vortex. But something less logical in me sensed a message in the pulse.

I raced out of the vortex and spent the next hour putting my hands inside my sweatshirt and wrapping them around every other metal railing I could find at Esalen. But there was no pulse. Not one. Slowly, sheepishly, I returned to the bridge. I stared at the railing. Then I wrapped my hands inside my sweatshirt and placed them back where they were. And there it was. Boom boom boom. The pulse, still thumping away.

I stood there, in that energy vortex, feeling my own heartbeat in sync with the very heartbeat of Mother Earth, and I heard the little voice again, even more insistent than when it told me I had to go to Esalen.

The voice said, "Darling, you're needed back in medicine."

I wept because I knew I simply couldn't go back. I couldn't sacrifice myself that way anymore, selling out my body, my relationships, and my soul. But at the same time, I also knew that I must. I cursed the voice. I cursed medicine. Why? Why? Why?

I had been called to medicine only to discover that medicine had lost its heart, that medicine wasn't about healing; it was about traumatizing everyone—the doctors, the nurses, the patients, even the alternative medicine practitioners. How had we gotten so far off track? Medicine was so broken. We had lost our way, and I felt helpless, hopeless, betrayed, and royally pissed off.

I didn't want to go back. I had devoted my life to medicine, but medicine had broken my heart.

But the voice was insistent. "Medicine needs to be healed. You will help to heal it."

No! Not me! Please, anyone but me.

I didn't want to go back, but the voice in the energy vortex was gentle and reassuring. "You will be protected. They can't hurt you this time."

I had no idea how this might look. What did the voice mean? How was I supposed to help heal medicine? What would be asked of me? I didn't know. I shuddered at what I might be expected to do. It would have been so much easier to just say no, to hang the phone back up and plunge into something that felt safer, like my art.

But something in me knew that I could trust this voice and that it would guide me if I paid attention and let it lead. With my hand on my heart, my hand tingling, I felt my own pulse, and curling into a ball, rocking myself, I breathed in and out. Feeling humbled and scared, and not really knowing what I was agreeing to, I finally stopped rocking, got on my knees, and bowed forward, putting my forehead on the bridge. Right there, I accepted the call.

You will accept your call, too, when the time is right. Your calling may begin as dreams, visions, or a direct knowledge about something that wants to be born through you. Often, you will feel a sense of urgency about bringing what you sense into form. When you're in the space between stories, those dreams may percolate and bubble up as desires. Perhaps you made it through hell and back as a survivor of a life-threatening illness, the loss of a loved one, a violent crime, divorce, financial hardship, or sexual abuse. Maybe because you learned how to survive and thrive, you now feel called to help others who are still experiencing the kind of pain that once caused you to suffer. This pure desire to serve may inspire you to start a nonprofit, write a book, plan a workshop, prepare a speech for the TED talk you hope to give, open a one-on-one practice, volunteer, or travel overseas in service to those in need. Maybe your husband died and now you want to work with widows, or you miscarried and now you want to help others who lost babies. Maybe you survived cancer by healing your thoughts, or you found a way to transmute that horrifying rape into soul growth, or you learned how to use art to heal from the effects of child abuse. Maybe you feel called to help transform the atrocities of the planet by serving the rainforests or raising consciousness around human trafficking or helping feed the hungry.

Your passion may lead you to jump to conclusions about the nature of your calling. But callings aren't always so simple. Martha Beck says that finding your calling is like tracking a wild animal. First you follow one "hot track" and then another. The wild animal may veer left, then right, and then it may walk in circles for a while. The mind hates this. It wants you to pursue your calling as a nice, straight line. But callings don't tend to operate this way.

Your "crazy ideas" and desires may lead you to your first hot track, but that track might not be the final destination of your calling. Because the Small Self craves certainty, it will sometimes try to project all the way to the end result of your purpose, focusing on a goal that may not be your true path. But even if your Small Self initially leads you astray, you can trust your process. Sometimes we wind up in the right place for all the wrong reasons. If you're brave enough to say yes when that first call comes and you're committed to following one hot track at a time, you'll find yourself smack-dab in the center of your purpose.

Trust that it's safe to say yes when you are called. Trust that you will be guided if you follow one hot track at a time. Stay open to the mysterious flow that will carry you, as if by magic, when you open yourself to that which wants to be born through you. Keep your mind and heart open to instincts that may not make sense to your mind. When you do, the Universe smiles.

HERO'S GUIDEPOST:
Stay Open to Mystery

It's easy to think we can understand the world and how it works. But then, if things happen that we can't explain, it can lead to discomfort, disorientation, or even denial. When something happens that disrupts your story of how the world works, be curious. Don't worry too much about explaining your experience. The need to know arises from the mind, which can't begin to fathom what your heart knows is possible. What if "How" and "Why" were not the most important questions, the ones that actually help us live? When you're willing to stop being an expert on life, you open yourself to magic. You let life be the teacher and humble yourself as the perpetual student. That's when the real fun begins.

HERO'S PRACTICE:
Disrupt Your Story

Has anything mysterious ever happened that left you questioning how the world works? Maybe you just knew someone was about to call right before the phone rang. Maybe you had a spontaneous remission from a seemingly incurable illness. Maybe you had a dream that predicted the future. Maybe you saw a vision in your mind that quickly came true. Maybe you had a near-death experience that gave you a glimpse of the other side. Maybe you had a thought and someone else seemed to pick up on it, as if by telepathy. Maybe you wished the rain would stop—and then it did. Maybe you set an impossible intention, and then the Universe rolled out the red carpet and brought it into being in seemingly miraculous ways. Maybe you knew something you shouldn't have known in a way that protected you or someone you love. Maybe a psychic told you something that came into being, or a medium channeled your dead grandmother and gave you information nobody else could have possibly known.

All it takes is one intense data point to disrupt your story of how the world works. When this happens, something cracks the shell of the ego and makes miracles more likely. Such things happen all the time, but once it happens to you, you suddenly have the eyes to see and the ears to hear. If you've already experienced encounters with the unknown that leave you open to mystery, write them down and post them somewhere you'll see them often. Remind yourself every day that miracles are possible. Then become One with mystery. Invite yourself to merge with synchronicity itself. Be the miracle, and watch, in awe, as life reveals itself to you.

CHAPTER 7

Accept Blessings

Like many heroes on a journey, I hoped that once I answered the scary call, my next set of instructions would be obvious. But that's not what happened. Instead, the signs from the Universe led me down many cul-de-sacs of confusion peppered with dark nights of the soul. I had embarked upon the classic hero's journey phase, the Road of Trials, after the hero accepts the call and journeys onward, only to discover that nothing is as easy as the hero hopes it will be.

As long as the sun was shining and I attended to the daily bustle of raising a toddler, I could stave off the worst of the fear voices, which I called "the Gremlin." I could muster up an air of false confidence so my family and friends didn't freak out about the fact that Matt and I were spending all of our money. During daylight hours, I could keep busy and look productive and brainstorm about what the future might hold. I had written a book, *I Don't Do Men*, hoping to get a book deal that might at least put a plug in the dam of our hemorrhaging bank account, but all the agents I submitted my book to had rejected me. I was brainstorming ways I might go back to medicine without selling my soul, but every lead that gave me hope led to closed doors.

I could hold it together during the daytime, but in the inky darkness, after everyone else had fallen asleep, the Gremlin would attack.

Who the hell do you think you are, posing like you're qualified to do anything but blow through Pap smears and deliver babies? You have no talent, and you'll never publish anything. You might as well just put your tail between your legs and crawl back to the hospital. You think you might start some revolutionary medical practice that others might emulate? You really think you're going to heal health care? Look how stupid and careless you are. You took a perfectly good career with a stable paycheck and a big fat retirement account that would have taken good care of you and your family, and you threw it all away because you wanted more. Grow up, Lissa. You've spoiled yourself with a very expensive sabbatical. It's time to throw in the towel, accept that this is as good as it gets, beg for forgiveness from the people you got all high and mighty with, and get back to what you're good at—delivering babies in the hospital. Stop being reckless and do what you must to clean up this mess you've made.

My Gremlin is a vicious son of a bitch. I suspect yours might be, too.

Fortunately, my Inner Pilot Light never abandoned me, even in the midst of those dark nights of the soul. Although the gentle, loving voice was nearly drowned out by the cacophony of my Gremlin, I could still hear the whispers that said, "Carry on, Lissa. You're on the right path, even though you don't know where you're going." That became my mantra during this challenging time. *You're on the right path, even though you don't know where you're going.* The greatest gift I was granted during this painful part of my hero's journey was the steadfast reassurance of my Inner Pilot Light, which never abandoned me, even when I was most scared. That voice became one of my most trusted mentors, but it wasn't my only guidance.

In the classic hero's journey, magical mentors appear to arm the hero with the necessary tools for the long, arduous journey that lies ahead. And that's exactly what happened to me. My Inner Pilot Light reminded me to follow up on all the names of people I discovered at Esalen. I looked up Dr. Rachel Naomi Remen first and discovered that she had written two books. Along with the six million other people who had read them, I gobbled up *Kitchen Table Wisdom* and *My Grandfather's Blessings*. Both collections included true wisdom stories about medicine and life drawn from her long relationship with her patients as a doctor and her rabbi grandfather as a child. These books were like oxygen for me. If there was even one doctor like Rachel out there in the dark, broken world of medicine, I knew I had to breathe her air.

From her Web site, I discovered that Rachel taught several workshops each year for doctors and other health professionals in Mill Valley, California, a 2-hour drive from where I was living. I knew it was a sign. I registered for one of them right away, in spite of the Gremlin voice that told me I was being reckless for putting the fee on a credit card I wouldn't be able to pay off anytime soon.

I arrived at Rachel's workshop along with 80 other doctors. Almost 2 years had passed since I had been in a hospital. I hadn't been in a room with so many doctors since I was in medical school doing morbidity and mortality (M&M) rounds, when we gathered to discuss cases that ended badly. Usually the focus was a death, a disability, or a surgical complication. The stated goal of M&M was to determine what went wrong, who might be at fault, and how to prevent such negative outcomes in the future. It's a noble goal. But in actual practice, M&M was often a bloodbath of blame and shame, full of finger-pointing, second-guessing, one-upmanship, ego, guilt, and grief.

When something bad happened in the hospital, especially when it was on my watch, I felt sick to my stomach. When a young mother died unexpectedly, or when a newborn started seizing in the delivery room, I replayed every moment of what happened in my head, not only in waking hours but also in the dreams that haunted me. Those experiences already dredged up my deepest fears, that I was inadequate, that I was a fraud, that I wasn't really qualified to hold life and death in my feeble hands. As if the grief and guilt that accompanied a negative outcome weren't enough, I was also terrified of getting sued.

Seeing all of those doctors sitting together in one room at Rachel's workshop brought back all the M&M trauma. I nearly had a panic attack. My heart raced and palpitated. I could hear my blood rushing in my ears. I felt short of breath and nauseated.

I could tell it wasn't just me. I saw the worry in the eyes of another young doctor who was about my age. I introduced myself to her, and she said her name was Heather. Sensing that Heather was one of the safe ones, I confessed to her that I felt nervous. Heather seemed visibly relieved. She too had left medicine and had come to the workshop to figure out what to do next. For both of us, our relationship with medicine was like a dysfunctional love affair. We couldn't possibly stay in the relationship, but we couldn't bear to leave. Heather and I sat in the very back, right near the exit, just in case we needed to make a quick run for it.

When Rachel entered the room, everyone hushed. Rachel's presence commanded silence. She was tall, slim, and regal, with pure white hair, silver and turquoise jewelry, and very white teeth that gleamed when she smiled, which was often. She was 70 years old and had lived with a chronic illness for most of them but showed little evidence of that. Greeting familiar faces, she moved to the front of the room and picked up the microphone. Speaking slowly and softly, requiring all of us to stop our fidgeting and rustling, and relax into attentive silence, Rachel welcomed us. I knew instantly that Rachel was a doctor I could trust.

Over the next few days Rachel offered us many reflections and exercises to enable us to remember our true selves. One of them started with a simple question: "How old were you when you first realized that the needs of a living thing . . . a plant . . . an insect . . . an animal or even a person mattered to you? How many people were between 20 and 25?" None of us raised our hands.

"Between 15 and 20?" Still no hands.

"Between 10 and 15?" Three or four hands were raised.

"Younger than 10?" Nearly every hand in the room shot up.

Rachel invited us to look around the room at all the hands in the air. We did not start to be healers the day we entered medical school, she told us. We had been responding to the needs of others and trying to make a difference since we were very young. She asked us to share some of our early memories from the long ago time when we did not have the tools of medicine to make a difference in the lives of others.

I raised my hand and told the story of my baby squirrels. Others followed with stories about turning the lights on in their nursery after they were put to bed so their dolls would not be afraid in the dark or their worries that their stuffed animals were hungry or lonely.

As the impulse to serve the needs of others was revealed to be present in each of us even when we were very young, I was deeply touched. So were many of the other doctors in the room. Rachel was showing us our truth. Perhaps we were actually born to be doctors and healers. Yet the impulse to preserve the lives of others led us into a medical training model that systematically asked us to violate the very thing that called us to the profession in the first place. I, for one, felt duped, betrayed, violated, angry, and confused. What was I supposed to do with the impulse to preserve life when I wasn't willing to sell out in order to practice that impulse?

It wasn't until Rachel's workshop that I stopped blaming the Squirrel Girl and my father for misleading me. I realized that I'd been a doctor for as long as I could remember. This was my true nature, not some social construct that brainwashed me. It was a revelation. As I became increasingly disillusioned with our health care system, I had convinced myself that I only went to medical school because my father was a doctor, that I had been influenced by a man I loved and wanted to impress, rather than being fueled by a true calling. I told myself that it was only because I yearned for my father's attention that I spent my childhood in hospitals, scrubbing in on my first surgery when I was 12 with my father's surgeon friend because I was so fascinated and curious. I volunteered as a candy striper when I was 15 and got my first job as a phlebotomist when I was 18, but surely, I rationalized, it was only because I wanted my father to love me and be proud of me. I had been telling myself the story that being a doctor went against my true nature, that perhaps my true nature was more suited to being an artist or a writer.

In that moment, sitting among those 80 doctors, I felt the plunk of my original calling coming back home. I hadn't made some egregious mistake when I felt called to medicine at the age of 7. I was still the Squirrel Girl. It's just that I had become confused by a system that twisted my natural impulse to preserve the lives of other living beings, and I felt helpless and powerless to reclaim the impulse that was rightfully mine.

Rachel's workshop not only inspired me to stay true to my calling but also awakened a reclamation of my own power. I hadn't realized how much I had allowed myself to fall into the role of victim. The story I had been telling myself was that "they" did this to me: "They" hurt me, "they" abused me, "they" never showed compassion when I lost a loved one or allowed me to grieve the trauma of delivering four dead babies in one night. I blamed "them." I made "them" wrong. Until that workshop, I had never owned that I was there by choice. Nobody held a gun to my head to keep me in the hospital. I chose to stay because of that impulse to preserve the lives of others. I thought I had no other choice, but perhaps I could stay true to that impulse without submitting to the traumas of the system. I had no idea what that would look or feel like, but I felt it in my bones.

When I first walked into that room of 80 doctors, I was firmly entrenched in "us" and "them," with "us" being the good guys, the doctors like me and Heather, who would rather leave the system than let it break us, and "them" being the bad guys, the abusers, the ones who did the hazing, the ones who stayed. I had let my Small Self polarize "us," and in doing so, I had compromised my ability to feel compassion for those doctors who, like abused children that go on to abuse their own kids, had been broken by the very system that was meant to help them.

Among those 80 doctors were academic doctors responsible for residents and medical students, community doctors in private practice, students and residents still in training, and doctors like Heather and me, who had left the system but were feeling the call to come back. Many of us had beefs with each other, but the loving, compassionate way Rachel led her workshop allowed us to see the humanity in one another, not as "us" and "them" but as human beings, called to service, doing the best we could.

When I spoke to Rachel after the workshop, I expressed my frustration with health care as it was and asked for her guidance. Rachel said, "Lissa, don't join something. Build something." I wrote it in Magic Marker on the wall of my home office.

Shortly thereafter, Rachel invited me to join a small group of doctors who met in her living room in Mill Valley to uncover and explore the deep meaning in our daily work. I started attending these Finding Meaning in Medicine meetings regularly, and they became *my* medicine. I have now been sitting on that floor of Rachel's living room for almost 8 years, but for the first 2 years I pretty much cried through every gathering. I had never felt safe in a room full of doctors. Never before had I been surrounded by doctors who simply wished me well. I could barely receive such a shocking gift.

It took years of crying on Rachel's floor to realize how much I had gotten stuck in my victim story. Back in my twenties, I spent a lot of time writing in my journal, usually about men. Then I had an epiphany. I realized that the quality of my relationships with men was inversely related to the amount of time I spent writing in my journal. If the relationship was healthy, I was off happily living my life, not sitting on my window seat writing about how happy I was. But if the relationship was dysfunctional, I wrote . . . and wrote . . . and wrote. And when I look back now at those journals, I have to laugh at myself because every whining, complaining story I told had me as the heroine of my "poor me" story. The guy was always a liar, cheater, loser, wimp, alcoholic, abuser, narcissist, or jerk. They were all WRONG. But me, I was always right.

In my twenties I was a hot mess who blamed everyone else for the messes she was creating, not only with men but also with my medical training. It embarrasses me now to reflect back upon how married I was to my medical victim story when I sat in a circle with that group of doctors. I have to remind myself to be compassionate with myself when I think back to how violently I blamed the system, how helpless and powerless I felt, how woeful my pity party had become, how much I suffered at my own hands unnecessarily.

I remember sitting on Rachel's floor in that circle of doctors, crying over the Dr. Jacksons of my medical training. I judged these doctors as insensitive dolts while I sat on my high-and-mighty throne of self-righteousness. I rewrote the story about how Dr. Jackson could have gotten the whole thing right. Imagine, I told myself, if Dr. Jackson, seeing me in tears, had knelt to the floor with the midwives and confessed that he too had cried when someone died, that it was natural to feel loss, that the heart is tender and something to be cherished. Imagine if Dr. Jackson had promised to take responsibility for covering labor and delivery to give me a few moments to digest what had happened. Imagine if I had been invited to share with my professor how I was feeling, if it had been safe to be vulnerable. Had I been allowed to heal, that night might not have led to a decade of nightmares and flashbacks. But because of the shaming, the message I received was that to become a good doctor, I needed to stop feeling, and that seemed not only impossible but also undesirable. As a woman, I was an emotional, empathic creature, and I felt things deeply. In essence, I was being asked to deny the very feminine essence within me.

But what if I wasn't a victim of the Dr. Jacksons of my medical training after all? After years of spending time with Rachel and the other doctors, I woke up to the realization that Dr. Jackson was probably doing the very best he could given his own traumas during his childhood or his medical training. What if his teachers had told him to "Buck up, Jackson" and he had internalized this message as his own, when really he once cried too when babies died? What if he genuinely thought he was shaping me into the best physician he could help me become? What if his intentions were not malicious at all? What if he was genuinely doing the best he could?

What if he was even giving me a gift on that night of four dead babies? That night marked a turning point in my life as a doctor. I made a promise to myself on the floor of that locker room that I would never, under any circumstances, sell my soul in order to be a doctor. I vowed to leave medicine before I let medicine break my spirit. I committed to keeping my heart open, no matter what. I wasn't always successful in my intention, but the influence of teachers like Dr. Jackson grew me into the doctor I became. Perhaps he was the perfect teacher to cement within my consciousness the life-altering lesson I learned that night. Perhaps I should be thanking him rather than judging him.

I'll be forever grateful to Rachel and the doctors who encircled me with their love during those formative years after I left my job in the hospital. They healed my victim story with their compassion without once judging me for it. Later, when I felt embarrassed by how unconscious I once was regarding the blaming, shaming, and judgment of my victim story, I bowed my head and admitted how I felt to Rachel.

She smiled at me with boundless love and said, referencing my youth as compared to the others and the preciousness of my own daughter, "Lissa, you were our Siena. We love you."

I can only imagine that God might say the same thing to us all.

Most of us have been traumatized by our own version of Dr. Jackson, and it's natural to feel like a victim when you're feeling pummeled by life. As spiritual teacher Jeff Brown posted on Facebook, "I am so tired of people saying 'You are exactly where you are supposed to be,' no matter what someone's life circumstances and challenges. Yes, there is no question that we can often learn something of value wherever we are on the path, and yes, we may have, in some situations, attracted the exact challenge that we need to grow, BUT that does not mean that we are ALWAYS where we are supposed to be or that we chose our every reality. Telling that to someone in every situation—even when they are ill or suffering tremendously—is arrogant, and adds insult to injury. Sometimes we need a kick in the ass, and sometimes we are just a victim of terrible circumstances. Sometimes our suffering is needless and the result of other people's wrongdoing. Compassion demands that we hold the space for other's challenges with a wide-open heart. Let them decide if they are exactly where they are supposed to be. It's not for us to say. There are many victims on this planet. Many. And the more we dismiss legitimate victimhood, the more we perpetuate and enable victimization. I really get that many of us reach a stage where it is essential that we move beyond victimhood and, in certain situations, recognize how we may have manifest our circumstances. But this is not true for everyone, nor is it true in every situation. For some of us, it is essential that we own our victimhood, that we are seen in our victimhood, and that we do not reframe our suffering in positive terms unless and until we feel it is true for us."

All of us heroes are offered the opportunity to rewrite our victim story, but not until we are ready to do so. Sometimes we need to stew in our victim story for a while, marinating in the pain we feel, milking our stories for all they're worth, until the day comes when we're ready to release the stories. Until then, it's natural to get angry at those who hurt us, feel sad about what we've lost, or blame the Universe for cursing us. After all, we're human, and we're prone to suffering from thoughts, feelings, and beliefs that arise in the midst of painful experiences. Whether your traumas arose during your childhood or caught up with you later in life, it's understandable to feel like the victim of bad luck, bad genes, or bad people.

But as the Buddhist proverb says, "Pain is inevitable. Suffering is optional." We may not be able to avoid the traumatic events that happen in our lives. No one knows why bad things happen to good people. Perhaps such tragedies are Divine appointments between our souls and the Universe that are scripted out on the spiritual plane before we are even born. Perhaps they're the result of karma created from past lives. Maybe we unwittingly create them with the unconscious beliefs that get downloaded into us when we are still innocent children. For all we know, we're simply spirits in human bodies playing a holographic video game, and we write such challenges into the game because we wouldn't know ecstasy and bliss if we didn't have pain and grief as contrast. The game wouldn't be as much fun if we couldn't experience life in its extremes.

I certainly don't claim to know the secrets to life, but I can say that we all experience painful human curveballs, especially those of us slated for a particularly hairy hero's journey. Many heroes were sexually abused in childhood, or we experienced the death of a loved one, or we were abandoned by a parent, or we got slammed with a serious illness or disability, or we were betrayed by someone we love. Some heroes meant to skyrocket to spiritual leadership have endured all of the above. The training for such spiritual service can be a bitch, but when we're able to move beyond our victim story, experiences such as these catapult us onto the spiritual fast track and get us ready to fulfill our missions. We need to be compassionate with ourselves and each other when we're feeling victimized, but we also need to avoid coddling our victim story in a way that gets us stuck.

We all have our own traumas, and they serve as initiations if we're willing to cull from them the lessons that help us love radically and strip away all that is not who we really are. If you're brave enough to learn the lessons from your traumas while choosing to free yourself from your victim story, your heart will open, your hero's journey will accelerate, and you will be rewarded for your courage.

Many of us have professional frustrations similar to what I experienced in medicine. Like I did, you may feel victimized by an industry that threatens your integrity and leaves you feeling out of touch with your calling. You may have been called to your career the way I was called to mine, but then something went awry. You became a teacher because you believe that children are our future and a loving, nurturing, instructional education will empower them to evolve our world. Then you wound up buried in bureaucracy and politics and standardized test expectations and rules that keep you from hugging your students, and you may feel that such things keep you from being the teacher you know your students need. Or you went to law school because you believe in upholding a just society, but you discovered that there is nothing just about our legal system, that it's all about arguing for your client's position, whether it's just or not. Or you got into politics because you were called to be the loving, caring voice of the people, shaping public policy, only to realize that politics is not about democracy; it's about who spends the most money, kisses up to the lobbyists, or launches the best smear campaign. Maybe you took a job in publishing because you believe in helping visionaries spread their messages, but you feel like it's all about the almighty dollar and your ability to amplify a spiritual message has gotten corrupted. You may have moved up the corporate ladder because you bought into the American dream and wanted to provide a better life for your children than you had, only to discover that what you sold out in order to get ahead wasn't worth the sacrifice.

I suspect you began your journey the way most of us do. Maybe, like many doctors, you were young when you recognized that the life of another being mattered. Or maybe you were a lawyer who, early on, fought for the underdogs and stood for what was just. Back then, you were young and idealistic and you believed you could make a difference. And then the others— the ones who haven't yet discovered their inner superheroes—threatened to break you.

But you can't ever be broken. You are a hero, and even though you might fall to your knees on a bathroom floor under the pressure of it all, you will rise, like a phoenix from the ashes, and you will stay true to the integrity of your calling. You will muster up the resilience to forgive those who hurt you, to accept what has happened in the past, and to find in your cracked-open heart the grace to thank those who taught you everything you need in order to fulfill your mission.

Yes, you've been hurt. Yes, life might have been easier if you hadn't endured what you did. Yes, all of your fellow heroes have deep compassion for the pain of what you've experienced. But we know that everything that has brought you to this point has been training you for this mission you have been called to fulfill. Everything has grown you. Everything has been purposeful, even if you don't fully understand why you had to endure what you did.

What if everything that has happened is for a very specific reason? Even if you're mired in an industry that isn't working anymore, what if things are falling apart perfectly as part of a cosmic plan to disrupt the status quo, uprooting your profession from the chains that bind it so you can sweep in with angel wings and reform it with a revolution of love? What if you are exactly the person to shift consciousness in your line of work? What if you've been training your whole life to be just such a hero?

HERO'S GUIDEPOST:
Release Your Victim Story When You're Ready

It's only natural to feel hurt, angry, or frightened because of the challenges you've faced, especially if these traumas were perpetrated by another person. But at some point on your hero's journey, you'll realize that your ability to accomplish your cosmic mission will be impeded by any blaming, shaming, and judgment that arises from your victim story. In other words, there's a statute of limitations on your victim story. Hold onto it as long as you must, but when you're ready to step into your power and take the next brave step on your hero's journey, you'll be asked to let it go. Be gentle and compassionate with yourself. Seek support from others who understand this process. Then do what you must to transmute your pain into fuel for soul growth. As spiritual teacher Ram Dass says, "Suffering is the sandpaper of our incarnation. It does its work of shaping us." Let life break you open and shape you into the hero you are becoming.

Are you ready and willing to do what you must to turn your blame and judgment into acceptance or even gratitude? Can you let go of feeling like you're a victim of evil people and a hostile universe? Can you accept that maybe your soul signed up for even your most painful traumas because these experiences taught you valuable lessons that grew you and strengthened your resilience? Are you ready for the next phase of your journey?

HERO'S PRACTICE:

Question Your Thoughts

If you notice a painful emotion bubbling up and feel like you might be stuck in a victim story, let yourself notice the emotion. Maybe you feel anger, fear, shame, disappointment, or grief. Close your eyes and allow yourself to simply feel the feeling, without judgment. Visualize the situation where you feel hurt. Where are you? Are you sitting or standing? Whom are you angry or upset with? Be very gentle with yourself.

See if you can identify the thought that creates the stressful feeling, the thought that makes you feel like a victim. Maybe you're thinking, "John is acting like a jerk" or "John shouldn't have said that" or "I need John to listen to me."

Question the thoughts that cause you stress using spiritual teacher and author Byron Katie's The Work. First, ask yourself these four questions about the thought you've been believing.

1. Is it true?

2. Can I absolutely know that it's true?

3. How do I react, what happens, when I believe that thought?

4. Who would I be without the thought?

Then, turn the thought around by finding an opposite. For example, "I need John to listen to me" can be turned around to "I don't need John to listen to me," "I need me to listen to myself," and "I need me to listen to John." Find at least three specific, genuine examples of how each turnaround is as true as or truer than your original thought.

For specific instructions on how to free yourself from suffering by questioning your thoughts using The Work, visit TheWork.com.

CHAPTER 8

NOT ALL WHO WANDER
ARE LOST

Back when I was pregnant with Siena, I had started The Woman Inside Project. The idea came to me because of Janie, a patient of mine who was diagnosed with breast cancer in her third trimester of pregnancy. I was almost as pregnant as she was, and a physician friend had sent me a belly-casting kit to memorialize my very pregnant form. I laughed when I realized that the fancy kit was nothing more than medical-grade plaster bandages, the kind we use to cast fractures, which I could have easily swiped from any emergency room. Matt had used the kit to make a sculpture of my torso the week before Janie was diagnosed with breast cancer, and because she was going to need a bilateral mastectomy as soon as we induced her labor and delivered the baby, I had the idea that I could invite Janie to my home so I could cast her belly and breasts the way Matt had cast mine, to memorialize her body in its present state.

Too young for routine mammograms, Janie had been getting yearly breast exams and religiously checking for lumps in the shower. She noticed a new lump during one of those shower exams, so she came to see me, and I felt what she felt. Radiology studies uncovered concerning calcifications, and before she knew it, an orderly was whisking her off to the operating room for a breast biopsy, only 2 months before her due date. She received the biopsy result the day her girlfriends threw her baby shower. Although she was devastated, the news didn't surprise her. Although she had no family history of breast cancer, she somehow always knew she would get it. A psychic had confirmed her suspicion when she was in college.

It took me a while to create the mold of Janie's torso, and while I sculpted her body, I had the opportunity to talk to her, woman to woman, in a way I never could have during my rushed office hours. I asked her to tell me about her baby, her life, and her feelings about the breast cancer diagnosis. She told me she was very frightened—afraid of dying, afraid of abandoning her baby, afraid of the surgery and the deformity and feeling like less of a woman after treatment.

After Janie left, I painted the plaster cast with pigmented molten bees-wax, which is very skinlike. And I wrote a first-person narrative of the beauty I saw within Janie. When I sent Janie the story, she cried and said, "No doctor has ever seen me or touched me the way you just did."

It felt so meaningful, so precious, to create this work of art and write this story that honored this beautiful woman. It touched something in me, some-thing that felt real and true about what originally called me to medicine.

After casting Janie's torso (which you can see at LissaRankinArt.com), I invited other patients of mine to come to my house to do the same. While they were naked in a lounge chair, I covered their bodies with warm, lavender-scented bandages, recreating a likeness of their figures from the chin to the pubis. While casting these women, I asked them to tell me their breast cancer stories. They usually started with the clinical details: the diag-nosis, the staging, the surgery, the chemo, the radiation. But invariably, the women strayed into the stories of what else was happening during their breast cancer treatments: the skateboarding accident that landed her son in the ICU right after her mastectomy, the betrayal of the husband who aban-doned her after her diagnosis, the spiritual awakening that accompanied facing her own mortality.

When I completed the casting, I'd hold up the sculpture and say, "This is what the world sees of you. Now tell me about the rest." Then I'd listen to the stories for as long as it took each woman to reveal "the woman inside." When they were done telling their stories, I painted the casts and handwrote their stories onto scrolls of waxed rice paper.

The first few women I included in the art project were patients of mine from my practice in Southern California, but after I left my clinical practice, I started getting referrals from other people who had heard about the proj-ect. It took casting almost 20 women before I finally realized what I had really been doing with The Woman Inside Project. I scheduled all the casting sessions on weekends when I could block off the whole day to spend time with my models. During this time, I gave each woman my complete attention for as long as the process took. It's as if I had been making amends to my patients for having given them only 7½ minutes in the office, and in doing so, I was also healing myself from the wounds to my integrity. My patients told me that for the first time in their lives, they felt truly heard, truly seen, truly witnessed by a physician, not only as a diagnosis but also for the beauty of who they were as a whole person.

As I prepared to exhibit The Woman Inside Project, I found myself thinking a lot about the shamanic journey where I received the vision of the stethoscope with the pink paintbrush on it. The exhibition of this art show felt like the culmination of something that had been birthed there in Big Sur, a manifestation of the journey of integration that had been spawned by that gift. Getting ready for that exhibition, I had an epiphany. *I had been painting my patients.* I finally understood the gift I had given myself. It was the gift of integration, the gift of bringing all the facets of myself—my doctor self, my writer self, my artist self, my healer self—together into my heart.

I was trying to birth my career as a writer. I had spent a year devoting myself to writing a memoir I called *I Don't Do Men: Confessions of an OB/GYN.* I knew nothing about how to become a published writer, but after scouring bookstores and reading a book called *Writer's Marketplace,* I found a bunch of literary agents willing to accept queries from wannabe writers. I dutifully researched how to submit a book to agents and sent cold-call letters to dozens of them. With butterflies in my belly, I waited. And waited. And waited. Finally, the rejection letters started pouring in. Each rejection was a scalpel to my heart. The Gremlin would rear up with each one and begin its diatribe. Each time, I had to armor up my faith bubble, calming the Gremlin with little cooing noises. But on dark nights, after Matt and Siena had fallen asleep, I would question whether I was just delusional. Maybe I really didn't have what it takes to be a published writer. Maybe I was simply overconfident and living in a fantasy. Maybe I needed to throw in the towel, admit defeat, and go back to the hospital, where I was an expert with a valuable skill that helped people and could make money.

Around the same time as I was living in Monterey and trying to get my book published, the economy tanked and my previously lucrative art career fizzled. I thought I could help support us by spending more time in the art studio and increasing sales of my art, but although I had several galleries representing my work, few were selling much. And two of them went under, one of which took my art with it when the gallery folded.

Matt and I had also discussed the possibility of having him go back to work in order to help ease the financial burden. I was starting to feel panicked about how we would pay the bills. All of our savings and the money from the sale of our house went towards medical school debt and paying what it cost to untangle myself from my practice. Although Matt and I were both blessed with skills that made us highly employable, both of us felt that using these skills would require us to pay a price we were unwilling to pay. We could have recreated financial security if I went back to the hospital or Matt returned to corporate America, but we would have done so at the expense of our souls.

Because I once brought in a secure salary and because the decision to give it up had been my choice, I felt guilty and responsible for the financial mess I had created. Thinking I needed to remain the perpetual optimist, I didn't admit to Matt that I was losing faith in myself, that I was feeling weak and scared, that I needed him to rally with me, to approach the situation as a team, even if it meant both of us would become baristas until something else came through. A year had passed since I had left medicine, and failure looked imminent.

I prayed that the Universe would help me catch the attention of a literary agent so I could finally publish the book I'd spent a year writing. After a rush of rejection letters from literary agents, Barbara, a young, peppy literary agent from an agency in New York City, called to say that she would get in a "monkey knife fight" to have the opportunity to represent my book. I swooned. A New York literary agent wanted to represent me! I was going to be a writer! Matt and I splurged on expensive champagne.

Such turning points can be very confusing to a hero on a journey. Was getting my book rejected a Cosmic No from the Universe, trying to redirect me back to the hospital? Or was it a test of my commitment, a measure of my faith, or a purposeful blow to my well-defended ego? Was the Universe sending me a message that I wasn't meant to become a writer? Or was I meant to learn to trust the strong intuitive feeling I couldn't shake, which told me that I would write many books one day? Was I supposed to write *I Don't Do Men* as part of my healing but not have it published? I felt very confused, frustrated, frightened, and disappointed at the time, though in retrospect, I'm grateful for how things unfolded. It all makes sense when I look back on it, as journeys so often do when you're on the Road of Trials.

Many heroes will be tempted to throw in the towel when they're on the Road of Trials, where the path is never smooth and things rarely go as planned. I was no different. I endured a painful crisis of faith, questioning everything and doubting myself. I felt confused and lost. I didn't know what to do next. I needed help, so I did what I had done many times over the past few years. I drove down to Big Sur looking for answers. I had been avoiding going to Big Sur since the fire there in 2008. Months earlier, I had been delighted by the flashes of light and jagged Zs of fire dancing between clouds during a freakish summer electrical storm. Thunder rolled through Carmel Valley, shaking the earth, while ominous clouds swirled into ever-darker clusters. Light rain fell, but the glorious monsoon we awaited eagerly, with hopes it would cool the air, never came. As quickly as it arrived, the storm passed.

Hours later I read the headline news that the breathtaking display of lightning had sparked more than a thousand wildfires in Northern California, including two in Big Sur. Within days, the two fires merged to create the largest threat to the idyllic resort town in decades. I slept restlessly, dreaming of firestorms and bolts of lightning, scary, apocalyptic images that haunted me long after I awoke.

To think of my soul's home in flames, with redwoods toppling into embers and historic structures threatened, left me feeling unrooted. During this time, I heard rumors of the devastation. They closed a long stretch of Highway 1, and all of my friends from Esalen were evacuated. The deer and condors and mountain lions of the Ventana Wilderness were running for their lives into town. The house I had rented many times as an art villa and vacation home burned to the ground. Julia Pfeiffer Burns State Park, the site of the rock I had visited many times in search of the wisdom I seemed to find there, was closed indefinitely.

I knew things wouldn't look the same when I finally mustered up the courage to make my postfire pilgrimage back to Big Sur. But I wasn't prepared for the emotional reaction that hit me like a bullet when I witnessed the devastation to the land I loved so much. The usually bright green, spectacular vista to the east had morphed into blackened, barren hills for as far as I could see. When I pulled over on the side of the road to digest what I was witnessing, I could barely breathe. The heavy odor of burnt earth, like old cigarette smoke in an ashtray, permeated the air, replacing the usual scent of eucalyptus and pine. Nothing but ash and charred bits of bramble and brown stumps filled the vista, mile after mile.

I was too shocked to cry.

I kept driving, past Big Sur Bakery and Nepenthe restaurant and Hawthorne Gallery and Deetjen's Big Sur Inn. Driving south, if I didn't look to the left, not much had changed. Highway 1 acted as a natural firebreak, and the firefighters worked tirelessly to protect historic structures, homes, and resorts on the western side of Highway 1. But then I'd round another corner and discover that the fire had burned acres and acres, all the way up to the road. It was a seared wasteland.

I was about to lose it, but I talked myself out of a meltdown. It was okay. I still had Esalen, which others had told me was unscathed. I could go back to the energy vortex and restore my faith. When I arrived, Esalen appeared as it always had, idyllic and dreamy in its signature campy style. I headed straight to the energy vortex, deep in the canyon, just past the meditation center. Walking down the hill, I felt my heartbeat begin to slow down and my breath deepen. I was almost there. When I finally got to the energy vortex, I planned to wrap my hands around the iron bar where I had felt the pulse the day I accepted my calling. I knew that if I just got quiet and listened, I would find comfort there.

But when I arrived at the gate that separated Esalen property from the wilderness, strips of yellow tape closed the gate, like a taped-off crime scene. A huge sign blockaded the gate, saying "EXTREME DANGER. KEEP OUT!"

My heartbeat quickened, and I felt myself hyperventilating. What now? I had come all this way. I felt like the Universe had betrayed me.

I could feel the part of me that was about to melt down even further into my "poor Lissa" story. But just then, I noticed the meditation center right behind the "Keep Out" sign. Although I had not been to Big Sur since the fire, I had been to Esalen many times since my original visit. But I had never entered the quiet sanctuary of the meditation center. The sign on the door had scared me away in the past; it read, "No reading, no writing, no napping, no yoga. Only meditation."

But not this time. I had the meditation center all to myself when I arrived.

I took off my shoes and padded inside. Squaring myself into the lotus position on a circular pillow, facing out toward the ocean, I closed my eyes, and my mind raced, the Gremlin having a field day with the silence. I didn't know anything about meditation. Aside from the occasional guided meditation in a workshop, I had never meditated before. I had been trained to be hyperproductive. Meditation felt like a stupid waste of time to me.

As I sat there in silence, I felt the first waves of panic begin to rise, but I sat with them, and the waves passed. Memories of Dad dying welled up. Then images of my dog Ariel flashed by. Feelings of loss and sadness washed through me, bringing swells of buried grief. But the grief passed after a few minutes. Anger arose, too—the failure of my book, Matt's unwillingness to get a job, the blocked entrance to the energy vortex. But the rage didn't last long either.

After the tides of emotion had passed, I felt something unexpected, something new. My mind stilled and moments went by without thought or feeling. When I looked at my watch afterward, I realized that time had elapsed, and I hadn't been bored. In fact, I felt unusually calm and peaceful.

That's when I had an epiphany.

Maybe the Universe was trying really hard to tell me something, but I was being dense. Maybe I was being guided along my hero's journey, but I wasn't attentive enough to notice the subtle signs. Maybe I needed to spend more time in silence, deal with the discomfort that arose when I got quiet, and let myself tune into Divine guidance. I made a promise to myself to begin a meditation practice, a promise I broke many times before making it a regular part of my life. I vowed to spend just 5 minutes every day sitting in silence and praying for guidance. It took me years to work up to 20 minutes a day, then 30, then sometimes an hour. I still fall off the wagon. But when I do, I try to sit back down on my meditation pillow in front of my home altar and still myself.

As I nursed my bruised ego in the wake of my failed book, Barbara encouraged me to start a blog. She said it would give me the platform I was missing as a writer. She explained that if I wrote a successful blog, and lots of people started reading it, it would be easier to sell my memoir. Memoirs written by successful bloggers, she told me, sometimes sold for a million dollars! If my blog was as juicy as my book, she assured me, I would have the platform I needed in order to publish *I Don't Do Men*.

I had never heard of a blog. The only Web site I'd ever used was the template Web site I used for my fine art. I had never read anybody else's blog. I barely knew how to check my e-mail, much less start a blog. I didn't even know what to blog about. I felt lost.

So when my friend Vera called to invite me to meet her and her fiancé Scott for lunch in Big Sur, I interpreted it as a sign. The Universe was sending me help!

Vera and Scott worked for an Internet company in Silicon Valley. Scott was a computer coder and Vera worked in marketing. The fact that Vera had called left me feeling like the Universe hadn't abandoned me after all. I felt transfused with a burst of hope.

At lunch, when Vera and Scott asked what my blog would be about, I said, excitedly, "Everything!" I'd thought a lot about it, and I figured I could use this blog to write about everything I was passionate about. Sure, I was a doctor, so it would be easy to write about health, but I didn't want to limit myself to writing about hormones or nutrition or the best supplement for treating PMS. I'd write about the things that make a person whole—creativity and relationships and spirituality and sexuality and parenting and business and money and the environment . . . you know, *everything!* My blog would be more than just a health blog because I'd redefine what it means to be whole and healthy. I could frame it all under the guise of "health," but it would be a larger definition of health than what I'd been taught in medical school. I'd call it "whole health," and this would give me an opportunity to explore some of what had been lighting me up since my transformational experience at Esalen.

Something fundamental had shifted in me since the writing workshop I had taken at Esalen. Between the people I met as a result of that workshop, the mystical experience that happened in the energy vortex, and a series of synchronicities that unfolded after I left Esalen, something previously closed-minded and skeptical had opened up within me in a way that surely would have left my father rolling over in his grave. I became curious about things I would have previously dismissed as nonsense, including all things mystical and spiritual. I read dozens of books, including everything Martha Beck had ever written. As I brainstormed about what I would blog about, I realized I felt inspired to share some of what I had been learning on my blog, but I didn't want to be the only one blogging. I had met some extraordinary people, and I wanted to curate and showcase these gifted individuals in a way that perhaps lent credibility to some of the arguably woo-woo things they were teaching.

I'd create a community blog of doctors, spiritual leaders, alternative health care providers, life coaches, psychologists, artists, sex therapists, and career counselors. I'd invite my Esalen friends, workshop leaders, motivational speakers, and self-help authors to be guests on my blog. Because I was a gynecologist who had just written a book called *I Don't Do Men*, I figured I'd attract a community of women, who, united by one vision, might uplift the world. I would name it after a popular art series I had made called Owning Pink. It would be about *owning* all the facets of what makes us whole as women.

By the time I was done describing my vision to Vera and Scott, I was a woman on a mission. But viewing the whole thing through her marketing lens, Vera wasn't so sure this was a great idea. She encouraged me to focus, thinking it might behoove me to narrow down what my blog would be about, maybe pick one of those topics from my running list. Health *or* creativity *or* relationships *or* sexuality *or* money, but not the whole kitchen sink. She felt that, because I was a doctor, writing about health would be a respectable place to start.

I now know that Vera was probably spot-on to give me that advice, and I'm grateful for her guidance, though I didn't really heed it. Branding companies have since used me as an example of how *not* to brand your business. But at the time, I felt like Vera's advice was yet another limitation of the culture that was trying to shove me back into my white coat, which felt like a straitjacket, too tight to contain me. I wanted to feel free to write about whatever inspired me. After all, I'm a doctor, but I'm also an artist, a patient, a spiritual seeker, a mother, a lover, and a career woman. I felt qualified to write about all of those varied topics. Why should I limit myself? I saw it as the perfect opportunity to stop squashing myself into a doctor box or an artist box or a Mommy box or any box at all.

I explained my rationale, trying to articulate what was bubbling up inside me. Flapping my arms wildly and raising my voice a bit too loud (even for the rowdy inn), I noticed how triggered I felt and how passionate I was about breaking free of the constraints of that doctor box. I explained how this blog would give me the chance to fully integrate all the previously fragmented parts of Lissa. I would blog about being *all me, all the time*. I would stop caring about what everybody thinks and just let the chips fall where they may. I would strip off all of my masks and just be unapologetically ME, without worrying whether my behavior was appropriate for a respectable doctor or a good mother or a successful artist. I would make my blog my

public "coming out" party. I would show the world the real Lissa—my triumphs and my tragedies, my strengths and my weaknesses. I would let go of
this prison of perfection I had created for myself and just let my freak flag fly.

I was quite worked up as I told Vera and Scott the story of how this decision to start blogging felt like the culmination of everything that had been
happening to me since my Perfect Storm. I told them about my shamanic
journey in Big Sur, detailing the whole story about the stethoscope with the
pink paintbrush on it and how it represented integration for me, how I met the
Squirrel Girl in the chamber of my own heart, how I longed to reconnect with
that joyful part of me, how my blog would give me a chance to live out the joy
of wholeness I had sensed during that shamanic journey. Vera had been one of
my models for The Woman Inside Project, and I explained how that art project felt like the first manifestation of the stethoscope with the pink paintbrush
on it. I had found a way to be a doctor and an artist and a writer—a whole
woman—and I had used the project to showcase the whole women who had
modeled for me.

The whole thing felt predestined, as if the hand of God had reached
down and scripted everything out just perfectly. This opportunity to blog
would be the next chapter in this cosmic script that would allow me to more
fully integrate all the previously fragmented parts of Lissa, and in doing so,
I would inspire other women to do the same. I was so impassioned—so on
fire, so smack-dab in the center of my purpose—that my eyes welled up with
a burst of gratitude.

I was literally midsentence, describing my shaman, the Kiefer Sutherland
lookalike, explaining to Vera and Scott how glad I was that I had decided to
do that shamanic journey on my wedding day, how it had changed my life
in a way that led me right to this moment.

And that's when I saw him—the same shaman who had guided me on
my wedding day. I hadn't seen him since then. It was one of those moments
that recorded in my memory in slow motion: I heard the river rushing by, a
Grateful Dead cover band playing, and kids squealing as they splashed each
other. I could only see part of his face, as he was sitting sideways at a table
on the edge of the deck, close to the river. His blonde hair, his blonde scruffy
beard. My mind doubted that it could possibly be him. It would have been
too big a synchronicity, too impossible to write off as chance. Surely, I must
have been mistaken.

I apologized to Vera and Scott, stood up, and walked in a stumbling daze
across the restaurant. When I approached the shaman, he looked up and

smiled. I must have been quite a sight, a strange woman interrupting his lunch, getting misty-eyed from the sheer awesomeness of the fact that the Universe had just delivered me one helluva big, whack-me-over-the head, hit-me-with-a-brick sign.

I asked, "Do you do shamanic journeys at the Post Ranch Inn?"

He smiled and nodded. He told me his name was Jon Rasmussen. He lived in Monterey and had a private practice as a shaman there. He led shamanic journeys at the Post Ranch Inn on Saturdays. He gave me his card.

As abandoned as I had felt recently, I took this run-in with Jon as clear evidence that I was not navigating this hero's journey alone. I was being guided, and after years of dead ends, roadblocks, and "Keep Out" signs, I felt like I was finally being given the green light. Surely this was the Cosmic Yes affirming everything I was saying to Vera and Scott. Surely I was finally on the right path toward my destiny. Surely the rest would be smooth sailing.

Or so I thought.

Once you finally leap into your hero's journey and cross the first threshold, you'll soon find yourself on the Road of Trials, filled with tests, allies, and enemies. You'll start meeting the people who can teach you the rules of your new world, the one so foreign from the Ordinary World you just left behind. Like Dorothy in Oz, this is when you'll meet your Scarecrow, your Tin Woodsman, and your Cowardly Lion. But you'll also meet the Wicked Witch of the West and her flying monkeys. You'll fall asleep, drugged in the poppy fields, and realize the trip to the Emerald City isn't going to be quite as easy as you thought.

When you cross the first threshold, you'll likely be dewy with possibility, excited about the leap you just took, proud of yourself for the courageous choice you just made, and optimistic about what lies ahead. Keep all of that! You'll need it. Optimism, confidence, trust, and faith in the process are essential to every hero's successful mission.

But be prepared for the initiation that lies ahead.

Every hero gets tested, not because the Universe doesn't have your back but because the initiation is an essential part of the spiritual development of a hero. It's where your mettle gets tested and you peel off layers of childhood patterning and ego traps that keep you from fully expressing the hero you really are.

Don't be discouraged as you embark upon the Road of Trials. Be excited. Be open to possibility. Try not to attach to particular outcomes, because the attachment can get you stuck in the reeds when you're meant to flow on the lavender-scented river. And most of all, keep the faith. Everything will unfold exactly as it must.

HERO'S GUIDEPOST:

When You Get Lost, Get Quiet and Pause

There will be times on your journey when you'll be perfectly guided, but there will invariably be times when you feel completely lost, as if the Universe has erected big, glaring "Keep Out" signs. When you feel lost, it's usually because of one of two things: Either you haven't gotten quiet enough to receive the guidance you'll need in order to move forward, or you're meant to have a pause in your journey. Sometimes things will move forward at warp speed. But sometimes you'll need to await further instructions. It's easy to get impatient when you feel lost, but the lost times are potent opportunities for practicing patience and putting your faith to the test.

HERO'S PRACTICE:

Be Still

If you feel lost, make sure you take time to be with yourself. Start a meditation practice, even if you're just spending 5 minutes in silence every day. If sitting meditation is too uncomfortable, find other ways to get quiet. Take walks in nature. Go on a personal retreat for a few days if you can. Get away to a hot springs resort. Go to Esalen, Kripalu, Omega, an ashram, or even just a little rental house in the forest. If you can't get away from home, take a day off and create sacred time for yourself. Set aside a small space in your house and make a home altar out of meaningful objects. Light some candles and incense. Put on some music that feeds your soul. Take a bath. Do a few yoga poses. Listen to a guided meditation, like the ones I recorded for you at TheAnatomyofaCalling.com. Be sure to ask for guidance if you're feeling lost. Open yourself to getting feedback in the form of intuition, sensations in your body, and external signs from the Universe. You just might be surprised at what bubbles forth when you make the space to turn inward and pay attention. If nothing arises, be patient. Trust that you'll be guided to your next step when the time is right. If you try to force a next step, you may wind up veering off course. Have faith and just sit with the discomfort of not knowing. The time for inspired action will arise in Divine timing.

CHAPTER 9

You Are Not Alone

After the extended, anxiety-provoking lull that followed quitting my job as a doctor, many things began to happen all at once. At the same time as I had been trying to publish *I Don't Do Men*, I had also been trying to conjure up a way to make good on my promise to the Universe that I would return to my calling in medicine in a way that felt aligned, joyful, and delicious. Shortly after I had returned from my first trip to Esalen, I crossed paths with Jo, a very wise and funny OB/GYN who was also a yoga teacher. Jo had quit practicing medicine because her treatment from breast cancer had left her partially disabled. I was drawn to Jo right away, and she became, in many ways, my first spiritual teacher. She lived near me in Pebble Beach, and our weekly hikes became their own sort of yoga class, as Jo mentored me with her spiritual wisdom, as well as her medical knowledge.

Like me, Jo dreamed of continuing to serve her calling as a doctor in a way that didn't require her to sell out her health or her soul, and we enjoyed scheming up what might be possible together. While I was brand-new to this whole "alternative gynecology" idea, Jo had experimented with fun, creative practice models before she was diagnosed with breast cancer. In her old practice, she had convinced her partners to turn their gynecology office into a sort of day spa. You could get a mani-pedi, a haircut, and a Pap smear in one fell swoop. The locals in town jokingly called it the "Pussy Palace," and artist Steve Hinton painted a notorious masterpiece spoofing the place. In the painting, a surly, old-school male gynecologist with a head lamp squats between a woman's straddled legs while Nurse Ratched looks on. As the doctor does the woman's Pap smear, a nail technician paints her toenails, an aesthetician applies a facial, and her fingernails soak in a bowl. The artist called it *A Day at the Daisy Dew*. Because it caused such a stir, the other doctors at the Pussy Palace purchased it, just to get it out of circulation. When Jo left the practice, they gave her the painting as a gift. It still hangs in her living room at home.

Jo was half joking, half serious about one day buying a pink RV and using it as a roaming Pap smear clinic. We giggled as she schemed about what she would call it. Maybe "Snappy Pappy at Your Cervix." Or "Pap & Lube." She wanted to deck it out with girly, frilly things and hang *A Day at the Daisy Dew* on the wall. I so wanted to be her Snappy Pappy partner! I could totally envision the two of us driving around Pebble Beach in that pink RV, past all the stuffy, uptight golfers, with Helen Reddy's "I Am Woman, Here Me Roar" blaring from loudspeakers, like some feminist ice cream truck.

We also threw around the idea of opening a clinic together in Monterey—a holistic women's health center that would give us a home base and allow us to collaborate with some of the alternative practitioners I had met at Esalen. We dreamed of inviting our patients to join us for women's health retreats in Big Sur. We'd gather women together in a sacred circle and talk about sex and relationships and health. We'd lead workshops about healing our wounded vaginas and our slashed-open uteruses and our cut-off breasts and all the other scars women bear. I could teach art and Jo could teach yoga, and we could integrate all of our gifts together to create something truly unique and beautiful.

But as much as she wanted to, Jo didn't feel ready to take any of these leaps with me. Since her breast cancer, she lacked the energy she knew it would take to start something from scratch, and she was afraid her numb hands wouldn't let her do a Snappy Pappy quite like she once did.

I was really scared to try to do it alone, but I investigated ways I might open such a practice. I put out a message on an online forum of doctors, met with other local doctors who might potentially partner with me, talked to landlords about rental spaces, and did my homework into the nitty-gritty behind opening my own entrepreneurial medical practice, something I had never done.

But every door kept slamming in my face. I grew increasingly discouraged, especially since I had been hit with closed door after closed door with my book-publishing dream. What was the Universe trying to tell me? I was losing my faith.

Taking a break from my efforts to find a way back to medicine, I visited one of my best friends, Cari Hernandez, who I had met via my art career. Cari and I had known each other for years, showing our art in some of the same galleries and teaching artists how to paint with encaustic together in several workshops. While I had lost some of my old friends since I embarked upon my hero's journey, Cari had steadfastly journeyed with me, always rallying to my side, no matter how crazy my choices seemed.

Cari lived in the San Francisco Bay Area, a few hours away from where I lived, and we were catching up while walking around the quaint village of Mill Valley when Cari literally bumped her hip into a metal box. We stopped and opened the box, and it was filled with brochures for an integrative medicine practice that was right upstairs from where we were standing. Cari handed me one. According to the brochure, the integrative medicine center, which I'll call Optimal Health, consisted of two MDs, an osteopath, a naturopath, a nutritionist, a psychologist, and a detox-cleanse expert. I had never seen a practice that looked exactly like what I had dreamed of creating with Jo and my friends from Esalen.

Cari said, "Lissa, why reinvent the wheel? What if you got a job here?"

I was intrigued. What if it was a sign? I felt like I was supposed to investigate further.

The next day, I wrote a letter to the medical director of Optimal Health—I'll call her Eve—to see if they might be hiring. Soon afterward, I found myself in an interview, sitting across a desk from a kind, generous, smart, movie-star-gorgeous woman.

She asked, "If you could build your dream practice here, what would it be like?"

It was such an expansive invitation that I found myself speechless. The very fact that there was a doctor in the world who would even ask such a question warmed my heart. In spite of the goofy fantasies Jo and I had tossed around, I didn't have a ready answer. All I knew for sure was that if I was going to come back to medicine, I needed more time with my patients—time to establish a heart-to-heart connection, time for true healing to take place. Eve promised we could make that happen and offered me a position at the center. I was overwhelmed with gratitude and accepted the job, which meant moving my family 2½ hours north from the Monterey peninsula to Marin County.

It was a good time to move. Nothing was keeping me, Matt, and Siena in Monterey now that Jo had declined my offer to partner with her. Even the magnetic draw of Big Sur had lost its appeal in the wake of the Big Sur fire. I had finally given up my hope of publishing *I Don't Do Men* and was scheming about how I might launch my *Owning Pink* blog, but I could do that from anywhere. In fact, proximity to Silicon Valley and San Francisco was appealing as someone about to embark upon a career as a blogger. The Universe was smiling upon us.

Or so it seemed.

For a few months before I started seeing my own patients, I shadowed Eve, learning how she worked with patients and picking her brain after patient visits about supplements, bioidentical hormone dosages, vitamins, and specialty labs that she ordered, the kinds of labs I was never taught to order or interpret during my conventional medical training. Eve recommended books for me to read, and she taught me natural ways to support conventional cancer treatments and her natural formulas for treating several chronic health conditions, such as adrenal fatigue, subclinical hypothyroidism, leaky gut, depression and anxiety, chronic Lyme disease, irritable bowel syndrome, and menopausal symptoms. I viewed a lot of what I was learning with a curious and open but skeptical and discerning eye. Much of what Eve was teaching me was in direct violation of what I had been taught in medical school, so I had a hard time reconciling my training in evidence-based medicine with the kinds of laboratory evaluations and supplement treatments that many functional-medicine doctors use. Many of these diagnostic tests and natural treatments are not covered by health insurance, so patients pay out of pocket. Yet many of these tests and treatments lack clear scientific evidence to back up their accuracy and efficacy.

The best part of my new practice was that I was able to spend a whole hour with my patients because they were paying out of pocket for my time. This allowed me to really get to know and love my patients, to really listen to what they were telling me, while also sensing what they weren't telling me. With so much time to tune into my patients, I discovered that sometimes I knew things about them I didn't have any business knowing. By reading into the unseen and unspoken, I could somehow intuit what might lie at the root of their illnesses. For example, a woman would tell me about her chronic fatigue and fibromyalgia symptoms, and I would just know she was getting beaten by her husband. Or a woman would talk about her severe food allergies and I would sense that she was allergic to her life, that her body was rejecting her whole lifestyle. I didn't share this information with my patients. I just used it to guide me to the most pointed questions, which I asked while making direct eye contact. I could tell when I asked just the right question, one that dug right into the heart of what wasn't being said, because most people would look away and start crying. In that moment, something would break through and we would both just sit with the uncomfortable truth, holding the truth with tenderness and compassion.

I didn't really understand what was happening at the time, and it left me feeling a bit insecure. I told Matt I must be doing something wrong since all of my patients were crying and none of Eve's ever had while I was shadowing her. I didn't feel completely confident billing myself as an "integrative gynecologist" without any prior education or experience as an integrative-medicine doctor. Was it fraudulent to call myself an integrative-medicine doctor when I had no experience or certification as such? I wasn't sure.

Another aspect of my new practice that confused me was that my patients were bona fide health nuts who had already received the best of what Western medicine had to offer. These people drank their daily green juice, ate a vegan diet, worked out with personal trainers, slept 8 hours a night, took 20 supplements every day, and had sought out the best doctors at places like Stanford and University of California, San Francisco, while also seeing acupuncturists, energy healers, and nutritionists. And yet, paradoxically, many of them were the sickest people I'd ever met. This made no sense to my doctor brain. Why weren't these people healthier? From everything I had learned in medical school, these patients should have been the healthiest people on the planet. But the majority of the patients who sought me out weren't sleeping well, suffered from chronic pain, were gaining weight, had no libido, felt depressed and anxious, had allergies and skin problems, experienced gastrointestinal problems, and had energy levels that were in the toilet. But why?

I questioned what I could possibly have to offer them.

Under Eve's guidance, I'd run specialized tests conventional doctors might not order, and occasionally, I'd uncover something that would solve everything. But often, the tests would come back normal. Or we'd find an abnormality through laboratory testing and institute a treatment to alter something biochemically, but the symptoms would remain. The patients who wound up under my care were a bit of a conundrum. In my medical education, we were trained to lump patients into one of two black-and-white categories. Sick people had abnormal lab tests, unstable vital signs, abnormal physical findings on examination, and abnormal radiological studies. Well people, on the other hand, had none of the above. If patients with physical symptoms demonstrated no abnormalities on a thorough workup, we figured it must be "all in their heads." We quietly slipped them cards for psychiatrists and hoped they never came back.

But these patients in my integrative medicine practice weren't crazy or malingering. They were clearly suffering, but I couldn't figure out why. If these people who took such good care of their bodies weren't optimally healthy, it was clear to me that, as doctors, we might be missing some essential piece of what predisposes people to illness and what really makes them feel vital.

My hunch led me to change my patient intake form. I started asking my patients very personal questions, questions that would force them to get real with me, like:

- Do you feel lonely, isolated, misunderstood, or disconnected?

- If you could break any rule without consequences, what rule would you break?

- Are you in a romantic relationship, and if so, are you happy? If not, do you wish you were?

- Do you feel like you're in touch with your life's purpose, fulfilling your Divine assignment here on this planet?

- Do you feel stressed about money?

- Do you feel spiritually connected?

- Do you feel free to be your authentic self?

My new patient intake form was 12 pages long, and what these questions revealed about my patients' lives shocked me. When combined with the intuitive information I sometimes received from patients, I started to get a sense of the link between their physical health and their emotional health. The two most illuminating questions I asked were:

- What is your body saying no to?

- What does your body need in order to heal?

I started prefacing these questions with an explanation that the physical symptom might be arising from something purely biochemical that could be easily fixed, like a bladder infection that needs an antibiotic. But I asked my patients to humor me and consider that perhaps the physical symptom was an indication not only of a biochemical imbalance but also of an emotional imbalance.

For example, one woman had strep throat. It was clear that the biochemical reason behind her infection was the streptococcus bacteria. But I asked her to consider that perhaps when she was exposed to this bacteria, she was in a room with a hundred other people, and perhaps only a few of them got strep throat. So why her? What might have been happening that could have weakened her immune system and made her susceptible to that bacteria?

She went on to tell me that she had been in a business meeting a few days earlier and was feeling out of touch with the direction the business meeting was going. She wanted to speak up. (She put her hand on her throat when she said that.) She felt the impulse to speak up. But then she silenced herself and wound up with strep throat.

Her infection got better with antibiotics, but the woman left with a commitment to speak more truthfully during business meetings. I said, "There. You just wrote your own prescription."

I found that when I asked my patients questions that tapped them into their own intuition, like "What does your body need in order to heal?" profound answers arose. My patients started prescribing major life changes for themselves, like:

- I need to leave my toxic relationship.

- I need to quit my job.

- I need to forgive my father.

- I need to finally write my novel.

- I need to get my mother out of the house and into a nursing home.

I'd say, "Okay. Go do it!"

Most of them would respond, "Well, I can't do that. That would be *crazy*."

Many of my patients didn't realize that those answers were their first calls to adventure, the very beginning of their own hero's journey. Many didn't know—and neither did I at the time—that answering the call was often the medicine they really needed, more than any drug, surgery, special diet, or supplement.

But a few of my patients tapped into their inner courage and started doing exactly what they had prescribed for themselves, while I watched in shock as some of them started experiencing unexpected remissions. All of a sudden, their health conditions started going away—*without medical treatment.*

To say that I was blown away by what was happening to my patients would be the understatement of the century. Yes, this was good news, but it also freaked me out. The very idea that a patient could get better not because of some pill or surgery or even alternative medicine therapy that I recommended but because they listened to their intuition and then did something brave rocked my world. After all, I went to school for 12 years ostensibly so that I would know patients' bodies better than they would, and then I'd have a toolbox full of treatments that could cure them. Nowhere in my highly skeptical Western medicine paradigm was there room for patients who were healing themselves by sensing what their bodies needed in order to heal and then making brave life changes. If that was possible, why the hell had I spent 12 years training to be a doctor?

This realization thrust me into a full-on ego meltdown. The small, scared part of me who was so sure she knew how the world worked was not happy to watch all of her seemingly solid beliefs about what makes a person healthy come undone. But I also had a belly full of butterflies. I felt like I was on the cusp of a shocking discovery. My Inner Pilot Light was delighted that I was finally waking up to a new truth.

Suddenly, everything I once believed to be true about medicine was up for questioning. Could the body heal itself? If so, what were the mechanisms? What facilitated such self-healing? Why did it work sometimes and not others? Were there certain kinds of illnesses that respond to self-healing and others that didn't? Was there any way to intentionally increase the chance of spontaneous remission? Or was it just luck? Were there commonalities among people who had remarkable recoveries, and if so, what were they? Why would one person get better when another would stay sick or die? Could positive emotions prevent or treat disease? Could negative emotions cause illness, and if so, how? Did fear cause disease? Did courage make people healthier? Was there any evidence to answer these questions? And if there was, what role should physicians be playing? Did we need to be not just mere health technicians but also therapists and spiritual guides, taking cues from the shamans of the indigenous people?

All of these questions arising from some curious place within me felt a bit like new age hooey. After all, I was a pragmatist. I was Dave Rankin's daughter, as well as the product of a decade of highly academic education, a by-product of a scientific age. I tried to stay open to new ideas, like any good scientist. But I was a big fan of data, preferring to back up new ideas with clean, solid evidence. Without such scientific discernment to prove that new ideas were reproducible and mechanistically explainable, we'd all be easy prey for charlatans and quacks, right? Sure, my experiences at Esalen and what was happening with my patients left me full of questions, but I wasn't inclined to jump to any unscientific conclusions. I prided myself on being open but not easily duped.

Given what was happening with my patients, my curiosity outweighed my skepticism, launching me down a research rabbit hole as I tried to find answers the only place I knew to trust, the bibles of modern medicine: the *New England Journal of Medicine, JAMA: The Journal of the American Medical Association*, and other peer-reviewed medical journals. My first inquiry led me to research what doctors call "spontaneous remissions." We use this term to describe patients who are cured either with no medical treatment or with medical treatment deemed by doctors to be inadequate for a cure. It's the phrase we use to describe medical mysteries, those cases we scratch our heads over and write up in the medical literature because we don't understand what happened.

As I dug deep into the medical literature, I uncovered the Spontaneous Remission Project, a database collected by the Institute of Noetic Sciences of over 3,500 case studies written up by doctors and published in the medical literature about patients who were spontaneously cured from a whole host of life-threatening illnesses. This database included patients who had spontaneous remissions from stage IV cancer, heart failure, kidney failure, even an HIV-positive patient who became HIV negative. The case studies didn't just include life-threatening illnesses. They also included autoimmune diseases, diabetes, chronic hypertension, gastrointestinal disorders, skin disorders, and many other conditions I had always considered incurable.

Were these flukes? Were these patients just lucky? Were they the product of something supernatural? Or had these patients done something proactive to be cured? If so, what might we learn from them?

That's when I came across the research of Kelly A. Turner, who studied at Harvard and the University of California, Berkeley, and did her PhD thesis on patients who had spontaneous remissions from stage IV cancers. As part of her research, Dr. Turner interviewed people who had recovered from stage IV cancer, as well as the healers who had supported them on their healing journeys. Her research was published in her book *Radical Remission*. What she found was that these patients shared nine characteristics in common, nine things they had done to be proactive about getting better. Only two of them were the sorts of things a forward-thinking doctor might have prescribed.

The nine things included:

1. Radically changing your diet

2. Taking control of your health

3. Following your intuition

4. Using herbs and supplements

5. Releasing suppressed emotions

6. Increasing positive emotions

7. Embracing social support

8. Deepening your spiritual connection

9. Having strong reasons for living

None of these things were even touched upon in my medical training, but if there's a chance that such things improved the likelihood of being cured from cancer, surely, as doctors, we should educate our patients! But when was the last time you heard a doctor prescribe following your intuition, deepening your spiritual connection, or embracing support as treatment for cancer? Why weren't we including such things in a holistic cancer-treatment program? If such things could potentially lead to spontaneous remissions from cancer, shouldn't we be attending to these facets of a patient's health every bit as much as we examined surgery and chemotherapy, or even diet and supplements, as options?

Looking at the health of the body in terms of such psychospiritual factors just isn't part of the consciousness of most doctors. At least it wasn't part of mine prior to this point. It's not that most doctors have been exposed to this evidence and have chosen to ignore it. It's simply that we are unaware that such evidence exists. When I first read Dr. Bernie S. Siegel's pioneering book *Love, Medicine & Miracles* in 2012, I was shocked. This book was published in 1986, when I was still in high school. Millions of people had read this bestselling book, but I had never heard of it. How is it possible that this book was not required reading for me in medical school in the 1990s? How is it that, even now, your typical integrative cancer center might recommend a diet change and immune-boosting herbs and supplements for a patient but most of the doctors I knew wouldn't touch talking to cancer patients about such things as releasing suppressed emotions, increasing positive emotions, and maintaining the will to live.

Researching spontaneous remissions and witnessing them among my patients challenged my whole belief system. It reminded me of the story I had once heard about the 4-minute mile. For a long time, exercise physiologists believed that it was physically impossible for a human being to run a mile in less than 4 minutes. And nobody ever had.

Then something radical happened.

In 1954, Roger Bannister ran a mile in 3 minutes and 59 seconds for the first time in recorded history. Suddenly, the worldwide belief that running a mile in less than 4 minutes was physiologically impossible was shattered. Shortly thereafter, several other runners went on to run a mile in less than 4 minutes. Now virtually every runner who competes in a world-class event has run the mile in under 4 minutes. Today's world-record time for the mile is 3:43:15, more than 15 seconds under 4 minutes.

The data I was finding about spontaneous remissions became my own personal 4-minute mile. If there was this much data in the medical literature about miraculous cures from seemingly incurable illnesses, maybe it was our limiting beliefs that were holding us back from witnessing more medical miracles. Maybe, instead of labeling our patients as "incurable" or hexing them with statistics like "You only have 3 months to live," as doctors and patients, we needed to expand our capacity for what might be possible. Maybe there was no such thing as an incurable illness. Maybe we could even be proactive about making our bodies ripe for miracles.

I didn't realize it at the time, but I now understand that I had accidentally stumbled into the well-researched field of mind-body medicine. I wasn't practicing integrative or functional medicine the way the other doctors at Optimal Health were. I was practicing an intuitive form of mind-body medicine without even knowing such a field existed, and patients were responding with positive outcomes.

During this time, my stomach felt full of butterflies almost all the time. I had a strong suspicion I was onto something critically important about health, but my mind couldn't wrap itself around what my patients were experiencing and what I was uncovering in the medical literature. What I learned in my discovery process ultimately became the foundation of my book *Mind Over Medicine*. But, back then, I had no intention of writing a book about mind-body medicine. I honestly questioned whether I was simply losing my mind.

About a year after I began my practice at Optimal Health, I started to get signs that perhaps I would have to leave soon. I was just getting comfortable in my new job. I really didn't want to leave, but as much as I tried to convince myself I'd be better off staying put, I kept feeling like the quality of the patient care I was delivering was being compromised by limitations in the practice. The lab tests I ordered weren't getting back to me in a timely fashion. Prescriptions I was writing weren't getting called in by the nurses. Policies meant to protect laboratory specimens weren't appropriately followed by staff members. And it wasn't just the operations of the practice that left me feeling uncomfortable. Conflict was arising with some of the people I worked with, and my best efforts to resolve the conflict weren't going smoothly. A few things happened that made me feel like I was compromising my ethics in order to justify the comfort and security of staying in my new job. I honestly believe those in charge of the practice had good intentions. Nobody intended to put patient care at risk, but when I brought quality-assurance issues to the attention of those who could implement new policies, nothing much happened. Once again, I felt like I was at the mercy of forces out of my control, and patient care was getting compromised, in spite of my best efforts. These circumstances triggered all the past issues I dealt with when I was working in the hospital and left me wondering whether it was even possible to practice excellent medical care anywhere. Maybe I was simply unrealistic in my expectations about the kind of exceptional patient care I believed was possible. Maybe this was as good as it gets, and I needed to simply quit my bellyaching, lower my standards, and suck it up.

As I was trying to make a decision about whether or not to leave Optimal

Health, I had a profound dream. In my dream, Eve invited me to go shopping with her. I agreed, and she asked me to follow her across a very primitive border, where we waited in a line amid chickens and goats and colorful crafts until someone ushered us ahead of the other people. Walking along a dirt road, heading south to the market, something caught my eye. I turned and looked.

To my left, across a canyon, were rolling mountains, green and lush, covered with wildflowers just like the ones that covered the Big Sur hills in the spring. On the hillside stood hundreds of thousands of people, all dressed in traditional clothing from around the world—headdresses and robes and a brilliant array of world-bazaar costumes. All of these people stood still, facing due north, and a radiant, golden light shone from above and glowed off of their multicolored faces.

I stopped dead in my tracks on the dirt road, in total and complete awe. Eve asked why I stopped, and I said, "Look!" and pointed to the left.

But Eve didn't see what I saw. She shrugged her shoulders and kept right on walking south, encouraging me to follow her to the market.

I felt torn. My loyalty ripped in two. Half of me wanted to follow through on what I promised Eve; the other half wanted to turn around and face north. Then, in my dream, I realized I had a choice, and so did Eve. It wasn't right or wrong to head north or south. It would be perfectly fine if Eve wanted to keep heading south to the market. But in that moment, I knew, without a doubt, that I needed to stop in my tracks, turn around, face north, and bask in the light.

When I awoke from my dream, I knew what I had to do.

The next day, I scheduled a meeting with Eve, and I spent 3 hours describing, in vivid detail, the kind of truly integrative way I dreamed of practicing. I finally had the answer to the question she had asked me over a year before. I now knew what my dream practice was like, and I wanted to invite her to practice with me in this radical, expanded way.

It was still a fledgling idea, and I hadn't sorted it all out in my mind. I wasn't even completely convinced that my idea made any sense. Part of it was still gestating, so I probably sounded pretty flighty when I tried to spell it all out for Eve, hoping she would share my vision and help me flesh it out. I explained as best I could that my vision for this new kind of medical practice would support patients on the journey to what I called "whole health." I delivered what I hoped was a passionate call to action, inviting Eve to join me in my new mission. I wanted us to help our patients transform, not only from sick to well but also from well to vital and thriving. I wanted us to call upon all the tools in our collective toolboxes—traditional Western medicine, integrative and functional medicine, mind-body medicine, psychology, and spiritual counseling—to help patients achieve whole health. I wanted to help our patients view illness from a place of empowerment, not from the perspective of the helpless victim. I explained to Eve that maybe illness wasn't just random bad luck. I wasn't trying to blame people for their illnesses, but maybe we participated with illness. Maybe our bodies mirrored what happened in our minds and spirits. When we experienced soul sickness, maybe our bodies followed, and as doctors, perhaps it was our responsibility to diagnose and treat not only the biochemistry of the sick body but also soul sickness. Maybe we needed to support patients as they moved beyond their victim stories so that, instead of feeling helpless and stuck, they could own and accept their participation with their illness and view illness as an opportunity for self-inquiry and spiritual growth. Most importantly, I wanted to reclaim the *heart* of medicine, to practice love, with a little medicine on the side. I told Eve that I had come to believe that when we approach our bodies with love, acceptance, and nurturing kindness, we pave the way for magic to unfold. I also admitted that I wanted to work in a practice that believed that the power to heal lies within us all. Rather than "fixing" patients, I wanted to empower them to partner with us on their healing journeys.

Sure, we would still balance their hormones, introduce them to the idea of green juice cleansing, help them implement exercise plans, and give them supplements when needed. But we could also offer them guidance with their relationships and careers, talk about their sex lives, ask how they expressed themselves creatively, touch upon the spiritual, discuss how they serve the planet, and help them get in touch with their life's purpose, all the things I was planning to write about in the blog I had launched in April of 2009.

I wanted to work in a practice where I wasn't the only one asking questions like "What does your body need in order to heal?" and "What's your body saying no to?" I wanted to offer patients more than just supplements and specialty lab tests. I wanted to offer them insight, so they could diagnose the real reason that they were sick, and I wanted to support them as they made the brave choices they'd need to make in order to make their bodies ripe for spontaneous remission.

Eve looked at me with big, watery eyes and said, "Can't it be okay if I just focus on helping patients manage their biochemistry?"

Of course it would be okay. Eve was an amazing doctor who knew way more than I did about the kind of medicine she practiced. But I felt so alone. Eve cried when I told her I had to leave. So did I. We hugged and made a promise to hike together after we stopped being business partners.

I started my own practice in a shared space with four acupuncturists, a psychologist, a nutritionist, a massage therapist, and a naturopath. When these already-established practitioners heard I was leaving Optimal Health, they invited me to move in with them. They confessed that they had never invited a physician to join them before because they didn't want someone getting all God complex on them, treating them as underlings down the totem pole. They said they sensed I wasn't one of those physicians, so they wanted to invite me to be an equal partner at what acupuncturist Susan Fox called "the healing round table," where all health care providers were on equal footing. I was genuinely touched and honored. It was exactly in line with my own philosophy of how health care should be delivered.

I once knew two doctors. One was a gastroenterology physician and the other was a naturopathic doctor. Both went to medical school for 4 years. And yet, they couldn't discuss medicine without knock-down, drag-out, screaming hissy fit fights. The gastroenterology physician thought the naturopathic doctor was delusional. And the naturopath thought the gastroenterologist was a closed-minded snob who was merely frightened of what he didn't understand. It made meals with them very awkward.

We had zero tolerance for this kind of hierarchical attitude at our practice, acknowledging the equality of all practitioners and respecting the patient as the one with the greatest power. We valued the patient's own intuition about her body and trusted that while we could be consultants to the patient, the patient was ultimately in charge.

I called my new practice the "Owning Pink Center," based on the name of the blog I had created. I fine-tuned my intake form even further so patients were screened with a full assessment of their physical health, mental health, spiritual health, creative health, sexual health, environmental health, financial health, work health, and relationship health using a model I described years later in my book *Mind Over Medicine.*

As a physician, I've been exposed to a variety of wellness models, most of them pie charts and pyramids detailing what it takes to be optimally healthy—a nutritious diet, an exercise regimen, enough sleep, etc. But something about these wellness models always left me feeling like something was missing. First, it was the format. A pie chart implies that you can take out a piece of the pie and still keep the rest of the uneaten pie intact. The same is true for a pyramid. If you take a strip out of a pyramid, you wind up with a shorter but still stable pyramid. None of the wellness models I had seen ever felt expansive enough or comprehensive enough, and none of them acknowledged the interdependency of all the facets of what makes us whole and how these life factors affect the health of the body.

Then one day, while I was still working at Optimal Health, I was hiking in coastal western Marin County up toward Mount Tamalpais, and I had a very graphic vision that appeared in front of me like a slide projected over the coastal landscape. The image that appeared before me was so vivid that I raced home and drew it on a large piece of watercolor paper. I called it the "Whole Health Cairn" and first introduced it in a 2011 TEDx talk titled "The Shocking Truth about Your Health," which has since had over a million views.

This wellness model was based on the image of a cairn, those stacks of balanced stones that tend to grace beaches and mark sacred landmarks. As an artist, I've always been drawn to cairns for their sculptural beauty, but I also love them because of their simultaneous strength and fragility. A well-built cairn subjected to ocean surf can survive a winter storm, but displace one stone out of balance and the whole thing topples. Most wellness models suggest that the body is the foundation upon which everything else is built, that in order to have close relationships or a successful career, the body must be healthy. But I've come to believe that the opposite is true, that the sum total of the health of all other aspects of your life is a sort of barometer of how balanced your body's health is. When your life topples out of balance, the body decompensates.

Your body begins by communicating via whispers—subtle physical symptoms, like nausea or a headache or a tightness in your chest or a pain in your back. But if you ignore the messages your body is trying to communicate through whispers, it begins to yell, and serious illnesses like heart disease and cancer can develop.

This is why the Physical Health stone is on the top of the Whole Health Cairn, as a reminder that if you're in a toxic relationship or you're not singing that song your soul longs to sing or you're stuck in a miserable job, your Whole Health Cairn is likely to become unstable, and as the most precarious stone on top, the body is likely to get sick.

So if the body isn't the foundation of your health, what is? I believe it's your Inner Pilot Light, that essential, unapologetically authentic, always radiant, never extinguished essence of your core. When we lose touch with this truthful part of ourselves, we wind up out of alignment, and as an extension of that core imbalance, we might find ourselves living lives we don't want to be living, feeling like victims of our lives rather than empowering ourselves to live more in alignment with the truth of our souls.

When I first saw this vision of the Whole Health Cairn on my hike, I had no idea whether what I was "seeing" was scientifically verifiable. Was there scientific proof that your relationships affect your health? Can your job really make you sick? Does expressing yourself creatively or enjoying an aligned sex life or tapping into spiritually really optimize your health?

What ensued was a study of the scientific data proving that every stone in the Whole Health Cairn affects your physical health, perhaps much more profoundly than you think. Each stone in the Whole Health Cairn has the potential to both heal you or make you sick. A healthy romance can cure you, whereas a toxic one can poison you. Making your art or writing your novel or creating your dream business can be medicine—but if you know what you long to do and aren't pursuing your passion, it can make you sick.

The key to preventing disease—or making the body ripe for miracles if you're sick—is determining what is out of alignment with your Inner Pilot Light and then being brave enough to take actions that will bring your life back into alignment with your truth. When you do, spontaneous remissions become more likely.

These are the sorts of healing practices we focused on at my new practice. Our motto was "We practice love with a little medicine on the side." The rules we practiced by included these 15 guidelines.

1. Listen.

2. Open your heart.

3. Make eye contact.

4. Take your hand off the doorknob and sit down.

5. Be present.

6. Offer healing touch.

7. Invite your patient to be your partner.

8. Avoid judgment.

9. Educate, but don't dictate.

10. Choose your words with care and remain optimistic.

11. Trust your patient's intuition.

12. Be respectful of other practitioners who are treating your patient.

13. Reassure your patients they are not alone.

14. Encourage stress relief and let your presence relieve stress.

15. Offer hope, because no matter how grim the prognosis, spontaneous remission is always possible.

Patients were not only getting extraordinary results because of what was happening in this practice but also healing me. I was blessed to get a whole hour with them, and I was getting at least as much nourishment from my patients as I hoped they were receiving from me. I felt truly grateful and fulfilled, thinking I had finally solved the dilemma of how to serve out my calling in medicine in a way that felt genuine, helpful, and enriching to both me and my patients. What I didn't realize at the time was that my life was about to fall apart *again,* which is typical when you're on the Road of Trials.

This phase of the journey tends to be full of false starts and unexpected dead ends.

When you're on the Road of Trials, you're likely to have breakthroughs, followed by breakdowns. You'll feel giddy with excitement and gutted with disappointment. You'll meet allies who may become enemies because you haven't yet grown into the hero you will one day be. The excitement you felt when you crossed the first threshold may start to wane. You're likely to doubt yourself. Things may even start to look hopeless. Then you'll meet a new ally, you'll regain your confidence, and you'll get back on the Road of Trials.

On the Road of Trials, there are traps to avoid, tests of your character to pass, and battles with your own ego. The longer it takes you to learn what you must, the longer you'll be on the Road of Trials. Because I was a slow learner, my Road of Trials was a *long* road. You might be a quicker study in the inevitable soul lessons you'll be called to learn. Either way, you must keep the faith. You wouldn't have been called to embark upon this mission if you didn't have within you everything it takes to complete your Divine assignment.

Try not to beat yourself up, even when you realize that many of the challenges you're facing are of your own creation. Try to be patient and to avoid rushing the process. Trust that it's all happening just as it must, because you are being groomed, and everything you are learning now will be required when you face what lies ahead.

There is no right way or wrong way to navigate a hero's journey. There is only your way, and you are right on track, wherever you are. Think of everything as fuel for your growth. Remember, it's not about the destination; it's about the journey. Everything, even the pitfalls, is divinely guided. Nothing is wasted. It is all happening in the perfect way, in the perfect timing. The outcome you envisioned may not be the outcome that wants to happen in Divine Will. But you will get where you must if you let go of attaching to what you desire and open yourself to what wants to become.

HERO'S GUIDEPOST:

You Are Not Separate from Other Heroes on Their Journeys

The feelings of loneliness, disconnection, and separation that can plague a hero on a journey, feelings that can also predispose you to illness, are born of a separation story created by the ego. The ego tells us we are separate from divinity, separate from each other, separate from love, when this is a bald-faced lie. We are all connected to divinity, to each other, and to the

Force that unites us, yet the ego needs to make itself "other" in order to feel relevant. The existential angst that arises from this tragic and artificial otherness creates suffering in us.

But you need not suffer. Notice any feelings that arise from this ego story, a story that demonstrates two sides of the same coin. One side feels like inadequacy, unworthiness, or negative comparisons and leaves you feeling inferior, judgmental, or jealous of others. The other side feels like specialness, superiority, arrogance, self-cherishing, or being better than others. Both are ego traps that separate you from divinity and from the other Divine souls with whom you are connected in a web of perfect Divine cosmic unity.

If this sounds familiar, don't fret. There's nothing to do other than notice your separation story. Become the observer of how your ego operates, without making yourself wrong or beating yourself up. The minute you realize your Inner Pilot Light is infinitely more powerful than your ego, you create distance from that separation story and realize you are not the small, lonely self your ego wants you to believe you are. Instead, you are this expansive, powerful, loving, connected Consciousness that is tied into your own Divine Essence as well as the Divine Essence of every other human being, animal, and plant on this planet.

HERO'S PRACTICE:
Tonglen Meditation for Compassion

Try this Tibetan Buddhist practice, which I described in *The Fear Cure*. This meditation practice of taking on the suffering of others and replacing it with your happiness, compassion, and peace through your breath has numerous benefits. It dissolves the self-protection, clinging, and fixation of the Small Self and opens the heart. It reverses the Small Self's tendency to avoid suffering and seek pleasure and liberates you from the prison of selfishness. In the beginning, you may find that you resist this practice. It may bring up all your revulsion, resentment, frustration, anger, and avoidance of suffering. If you experience these feelings, use them to deepen the practice. Let the poison of life's suffering become the medicine. By doing this practice, your heart will open more and more and you will become a vessel of compassion that heals others with your presence. Imagine a world in which we all practiced tonglen every day.

- Start by cleansing your emotional landscape. Sit quietly and focus on your breath as you allow your mind to become still. Using your breath, see yourself breathing in any negative emotions you might be feeling right now and then breathing out peace and joy. Purify your emotional landscape by repeating this process until you feel calm and clear.

- Next, cleanse yourself. See yourself as two beings—your Inner Pilot Light and your Small Self. As you breathe in, visualize your Inner Pilot Light breathing in all of your Small Self's suffering into its wide-open heart. As you breathe out, see your Inner Pilot Light sending your Small Self healing, peace, calmness, love, and compassion. In the compassionate embrace of your Inner Pilot Light, your Small Self responds by opening its heart, too, and all the suffering dissolves.

- Cleanse your wrongdoings by considering a situation where you didn't behave as your best self. Maybe you feel guilty or ashamed or regretful. As you think about this situation, accept responsibility for it as you breathe in, and then as you breathe out, acknowledge your wrongdoing and send forgiveness to yourself and offerings of love, peace, and reconciliation to the ones you harmed.

- Now that you've cleansed your emotional landscape and your Small Self's pain and moved into the energy of forgiveness and reconciliation, expand your tonglen practice for others. Start with just one person you want to help. Invoke the presence of the Divine in your heart, and then as you feel the pain or suffering this person is feeling, visualize the pain as grimy black smoke that you breathe in. As you breathe it in, this toxic smoke dissolves in the openness of your heart and purifies your heart of any of the Small Self's grasping, self-protection, or self-absorption that prevents you from sensing the Oneness of all beings. As you breathe out, see yourself spreading light, love, compassion, and happiness to the one in pain.

- Now expand this practice beyond one person into the collective. Breathe in the suffering of others, and then as you breathe out, see the rays of light, love, and compassion touching every soul on the planet. This practice can be very powerful, infusing the energy of compassion into the culture and connecting us in our web of Oneness.

- If you find yourself resisting this practice, notice any emotions that come up: resentment, fear, anger, sadness, terror, revulsion, feelings of revenge.

Also notice any physical sensations: tightness in your chest, gripping in your solar plexus, or a feeling of heaviness or darkness. As you breathe in, feel the Oneness with all the other people on the planet who are feeling just like you do. As you breathe out, send relief to all suffering beings, including yourself.

CHAPTER 10

RELEASE YOUR ATTACHMENTS

At the same time that I was finding my way back to medicine, first through my job at Optimal Health and then with my own practice, I still hadn't given up my dream of becoming a professional writer. Barbara had suggested I start a blog, and after my meeting with Jon the shaman, which I interpreted as a Cosmic Yes, I charged full speed ahead into figuring out how to start a Web site.

I wasn't planning to launch my new blog until May 1, 2009, about 6 months after I had started working at Optimal Health. But I wound up launching it on April 27, 3 days after my 40th birthday. The graphic design for my site wasn't even done yet. The Web site had a placeholder banner that said "I Am a Writer." I had yet to write my first post.

But terror about a swine flu outbreak was sweeping Twitter, and Sarah, the social media consultant I hired, advised me to get online and calm everyone down. After all, it was just a flu virus, not the plague. My very first blog post was titled "17 Ways to Avoid Swine Flu and Why Not to Freak Out."

I had never before written a blog post or posted on social media. I posted the link to my first blog on Twitter and Facebook, and it went viral.

Within a month, my blog was regularly getting a lot of traffic, and I had recruited 30 guest bloggers to help me create useful content under nine categories: physical health, mental health, relationships, creativity, work/life purpose, sexuality, spirituality, the environment, and finances. The thread that tied them all together was what we called our "strict un-guru policy." Our bloggers were invited to teach what they had learned as experts, but they were expected to be vulnerable and share how they had learned what they learned. Nobody was allowed to get up on a pedestal and talk down to people.

I wrote this mission statement for the blog.

We are committed to inviting you to explore your truth, knowing you are loved, safe, and nurtured. We believe that true healing comes from loving and nurturing both ourselves and others as whole beings. When we own all the disparate parts of ourselves, we tap into the Divine spark within us, allowing us to release limiting beliefs, overcome fears, and enjoy our lives more fully. Once we are in touch with our own divinity—shedding our masks, revealing our authentic selves, and being accepted just as we are— we can see with "magical eyes," gazing beyond the masks we tend to wear to see the unique and special humanity that lies within us all.

By engaging with our community, we hope you will feel inspired, get motivated to bring your authentic self out of the closet, and take steps that bring you closer to health, healing, and inner peace. If you have lost your mojo and feel you have little to give, we welcome you with no expectations. If you have lots to give in service to those in need, we invite you to share your gifts. Chances are good that you're all of the above—sometimes seeking, sometimes giving, always enough.

Regardless of where you are on your personal path of awakening, we welcome you. Let us bear witness to your journey, knowing that while each of us walk a unique path, we walk it in good company.

I had only been blogging for 3 months when Barbara called me giddy with news. At a recent conference, she ran into one of the editors who had loved my original book proposal. She had been following my blog and pitched Barbara on a book idea: She wanted me to write about vaginas. In all seriousness, the book would be a Q&A format self-help book about women's health, intended to help women love, understand, and accept their bodies. To get me started, the editor had collected the secret questions her girlfriends would ask if only they knew a gynecologist like me. When I read the list of questions, I laughed out loud. They were great questions, the same kinds of things the women in my writing workshop at Esalen had asked me: "Why do we have pubic hair?" "If I don't wear a bra, will I get droopy boobs?" "How long is the average labia?" "If I take my husband's Viagra, will I get horny?"

I had mixed feelings about the offer. Part of me jumped up and down with glee. Finally! A book deal! But another part was disappointed. I wasn't being offered to publish the book I'd spent a year writing. This would require starting from scratch to write a completely different kind of book, one that wasn't anything like the spiritual memoir that felt close to my heart. The premise for the book felt a little silly, much more juvenile than the meaningful memoir I had hoped to publish. But hell, it was a book deal! After more than 30 publishing companies had rejected *I Don't Do Men*, I figured I should be grateful.

Thinking back, I realize my Inner Pilot Light was telling me not to write this book. I didn't want to write about gynecology. I wanted to write about what I blogged about, which was more about my spiritual journey than my vagina. But I was still learning to cultivate my relationship with my Inner Pilot Light. By saying yes to writing this book, I allowed myself to be motivated not by faith but by fear. I didn't trust that another book deal would come along, so I was afraid to turn it down, even though it wasn't the book I wanted to write.

The book wound up going to auction, and four publishers all offered the exact same advance: $15,000. Barbara and I were both disappointed. This wouldn't even come close to paying off my rising debt. In fact, I would actually lose money on publishing my book. But because I dreamed of becoming a professional writer, I agreed to do it anyway.

My book *What's Up Down There?* was birthed into the world on September 30, 2010, and all the stars were aligned to make it a wild success. A corporate sponsor was sending me around the country on a college tour. An on-campus peer-to-peer health organization championed the book and helped arrange to get me in front of large audiences of young women who would be given the opportunity to anonymously ask me the kinds of questions you'd only ask your gynecologist if she were your best friend. The media was all over it. I was interviewed by national women's magazines, as well as on big Web sites like AOL, CBS News, and Oprah.com. I appeared on Oprah radio. I was even scheduled to appear on national television. I felt like a celebrity!

As all of this was going down, I was given countless opportunities to witness, first with horror and revulsion and then eventually with a gentler humor and self-compassion, how my ego operates. Up until this point, I thought I knew myself. After all, I had been in therapy. I had been to Esalen.

I was reading self-help books. But I was a spiritual newborn who was blind to the fact that my ego had been running the show for most of my life.

I'm not talking about the ego Sigmund Freud references. I'm also not talking about the garden-variety use of the word "ego," or "egotistical," used to mean vain, selfish, or opinionated. I'm talking about the ego as it is defined in the book *A Course In Miracles*, which describes it as the illusion of separation, the idea that we are separate from the Divine and separate from our interconnectedness in Divine Oneness to all other living beings. In his Integral Enlightenment teleclass series, Craig Hamilton describes the ego as the part of you that has an emotional investment in your self-image. He explains that there's a part of us that has a need to see ourselves in a particular way. The ego has a story about the kind of person we are, the kind of person we're not, what we're good at, what we're not good at, what we're capable of achieving, what we're not. The ego is your Small Self, the part that can't allow itself to be as expansive as your soul longs to be. It tends to make you "better than" or, even more frequently, "less than" others. Whether you feel superior or inferior, more worthy or less worthy, smarter than or stupider than, prettier than or uglier than, it's all ego.

The ego has a compulsion to have a coherent story about who we are, and if these inherent qualities about ourselves that we believe to be true get challenged, we get defensive. The ego is always trying to resolve any inconsistencies between belief and reality. For example, if you believe you're not good enough to achieve something, you'll unconsciously self-sabotage in order to make sure that your reality is consistent with your belief.

To explain what I mean, let me introduce you to my ego, whom I lovingly call "Victoria Rochester," because that's what I wished my mother had named me when I was a little girl. Victoria is a doctor, an artist, an author, a blogger, a mother, and an online entrepreneur. She's a serious overachiever who, motivated by an underlying sense of unworthiness, continues to doggedly pursue external validation as a way to feel more valuable in the world. She has a savior complex, having been raised in a family full of doctors and missionaries. Nothing lights her up more than e-mails from people who swear she saved their lives. It's part of what drew her to medicine in the first place, this impulse to be of service, motivated in part by the impulse to spread love in the world but also by the feeling that she's not good enough unless she's giving until she's depleted.

Victoria is always striving to prove herself, to do it better, to help more people. She has a hard time feeling satisfied with who she is and what she's achieved. She wants to save the world, and she'll do whatever it takes to make it happen. If anyone suggests she can't have what she wants, she'll belt out, "Just watch me." Then she'll go get it. After learning to protect herself during many years of medical education, Victoria is a tough cookie. If you're standing between her and what she wants, she might run right over you, without an ounce of malice, but also without an ounce of awareness that she hurt you when she bulldozed through.

When Victoria is relaxed and feeling secure, she can be confident, generous, curious, compelling, compassionate, smart, and loving. Under pressure, though, she can be bossy, intolerant, controlling, judgmental, and entitled, like your stereotypical surgeon. If she feels threatened, she'll put you in your place so fast you might get knocked over with an elbow. When she falls into a negative pattern that has repeated itself many times in the past, Victoria can be what my therapist calls an "incinerator." (She also *really* doesn't want me telling you all of this negative stuff about her because she wants you to approve of her!) Egos thrive by staying under the radar. They do not want to be illuminated, because when you shine light on how the ego operates, the ego is busted.

Victoria is a creative flame, a font of inspiration and talent that pours through, seemingly without effort. Because of her creative fire, she appears as a bright light illuminating the darkness. Others are drawn to her like moths to the flame, but for those who get too close—look out. Victoria may burn you. Then she feels awful because she has a tender heart and shames herself if she hurts people unwittingly.

A book tour is right up Victoria's alley. She likes to get dressed up and attract attention. She's into glamour shots, fashion, and seeing her number of Facebook "likes" grow. She loves hanging around famous people. It feeds that underlying sense of unworthiness and makes her feel important, like she matters, like she belongs. Victoria struts out her intellect when she feels insecure and boasts about her accomplishments when she's feeling like she's not enough. She fusses when someone recognizes her in a crowd, claiming, with false modesty, that she wants to remain anonymous. But then if nobody is paying attention to her, she'll start name-dropping like nobody's business. She feels right at home on stage and on television, amid lots of applause. If 100,000 people read her blog, she wants 200,000. She has big energy and fills up a room without meaning to. But she's clueless about the effect she has when she decides to start flapping her butterfly wings.

Until I went on my book tour, I thought I was Victoria. But as I grew in my spiritual development, I realized that Victoria was only one part of Lissa. As the blind spots of my ego were illuminated, I started to wake up to another part of myself, an infinite dimension within me that was not limited by the stories I'd created about myself. This expansive part of me, this infinitely loving spirit of me, was my Inner Pilot Light.

My Inner Pilot Light is the part of me that sometimes flares and sometimes grows dim but that will never be extinguished, not even when I die. She was there before I was born and will survive the physical incarnation of me. This part of me is older and wiser than Victoria, gentler, kinder, less driven, more loving, more mindful, less frantic, more still, more compassionate. My Inner Pilot Light never judges, finding equanimity with everyone, even if someone behaves in a way that might seem hurtful to Victoria, who can act like a hurt little princess when she perceives that someone wrongs her. My Inner Pilot Light operates from a wide-open heart and makes decisions not from the mind but from intuition, guided by the heart.

My Inner Pilot Light trusts that the Universe has everything handled, that there's no need to control every outcome, and that the Universe is a friendly place with its own universal intelligence. She doesn't care about fame or accolades, and she has nothing to prove. She knows she's worthy, not because of achievements, helpful acts, intelligence, beauty, or popularity but because she is a spark of divinity, and that makes her inherently valuable. She knows she's special but also not special. She's special because of this spark of divinity dwelling within her, but she's not special because that Divine spark resides within every living being.

My Inner Pilot Light thrives on long walks in nature; quiet time in meditation; intimate, respectful, deep connections with loved ones; and the joyful sense of communion with the Divine. My Inner Pilot Light loves everybody. When you look into her eyes, you see sweet, soft, pure, unconditional Buddha eyes that channel Divine love. This part of me doesn't get tempted with a savior complex, but she does respond to the impulse to serve, not because she's not good enough if she doesn't help others but because the inclination to love launches her into action. This kind of service is not about self-sacrifice, because my Inner Pilot Light is so interconnected to all things that there's not much "self" to sacrifice. What serves my Inner Pilot Light serves us all, so there is a generosity of spirit that never keeps score or expects reciprocity, although love breeds love.

My Inner Pilot Light is almost unshakably calm and fearless. Even if her life is in danger, she knows that she will survive death and is therefore not at risk. This gives her an almost superhuman capacity to love unconditionally and be a vessel of service, even in the direst of circumstances. She can keep her heart open, even when others threaten to break it. My Inner Pilot Light is kind, compassionate, self-nurturing, and nurturing to others, because we are all One, and she knows that the only way we will survive on Mother Earth is if we nurture one another. She never sees herself as a victim, understanding that she is always co-creating her reality, and therefore, it is within her power to change her perception of her circumstances at any moment. She has to be patient and gentle with Victoria, though, who loves to stew in her victim stories and make everybody else wrong. She has learned not to judge or punish Victoria, because when she does, Victoria only acts up, like a naughty child. Victoria responds better to love and clear boundaries. When Victoria feels safe, she can relax and let my Inner Pilot Light take the wheel, but if Victoria feels threatened, rejected, punished, bullied, or judged, she tends to throw a fit.

If only my Inner Pilot Light ruled the vehicle of Lissa 24/7, my life might be much easier. But Victoria still grabs the wheel from time to time. Because she is afraid of getting called out on her shenanigans, Victoria is unspeakably threatened by my Inner Pilot Light, even though my Inner Pilot Light treats her with a firm hand and compassion, like you would treat a beloved child who's acting up. When aspects of Victoria are revealed, she gets defensive and argumentative because she is emotionally invested in her own relevance. Victoria can't stand the idea that, as I navigate my hero's journey, my Inner Pilot Light might take the driver's seat more and more, influencing Lissa's behavior. Victoria is not happy sitting in the backseat. But my Inner Pilot Light is grateful when light shines on how Victoria behaves and operates. Once my Inner Pilot Light recognizes these Small Self patterns, it's easier to avoid letting Victoria go rogue and grab the wheel, steering the vehicle of Lissa off course. Over time, my Inner Pilot Light has learned how to drive more often. But that doesn't mean Victoria isn't at risk of taking over any time she gets triggered.

I am not the only being with an Inner Pilot Light. We all have this infinite "unself" within. It's the part of us that is pure Consciousness, which is inextricably linked with the Inner Pilot Light of every other living thing. Some of us are more in touch with this part of ourselves, while others can't yet hear the quiet, subtle whisperings of this wise inner teacher. The journey deepens our relationship with this wise being that inhabits us. It is a choice we make, to be brave enough to examine our inner Victorias, not to judge or criticize but to recognize the way we create our own suffering, so we can wake up and be more conscious about how we align our energy, how we make choices, and how we behave.

Once I was aware of these various parts of my psyche—Victoria, my Inner Pilot Light, and my Gremlin (who is also a part of my ego but speaks with a different voice than Victoria)—I was able to distance myself enough to view those voices as an outside observer. This helped me grow as I watched Victoria unravel during my book tour, which was not going as planned.

The national television show that initially booked me asked that I use the term "passion flower" instead of "vagina" and then ultimately cancelled my appearance after I refused to use the term. I had been commissioned to write an article by CBSNews.com, titled "15 Crazy Things about Vaginas," which headlined on the front page of the Web site for about an hour, until men in suits demanded that it be taken off the site. The Oprah radio show host who interviewed me kept getting bleeped when she talked to me about vaginas during our interview. Victoria was not happy.

I was scheduled to be in New York City for 6 days of my book tour, under the assumption that I'd be booked with media appearances, speaking gigs, and interviews. I'd be doing live events, if not in big auditoriums on college campuses, at least in funky bookstores. But when I got to New York and looked at my calendar, I realized that nothing had actually panned out. I had a mini entourage with me: Lauren, who managed my logistics, and Jayne, who was shooting video of our events. But the only things I had scheduled were lunch dates with friends. Because she tends to take over when things feel out of control, Victoria took the reins and tried to force things back on track in her self-righteous, indignant, bulldozing, victim story–laden way.

I was walking through the East Village in New York with Regena Thomashauer, also known as "Mama Gena," when Victoria started bitching to Regena about how I was the helpless victim of discrimination by the media because my book was about vaginas. Regena, who was all about vaginas (she named her apartment the Pussy Palace), became incensed. She pulled out her cell phone as we were walking to her favorite coffee shop, and she scrolled through her contacts to ring up her friend Dr. Christiane Northrup, the pioneering women's health visionary who had written the foreword to my book.

Regena relayed the story of how the media was discriminating against vaginas. (The barista making our espresso perked up when he heard the word "pussy" repetitively.) Then Regena was silent. Christiane was obviously talking, but I couldn't hear what was being said. The barista handed us our espressos, and we walked through the East Village to the bookstore where Regena planned to beg the owner to hold an emergency book signing for *What's Up Down There?* We made it to the bookstore and Regena was still listening to Christiane. Finally, she hung up the phone.

Silence.

Regena said, "Well, that's not exactly the response I expected."

She went on to explain to me that Christiane could help me. Sure, she could mobilize her loyal troops, rally people on Facebook, call the people at *The Oprah Winfrey Show*, and tap into her New York City Rolodex on my behalf. But Christiane told Regena she wasn't going to do so because it was time for me to learn something essential.

The message, as I remember it, went something like this: "Lissa is brilliant at *doing*, but she needs to learn how to *receive*. Lissa needs to be less sperm, more egg. To be 'eggy' is to set goals but release attachment to outcomes, to surrender to what wants to happen rather than pushing for what you're trying to *make* happen, to put your desires out there without doing anything to bring them into being, to simply trust that when you move in the direction of joy, ease, peace, harmony, love, and the highest good for all beings, the Universe, like an army of sperm, falls over itself trying to bring your desires into form. Tell Lissa I know we had to be 'spermy' in order to survive 12 years of medical education. This 'spermy' strategy can be quite successful if your goal is world domination via sheer might and utter exhaustion. But the very thing that was adaptive at the time will become our downfall if we don't learn to operate in a new, more 'eggy' way. There's a more feminine way to achieving what you desire, and Lissa needs to learn it. Tell her I'm sorry things aren't going well, and I want to help. But I'm going to resist the impulse to fix this because this is Lissa's laboratory for this lesson her soul needs to learn."

When Regena relayed this message, Victoria pulled out her pointer finger and was all, "Sister did *not* just say that." I mean, come on! This woman wrote the foreword to my book, and she couldn't do me one little favor and dial up her friend Oprah to rant about what a travesty it was that The Man was discriminating against me, my awesome book, and vaginas everywhere?

Victoria was incensed, but my Inner Pilot Light felt the plunk of truth in Christiane's words. I sensed I had just been granted a precious gift.

As a doctor, I was firmly indoctrinated into a masculine approach to success. The rules, as I learned them, were:

Push.

Strive.

Put your ass in the chair until it's done.

Make it happen.

Go for it.

Chase it.

Put your nose to the grindstone.

No pain, no gain.

Grasp.

Clutch.

Cling to it like your life depends on it if it feels like it's slipping away.

If it's not going well, try harder.

Succeed.

Triumph.

But for the love of God, never let 'em see you sweat.

And for Pete's sake, don't stop and savor what you've achieved, because there's a bigger goal right around the corner.

But it's exhausting to be all sperm, all the time. When I heard Christiane's message, I took a deep breath at the very mention of being eggy. This bit of wisdom gave my Inner Pilot Light a chance to shine brighter, much to the chagrin of Victoria, who started melting down into a full-blown panic attack.

It was great advice, but I wasn't quite ready to be less sperm, more egg during that book tour. So I tried to sperm my way to success. Unsurprisingly, it didn't work. The next 5 months of touring took a toll on me. I wound up physically depleted, emotionally drained, and financially broke, wallowing in my "Poor Lissa" story without any consciousness around how I might have participated in creating my reality. I just wasn't ready yet to start accepting personal responsibility for everything that happened to me in life. I had graduated from spiritual kindergarten, but I was still in about third grade, doing the best I could but fumbling along, disrupted with feelings of inner turmoil.

By the end of my first year at the Owning Pink Center, I was in negotiations for my next book deal, and it became evident that I had a very important choice to make. Because I had been traveling the country instead of seeing patients, my integrative medicine practice had become a financial drain. Plus, I had alienated many of my existing patients with my extended disappearing act. I didn't mean to be gone for as long as I was, but speaking gigs kept getting added to my schedule, and because a sponsor was paying for my book tour, I felt obligated to keep sperming ahead.

I realized that if I wanted a successful medical practice, I needed to commit to being the best doctor I could be—or I needed to free myself from the duties of a brick-and-mortar practice so I could commit to writing and speaking full time, sharing the message of whole health I was just beginning to understand. I was conflicted about which direction to take. After all, I had made a promise to return to medicine on that bridge in the energy vortex at Esalen. I didn't want to abandon my calling, but when I tuned into what felt true for me, I realized that as much as I loved my patients, enjoyed this new type of mind-body healing work, and felt fulfilled in my practice, I felt more swellings of joy, passion, and pure service when I was writing and speaking than when I was practicing clinical medicine.

Plus, I felt like the signs from the Universe were guiding me to close my practice. The woman who helped me run my practice had been offered a better job while I had been gone. Many of my patients had understandably gone elsewhere during my absence, and I was having trouble filling my office hours. The laboratory I was using was changing its policies. And my overhead on the practice was about to go up, when I was already $200,000 in debt.

I wasn't quite sure how I would pay the bills if I closed my medical practice. But since my practice was costing me as much as it was earning, I wouldn't be sacrificing much income. I hoped that my writing would begin to pay the bills soon, since my debt was mounting, Matt still wasn't working, and I had gotten no royalty checks after my $15,000 advance for *What's Up Down There?* But I trusted that if I followed the spiritual guidance that left me feeling like I was supposed to close my practice, the money would follow.

Little did I know how wrong I was.

I had hoped to get another book advance for the new memoir I'd written, titled *Broken: One Doctor's Search for the Lost Heart of Medicine.* Always the optimist, I was, once again, hopeful that things would work out if only I clung to the unshakable confidence Victoria had in spades.

Barbara pitched my next book to my publisher and called me soon afterward, saying, "Good news! St. Martin's Press wants your book!"

Yes! It was finally happening! My book was going to be a bestseller! I was going to get to publish the kind of book *I* wanted to publish. My dreams of becoming a professional writer were coming true. All the risks I had taken by closing my medical practice in order to devote myself to my writing career were going to pay off!

I started to do a little happy dance, but before I could pop open the champagne, Barbara cut in. "The bad news is that they're offering $17,500."

Victoria had a tizzy.

What? My blogger colleagues, people with platforms no bigger than mine, were all getting six-figure advances for their books. What was wrong with my book? What was wrong with *me?* Forget that! What was wrong with my publisher for not recognizing my brilliance as a writer? Plus, I had tried so hard to prove myself. My blog readership had tripled. I had demonstrated my ability to rally the media. And I had shown commitment and follow-through on my book tour. I thought I had done everything within my spermy power to make sure we'd be talking big numbers this time around.

Now, instead of feeling victimized by medicine, I felt like I was at the mercy of an unfair publishing industry. Victoria loved blaming other people when things didn't go her way.

I asked Barbara whether there was any way to finagle more money out of the deal. Couldn't we shop it to other publishers? Wasn't there some way to demonstrate to the publishers how valuable my book was? Surely, we could get a six-figure advance somehow.

That's when Barbara got straight with me and told me that in spite of all the media hype, social media buzz, and large audiences of college students interested in getting their private questions answered, *What's Up Down There?* simply hadn't sold many copies. I was shocked.

"Maybe the publishers were right, Lissa," Barbara said in a resigned voice. "Maybe nobody cares about vaginas."

But how could this be? Half the population has one, and the other half wants to get in them. I felt nauseated. I thought I had spent 5 months making sure the world cared about vaginas. And it hadn't worked. I felt helpless, hopeless, embarrassed, ashamed, outraged, and extremely discouraged, wallowing in the misery of what my friend Christine Hassler would call my "expectation hangover."

I grudgingly accepted the book deal and tried to muster up an attitude of gratitude. I knew I should be thanking my lucky stars. Millions of people only dream of an opportunity like this, and here I was acting like a spoiled brat and resenting my book deal. I tried to rally my enthusiasm. My mother and I raised our glasses to celebrate the book deal. I did a half-hearted little happy dance with Matt and Siena. I announced the book deal on my blog.

I was going to publish another book. Yeah!

But deep down, I felt like crap. I felt shame. I felt weak. I was embarrassed to admit how worthless I was to my publisher. When my blogger friends asked about my book deal, I felt like a nobody. Over the next few days, my feelings of desperation, anxiety, bitterness, and worthlessness escalated. The bills were piling up. We had maxed out our credit cards and borrowed all we could from my mother.

I felt so sick to my stomach that I started losing weight. Then I got slammed with a wicked cold. I had lost my voice by the time the contract arrived.

I just couldn't make myself sign it.

I called Barbara with my raspy voice and confessed how I felt.

She said, "Lissa, no author should feel bummed about signing a book deal."

My eyes filled with tears. I felt like a failure.

Up to this point, my hero's journey had been a long and winding Road of Trials. But in that moment, when Barbara expressed compassion for my disappointment, I found myself facing the next phase of the journey: the approach to the Innermost Cave. During this part of the journey, the hero finally arrives at the dark, underground place where the object of the quest lies. It might be the headquarters of the enemy or the underground passage through which the hero must pass in order to make it to the promised land. The Innermost Cave is the most dangerous place in the Special World, the scary belly of darkness through which the hero must pass. For Luke Skywalker, it's when he's sucked into the Death Star. For Dorothy in Oz, it's when she's captured by the Wicked Witch of the West. For Indiana Jones, it's the Temple of Doom.

As I stared at that book contract and felt my body rejecting it on every level, I prayed for guidance. That's when I heard Victoria pitching a fit. And I heard the Gremlin telling me I would be crazy to reject any book deal when there was nothing else on the horizon. But loud and clear, more convincing than any of the other voices, the voice of my Inner Pilot Light said, "Darling. Don't. Do. It."

I called Barbara and turned down my book deal, and when I did, she told me she could no longer be my agent. She was quick to explain that it wasn't that she didn't love me or appreciate my writing. It's just that she felt like she had done everything within her power to please me, and it wasn't enough. I had to agree that she was right. She had been a wonderful agent, but I hadn't been able to write a book that would pay the bills.

We agreed to break up and stay in love.

I guess I had hoped that if I threatened to walk out, my publisher would fight for me and pony up more money and Barbara would decide to stay. But that's not what happened. St. Martin's was kind about my rejection. They relinquished me from any further obligation to them and wished me well. My editor said that if I changed my mind at any point in the future, she'd welcome me back with open arms. I was humbled by the reaction and grateful for the gentleness.

So there I was, no book deal, no publisher, no agent, and a lot of debt. On the outside, I looked quite successful. My blog was getting tons of traffic. My name was plastered all over national magazines and the Internet. I got hundreds of fan letters every day. But none of that translated into a paycheck.

I had been calling my blog "my business," but when I heard online entrepreneur Marie Forleo say, "If your business isn't generating money, it's a hobby, not a business," I felt like I had been kicked in the gut. My blog was not a business. It was some cute hobby that I thought would turn me into a professional writer. I might as well have just plastered a big red loser *L* on my forehead.

My online community had been following my professional journey with a sort of morbid curiosity, like a reality TV show you know you should turn off but can't. I knew they were asking themselves the same question I was asking: *Is Lissa an inspiration or a cautionary tale?* They wanted to believe that it was safe for them to follow my lead, to take leaps of faith and listen to their intuition and be unapologetically authentic and go after their dreams and stop compromising or selling out their integrity. I had told the truth throughout my journey, never sugarcoating it, always at least trying to be transparent about my triumphs and challenges.

As embarrassed as I felt, I knew it was my duty to come clean. My brave experiment had failed, and my community had a right to know that it wasn't safe to follow my lead. So I publicly explained what had happened—with my practice, my book deal, my agent, my publisher. I confessed to my shame and humiliation and feelings of failure. I told everyone how Victoria had gotten the upper hand on my book tour and sabotaged things. I explained that I was doing the best that I could and trying to be compassionate with myself, but the Gremlin was hard on me. I shared how badly I felt about myself, how my self-esteem had taken a big blow. I tried to stay optimistic, to rouse within myself the trust that no matter what happened, I would always land butter-side up.

But I was losing my faith.

I could tell that, for many of my readers, my vulnerability was hard to witness. They wanted to shield me, to protect me from what others might think about me, to armor up on my behalf. But that wasn't my journey. I had to walk that Road of Trials stark naked in front of everyone. Victoria felt intensely vulnerable with the public scrutiny, but my Inner Pilot Light was leading the way. Those in my online community were kind and generous cheerleaders, rooting for me even though I looked like the losing team. I could feel the love shining through, and it buoyed me against the harsh judge of the Gremlin.

It wasn't just me that was losing my faith. Matt was, too. He had supported me in my decision to quit my job. He was on board when we had to sell our house, liquidate my retirement account, borrow money from my mother, and rack up credit card debt. He understood why I had turned down the book deal and closed my medical practice, and he had put his heart and soul into helping me build the businesses that weren't earning enough income to pay off our debt. But we were both growing weary. We both craved comfort and security, and as we faced the genuine possibility of bankruptcy we had a hard time coping.

I tried to cocoon myself in a bubble of faith, so I could hold a steady optimism. But I was losing my faith. Fear and doubt kept seeping their way into my faith bubble, and I started to think I might have made a terrible mistake. I was a scared little girl who tried to put on a brave face when she was quaking inside, but I kept rallying to play the strong, competent cheerleader. My charade was falling apart, taking its toll on my body, my mood, and my marriage. It was a dark, dark time.

If you're struggling on your own Road of Trials, it's so tempting to let fear win. The Gremlin starts spewing, "Who are you to think you could have achieved this mission? You were delusional to even pick up that phone when your calling rang. There aren't any happily-ever-afters. Real life ends with you failing and everyone watching you."

What most heroes don't realize when they stumble on the Road of Trials is that *this is where you find your faith.* Your ego will do anything to cling to the illusion of certainty, to grasp at comfort, and to believe that you can control your life. The tendency to avoid uncertainty is rampant in our culture. Uncertainty is un-American. In reality, avoiding uncertainty is the goal of 90 percent of your ego's choices. The search for certainty is an addiction, and it's deeply related to the pursuit of comfort. We've been programmed since childhood to believe that if you're successful, you have comforts—big homes, good food, nice cars, a big nest egg for retirement. But what if we've been sold a booby prize? What if living a meaningful, fulfilling life is about recognizing that there is something beyond comfort and certainty, that uncertainty is a gateway to possibility?

When we make peace with uncertainty, we realize that anything can happen. When we cling to certainty, we limit ourselves, but if we're willing to venture bravely into an uncertain future, the doorway to mystery, wonder, and awe opens. What lies on the other side of the doorway invites you to explore. When you don't know what you'll discover, you might be surprised to find that the uncertain is even more wonderful than what seems certain. Whatever might come next is an adventure once you're no longer afraid of what you don't know.

Real faith requires letting go of everything you once thought was certain. The development of an ego, that false self who you identify with, the part that makes you separate from the Divine, emerged as part of a natural survival instinct gone awry. Your mind has a picture of who you are, which includes all of your strengths and weaknesses, your likes and dislikes, your achievements, your failures, how you look, and what other people think about you. But your mind is ruled by your primitive amygdala, that self-protective part of your limbic brain that is always on the lookout for danger. As Martha Beck says, "The mind is a two-bit whore." You can't trust it to be honest with you.

Craig Hamilton teaches that your ego has an emotional attachment to protecting and defending this mental construct of who you are. If the ego gets threatened, the body literally goes into fight-or-flight mode, as if your very life is being threatened, because the amygdala can't tell the difference between a threat to the ego's safety and a threat to your real body. The minute you start observing how your ego operates rather than functioning unconsciously from within it, your survival instincts get triggered. If you even question that perhaps something you thought about yourself might not be true, that there might be another part of you other than your ego, fear and defensiveness show up. When your ego is threatened, your body is not literally dying, but the mental self-image you have of yourself may be, so it feels like death.

The ego has an insane need to know and understand how things are. It is intolerant of change or uncertainty. It resists change and makes up all of these stories about why change is scary and impossible. The ego simply can't let go. It fights, rather than surrendering. It doubts. It prefers to withdraw into its little dream world of illusion. It simply can't have true faith.

Your Inner Pilot Light, on the other hand, is not invested in how others perceive you, what you achieve, how you look, or what makes you separate from others. Your Inner Pilot Light is infinitely curious, not attached to limiting beliefs or a set worldview. Rather than defending a mental self-image of who you are, your Inner Pilot Light merely wants to know the truth, to lovingly see all parts of you, including how your ego operates. Your Inner Pilot Light also craves truth in other people and truth in the world. It doesn't attach to how things should be, it doesn't resist what is. It just wants to know how things really are. Your Inner Pilot Light knows it is One with a vast, infinitely unknowable Universe, which is one big question mark. This part of you is perfectly comfortable with uncertainty and knows that the flip side of the fear of uncertainty is the excitement of possibility.

The ego will always choose fear over faith, and it will make up a whole fear story about why faith is not safe, why you can't trust that the Universe has a Divine intelligence, and why the Universe doesn't need you to be in charge. But your Inner Pilot Light knows the truth, that when things aren't going the way you hoped, it's time to turn your life and your problems over to Divine Will. Disappointment, sadness, frustration, anger, resentment, and fear are all manifestations of the ego's attachment to things being a certain way. The ego wants the ego's will, not Divine Will, and when the ego doesn't get its way, it's likely to have a tantrum.

I realize now that these trials were a necessary part of my spiritual evolution. Perhaps my soul perfectly orchestrated these obstacles as a way to learn the lessons I needed to learn in order to grow. Victoria was too attached to how she wanted things to be. She simply couldn't trust that Divine intelligence was ensuring that everything was going exactly as it was supposed to on my hero's journey.

You might doubt your journey, too. If that's how you feel, don't worry. It's all happening just as it should, in perfect timing, in the perfect way. Try to get your Small Self out of the driver's seat and know that it is safe to go along for the ride of your life.

HERO'S GUIDEPOST:

Make Peace with Disappointment

It's natural to get disappointed when you're on your hero's journey. It takes so much courage to even embark upon the journey, and when you do, there's excitement pouring through you as ideas, passions, and dreams reveal themselves. It's nearly impossible not to attach to such dreams. Of course you want your dreams to come true! Expectations result naturally. When what you hope for doesn't pan out, you may wind up with an expectation hangover. Such hangovers can leave you wallowing in a pit of negative emotions. You won't want to skip feeling these emotions. The "spiritual bypass" never works and can actually slow your healing process. But once you've allowed yourself to feel what you feel, it's possible to mine your expectation hangover for all that it's worth. Expectation hangovers are ripe times for soul growth, if you're brave enough to move through them consciously. When you do, you realize that any attachment to things turning out a certain way is merely the ego trying to assert its will. The Small Self always wants to be in the driver's seat. It doesn't want to believe that it's safe to release control. So it will have a hissy fit when it doesn't get what it wants. But your Inner Pilot Light is always there to calm your Small Self when it's melting down. Most of the pain of an expectation hangover stems from your resistance to what is. If you can, move into a place of accepting what is rather than resisting it, trusting that if you're not getting what you want, it's purposeful. You may even look back in hindsight and see that the Universe was actually protecting you with the Cosmic No. The Universe has your back, even if you don't understand its plan. When you trust this, inner peace can fill you.

HERO'S PRACTICE:
"I Accept" Meditation

Practice an "I accept" meditation. Close your eyes and allow yourself to feel all the disappointment about things that aren't going how you hoped. Let yourself feel the sadness, anger, frustration, hopelessness, fear, and embarrassment. Don't judge your feelings. Just feel them. Then repeat the mantra "I accept. I accept. I accept." Notice any inner resistance that bubbles up and keep repeating the mantra. Pay attention to any thoughts that refute your mantra, any things you feel that you can't accept. But keep going. "I accept. I accept. I accept." To be guided through an "I accept" meditation, download the free guided meditation at TheAnatomyofaCalling.com. For more help preventing and accepting disappointment, read Christine Hassler's book *Expectation Hangover*.

CHAPTER 11

GET RADICALLY CURIOUS

After closing my clinical practice and turning down my next book offer, I hung out an online shingle, having the nerve to call myself a "life coach," available for hire to do phone or in-person coaching sessions with my blog readers. April was one of my first clients.

Always wearing oversize clothing that covered most of her face, April revealed to me that she had been traumatized throughout her childhood with physical and sexual abuse. Her alcoholic mother, whose many boyfriends molested April, finally walked out when April was 10. Her father worked nights, leaving April and her brother home alone to fend for themselves. In addition to being autistic, for years she had suffered from post-traumatic stress disorder, a variety of phobias, obsessive-compulsive traits, and a mysterious blood disorder that had been worked up by a variety of hematologists, none of whom could explain why April became dangerously anemic, iron deficient, and exhausted in spite of the fact that she wasn't bleeding. She passed out frequently and was often short of breath. Every month she had to go to the hospital for IV infusions that brought her blood count up to normal, and by the end of every month, she was anemic again. Although the doctors couldn't explain what was causing the anemia, they assured her she would require infusions for the rest of her life. They couldn't identify any of the typical genetic conditions that cause anemia, such as sickle-cell anemia or thalassemia, but, apparently, April's mother suffered from a similarly misunderstood condition.

After being placed in foster care as a teenager, April wanted to become a cop, but her physical limitations kept her from qualifying for the police academy, so she trained to become a professional bodyguard, which only fed into her phobias and obsessive-compulsive tendencies. By the time I met April, she was so hypervigilant, always on the lookout for danger, that she slept with a gun under her pillow and could barely leave the house. When I asked her if she wanted to do our session over a hike, she told me we'd have to do it inside. Otherwise, she'd be forced to behave as my bodyguard, always on high alert. Even inside, she couldn't turn her back to me. For that matter, she couldn't turn her back to anyone, so she was always spinning in circles, looking over her shoulder, making sure nobody was approaching her from behind.

After a few sessions with April, I was out hiking on one of the coastal trails near my Marin County home when I had a vision, like a very detailed movie that appeared in front of me. I was in a room that smelled like sage, with a lit candle, a grayish black crystal shaped like a heart, an iPod playing the Mumford & Sons song "Awake My Soul," and a bottle of aromatherapy oil. I was sitting on a yoga mat that had been made into a nest with soft blankets, leaning against a wall. April was lying down between my legs, her back against my belly and her head resting on my chest, facing away from me so I couldn't see her face. I handed April the crystal and told her to hold it in her right hand, and then I anointed April's forehead and chest with one drop of the aromatherapy oil before pressing my right palm against her forehead and my left palm against her chest.

Then the vision stopped. Never having seen a movie appear in front of me, I got a bit freaked out. I kept hiking, thinking, "What does *that* mean?"

Since I had little experience—and a lot of skepticism—around the notion that we all have intuitive capacities, I initially dismissed it as a weird daydream. But the idea haunted me. The next day, hiking a different trail, the same movie flashed before me, and I heard the voice of my Inner Pilot Light say, "You're supposed to do this with April. Don't be afraid."

I couldn't do what I had seen in the movie. First of all, I didn't own a grayish black crystal shaped like a heart. More importantly, they taught us in medical school that there are boundaries that must be set. You definitely can't cuddle up on the floor with someone and start anointing her forehead with oil. Not to mention the fact that April had already told me she couldn't turn her back to anyone. There was no way she'd permit it.

That night, I dreamed that I was performing this strange ceremony with April. An angel wearing purple was sitting to my left. The angel said, in the most loving, gentle voice, "Don't be afraid," which was exactly what my Inner Pilot Light had said. When I woke up, I knew I had to at least discuss this with April.

As I stumbled through my explanation of what I was being guided to do, April surprised me by agreeing to try it. This meant I found myself in the bizarre situation of trying to find a gray, heart-shaped crystal. Now, I live in Marin County, so I thought it would be easy. But none of the shops I visited in Mill Valley sold crystals. I scouted out the touristy boutiques in Sausalito. Nothing. So finally, I asked on Twitter, and someone referred me to a store in Larkspur.

Feeling more than a little goofy, I approached the owner of the shop and confessed that I was a doctor, that I knew nothing about crystals and was frankly skeptical that they were capable of anything healing or mystical, but I was in search of a gray crystal, which I would be using with a client. She asked for more details, and when I confided in her what I had seen in my vision, she said, "Oh, you're clairvoyant."

I shook my head violently. "Oh, no. I'm not psychic or anything. I just daydream. Sometimes I see pictures or scenes in my head." I didn't tell her I talked to my Inner Pilot Light and it spoke back.

She said, "Sweetheart, that's what clairvoyance is. Don't be afraid of it. It's a gift. You're wise to follow up on your intuition." Then she led me to a special locked case in the corner of the room and opened it with a key. "These crystals are particularly high vibration." She pulled out a large grayish black crystal with irregular edges and sharp angles.

I blinked when I saw that it cost $1,299.

She said, "Actually, I'm going out of business, so I'll give it to you for 80 percent off."

I was about to pay this still-hefty price, when I spotted a ceramic bowl sitting on the checkout counter. Inside was a grayish black heart-shaped stone that looked exactly like what I had seen in my vision.

The shop clerk said, "Oh, that's hematite. Very grounding." It was only $10.

I bought the hematite instead and hid it in my purse, feeling strangely guilty, like I was smuggling drugs across the border of my sanity.

Before my next session with April, I felt a little crazy as I prepared the space, laying down a yoga mat, covering it with blankets, and making a little altar upon which I placed the hematite heart, a lit candle, a bottle of lavender oil I sometimes used as perfume, and an iPod cued up to Mumford & Sons' "Awake My Soul." Before April arrived, I burned some sage that I had bought at a metaphysical bookstore in San Rafael after asking the woman in the crystal store where to buy sage.

"Oh, for smudging," she said, as if everyone knew what smudging was.

I explained that I really wasn't the woo-woo type, and she laughed and said, "A clairvoyant who lives in Marin and isn't woo-woo. Now that's a first."

I had an impulse to meditate before April arrived for our session, but I wasn't good at meditating. I had tried before, mostly at Esalen, but I was so plagued with racing thoughts that I found it nearly impossible to settle my mind. Nevertheless, before April arrived, I sat in the space that smelled deliciously of sage and closed my eyes and prayed. I asked God and Jesus and Buddha and my Inner Pilot Light and all the angels, especially the one wearing purple from my dream, to join April and me in service to the highest good of all beings. I recited the prayer I always used before seeing patients at my integrative medicine practice, "Make me a vessel," and I felt the weight of the responsibility of what I was about to do.

Finally, April arrived. I had prepped her over the phone so she wasn't surprised. I assumed my straddle position on the floor and asked her to turn her back to me. She did, but as she reclined on the floor, she looked back at me over her shoulder. I instructed her to face away from me, and she lifted an eyebrow but finally conceded. As she crawled to the floor and leaned back against my chest, her body started to tremble.

I handed her the hematite heart and instructed her to hold it in her right hand. She gripped it until her hand turned nearly purple; meanwhile, I placed one drop of lavender oil on her forehead and one on her chest. Flipping on my iPod, Mumford & Sons filled the room as I placed my hands on April's forehead and chest. I held April in my arms, and I felt her body twitching the way you might when you're about to fall asleep. I ran my fingers through her hair like I did with Siena, feeling slightly awkward about the intimacy of the gesture, but also feeling like it was the right thing to do. I made little cooing noises and moved my left hand to her belly.

She started twitching more.

Then April started convulsing, like she was having a grand mal seizure, something I had witnessed many times with pregnant women who developed eclampsia, a pregnancy complication that can be fatal to both mother and baby.

I panicked. *What was happening? What was I doing? Should I abort my plan? Should I call 911?*

A voice in my head said, "Don't move. She's fine. This has to happen. All you have to do is love her and ground yourself."

I felt myself engulfed in something I can only describe as pure, unconditional love for April, but not just for April, for the crystal in her hand and the plant in the corner and the coyotes that started howling outside during our session. My friend Elisabeth had taught me what she called a "grounding meditation," so I practiced doing that, closing my eyes and visualizing a golden cord of light, like an electrical cord, coming from my heart and going down through my bottom, through the water table, through the rock and the magma, down into the core of Mother Earth, where it plugged into a big socket. I tried to steady my breathing and let myself be nourished by the earth as I allowed whatever was coming through me to flow right into the ground.

April convulsed for about 20 minutes until her shaking slowed. And then finally, blessedly, she was still. Her cheeks were flushed, and her arms and brow were laden with beads of sweat. I could feel her heartbeat racing under my hand, which was resting on her chest. April and I stayed like that for a while, until finally I asked, "What happened?"

April barely whispered, "My mother came out of my belly."

It was official. I had finally crossed over to woo-woo land.

When I tried to help April up off the floor, she was too exhausted to move. She crawled into the bed in my guest room, where we had done the session, and slept for almost a full day. I checked on her every few hours. When she finally awoke, she was so sore she could barely move. It took her several more days before she fully recovered from whatever had just happened.

Right after our session ended, after I had tucked April into bed, I realized I had a splitting headache, something that never happened to me. An instinct led me to call Jon Rasmussen, the shaman I had first met on my wedding day, then again in Big Sur. Jon and I had become friends, and I had a feeling he might have a better understanding of the mysterious event that had just transpired between April and me. I wondered whether he might have some explanation for her seizures and my headache.

Jon joked, "Lissa, you just practiced shamanism without a license!"

He said I had just perfectly executed a classic shamanic ritual, all the way down to the sage, the flame of the candle, the grounding of the crystal, and the healing touch. He explained that what April had experienced was a sort of exorcism and soul retrieval, where she released the possession by her abusive mother and brought back into her body, through Divine love, the piece of her soul that had been robbed from her as a child. He said that the convulsions were common and harmless, just a part of the release, that her physical exhaustion was to be expected but could be tempered if practiced by someone with more experience, and that the splitting headache was also common among inexperienced shamans who didn't know how to protect their own energetic fields and wound up "taking on" the pain that was being released. He promised to come to my house to teach me some tips, both to protect myself and to reduce the level of fatigue and discomfort April experienced afterward.

Three days later, April and I repeated the ritual with Jon's advice, only this time, she didn't seize, and instead of sitting in silence, I led her through a guided imagery session to help her visualize a fully healed version of herself at a point in the near future. She had the chance to see where she lived, meet her future self, ask her fully healed self any questions, and receive a gift from her healed self. Then her healed self hopped on a beam of light with her and entered her body in the present moment. I pronounced her whole, healed, and perfect, and then the session was over.

A week after she left California and returned to her home in New York, April wrote me this letter.

> Dear Lissa,
>
> I have come back with a clarity about exactly what I do and don't want in my life. It's almost frightening how clear it is. I do feel changed. I do feel free in a way that I never have. And I'm reaching for what I want without being timid.
>
> I am doing wonderfully—free and light as a bird—and I don't at all mind saying so. If I get anymore wide open than I am right now, I'll be inside out, and that's just fine, too. I spent the day with my friend yesterday and told her about what happened, how the weight of everything I carried is gone and the only person that dwells in me now is me. My mother's threatening and crushing presence is gone. The looming shadows of unknown men are gone. It's just me! And I love that I have myself back, or possibly even that I have myself for the first time at all, ever. My friend said the difference since she saw me last was more than remarkable. Life is so good.

As it turns out, the sessions April and I did together changed us both. Those sessions happened years ago, and April has not needed an infusion ever since. April wound up moving from New York to California to be the nanny for my daughter. She now lives in that same guesthouse where her healing was sparked. April's doctors never could explain what happened. Neither could Victoria, and Victoria did not like to participate in things she didn't understand. Victoria craved certainty. She was very uncomfortable with the idea of a spontaneous healing that arose out of a shamanic ritual that was downloaded to me in a vision. She wanted a scientific explanation of what happened, stat! For Victoria to accept that a shamanic ritual led to April's spontaneous remission, she'd have to question everything she believed as a doctor, and that was too uncomfortable for her to accept. If love and ritual really could heal, then what they taught me in medicine hadn't been the whole story, and that left Victoria feeling very unsettled.

While Victoria defended medical dogma, my Inner Pilot Light spoke something that felt more true. "Be open to the mystery, my dear. Just strap on your seat belt and let go of your need to explain and control. The Universe is capable of things science has yet to explain, and when it's in the highest good of all beings, scientifically inexplicable things, things you might call miracles, may happen."

As more strange, mystical, inexplicable things like this started occurring with increasing frequency—spontaneous remissions, clairvoyant visions, hearing inner voices—I started experiencing some glitches in my ability to effortlessly navigate the world. It started with these weird somatic freak-outs. I'd feel like my skin couldn't contain me, like it was literally crawling, like something inside of me was pushing on my skin from the inside. It was a physically uncomfortable feeling that was only soothed if I sat on the floor in front of my altar and rocked myself.

I sought out the help of my spiritual counselors because I suspected this physical freak-out was related to resistance from Victoria. I sensed that Victoria did not like the direction I was going on my hero's journey, because she had a sneaking suspicion that she was losing control of me, and she was not okay with that. My therapist and friend, one of my mentors, explained that my physical body was struggling to contain the higher vibration that was flowing through me in times of deep spiritual service. All I needed was to reprogram my beliefs and my body in order to hold higher vibrations of energy without discomfort.

So I contacted my friend Steve Sisgold. Steve is my go-to guy when I realize that a thought or belief is creating unwelcome patterns in my life and I'm ready to release it not only from my conscious mind but also from my body, where he says such beliefs are often held unconsciously. I suspected that by applying Steve's Whole Body Intelligence process to my resistance around spiritual growth, I might be able to identify what those limiting beliefs were and free up anything that was holding me back from my spiritual path. I suspected I had some limiting beliefs about bad things that would happen if I grew spiritually, things like "My life will be boring and I won't get to do anything fun," "I'll outgrow my loved ones and lose all the people I love," and "Letting my soul take the wheel instead of my ego will get me in trouble." Part of me yearned to stay committed to the spiritual path, but another part was very resistant. I sensed that Steve could help me.

Steve led me through some breath work and had me repeat the affirmation "I am an expansive spark of divinity" while addressing the physical symptoms that arose as I tried to embody this uncomfortable truth. For example, when I said "I am an expansive spark of divinity" and breathed with the words, I felt a gripping in my solar plexus, so Steve focused our attention on what this part of my body was telling me, and we gleaned it for its wisdom.

After just one session with Steve, I never again experienced the physical shaking that accompanied these high-vibration states. I still have a hard time integrating what comes through me sometimes. I still have a tendency to feel a little ungrounded during times of spiritual intensity. I sometimes need to take my shoes off and walk in the earth. But my body no longer resists the vibration that comes through me in such a physical way. For more information about Whole Body Intelligence, read Steve Sisgold's book *Whole Body Intelligence* or visit WholeBodyIntelligence.com.

It wasn't just my body that was rebelling against what was happening in my spiritual life. My mind was acting up, too. There was a war going on between Victoria and my Inner Pilot Light. Victoria wanted to claim credit for every magical, mystical thing that happened. She wanted to boost herself up, to use these miraculous experiences as evidence for her "I'm special" story. My Inner Pilot Light was always gently but firmly reminding Victoria that she couldn't claim credit for any of these miracles. Every intuitive gift, every spontaneous remission, every mystical experience belonged to Something Larger, and the human being of Lissa was only the vessel for what was coming through as I started doing the inner work to clean the channels, to let my Inner Pilot Light gently take the wheel of Lissa away from Victoria so

Something Larger could use me as an instrument of pure service, free of ego or agenda or attachment.

What Victoria didn't realize is that the gifts and miracles might very well stop if she didn't learn to not take credit for them. One of my mentors told me a story about a gifted spiritual teacher who channeled brilliant epiphanies in front of throngs of adoring fans. For years, the gifts flowed through her, unimpeded. Audiences got bigger and bigger, and the teacher was getting booked to speak all over the world. As the attention grew, so did her ego. She thought she was all that, and so did all of her fans.

Then one day, she stood up in front of thousands of people in a stadium, and when she went to open her mouth, nothing came out. She was mute. Doctors couldn't figure out what was wrong. There was no apparent physical abnormality. But for months, she couldn't utter a word. That's when she sought out help from another spiritual teacher, and she was told that she needed to remember that none of the gifts belonged to her—not the speeches, the messages, the brilliant words she wrote, the fans. They were God's speeches. God's messages. God's books. God's fans. When she humbly recognized the truth of this, her voice came back.

It's tricky to learn how to inhabit our brilliance—to let our lights shine unimpeded—without mistakenly letting it fuel the ego. On the one hand, what spiritual teacher and author Marianne Williamson writes in her book *A Return to Love* is true.

"Our deepest fear is not that we are inadequate. Our deepest fear is that we are powerful beyond measure. It is our light, not our darkness that most frightens us. We ask ourselves, 'Who am I to be brilliant, gorgeous, talented, fabulous?' Actually, who are you not to be? You are a child of God. Your playing small does not serve the world. There is nothing enlightened about shrinking so that other people won't feel insecure around you. We are all meant to shine, as children do. We were born to make manifest the glory of God that is within us. It's not just in some of us; it's in everyone. And as we let our own light shine, we unconsciously give other people permission to do the same. As we are liberated from our own fear, our presence automatically liberates others."

Every word of this rings so true, and yet, if misinterpreted, the ego can use this message as permission to run amuck. Owning your magnificence is essential to any hero's journey, because playing small is just one of the ways the ego can sabotage the journey. But the spiritualized ego can also block you from your mission. The key is to recognize that spiritual gifts, Divine downloads, miracles, and magic are all the result of Consciousness streaming through us. Our egos don't get to claim credit for any of it. But it is our responsibility to avoid blocking its expression through us.

As Joyce Carol Oates said, "I never understand when people make a fuss over me as a writer. I'm just the garden hose that the water sprays through." If there's anything we can pat ourselves on the backs about, perhaps it's the commitment to being who we must and doing what we're called to do in order to keep the sacred garden hose clean, which is no small task for most of us. When you live in a culture that revolves around feeding the ego and clogging up the garden hose, it takes mindfulness—and support—to stay in impeccable alignment with your intention to live with a clean garden hose.

I certainly needed Herculean levels of support from my magic mentors, because my garden hose was a clogged-up mess! But as my garden hose got clearer and clearer, the change within me began to disrupt many of my close relationships. My marriage was rocky, and many of my other close relationships began to fall apart. I started withdrawing from some of the people I had known for much of my life. It wasn't because I didn't still love them; it was because I was trying to break some of the patterns Victoria tended to slide into, and when I did, some of the people I cared about resisted the changes I was making in my life. It's like we had agreed to hook into certain patterns that supported our ideas about who we were, as if we were a lock and a key, matching up. When I stopped being the lock or the key, it was like these relationships didn't quite work anymore. Something had to change in order for these relationships to continue, as if there was a call to growth or a call to closure. The shifts in these relationships frightened me. I worried that I would wind up all alone, with nobody in my life who really loved me.

I didn't know that I was experiencing what Martha Beck calls the "empty elevator syndrome." When you embark upon your hero's journey and start doing the work required to unhook from your childhood patterns and ego programs, you raise your vibration. It's like leaving a party full of people to step into an elevator, and as you journey up a few floors, you may feel all alone, as if nobody understands the person you are becoming. You may be all alone in that rising elevator, but when that elevator door opens, you suddenly find a whole new tribe of people who resonate with your new vibration. When my own elevator door opened, I found myself surrounded by some strange but wonderful new people, people who talked to spirit guides, got psychic visions, studied with shamans, dreamed about the future, channeled spirits and angels, and trusted their intuition. It was a wild new world I had stepped into. I felt like Neo in the movie *The Matrix* when Morpheus says, "You take the blue pill, the story ends. You wake up in your bed and believe whatever you want to believe. You take the red pill, you stay in wonderland, and I show you how deep the rabbit hole goes." There were times I wished I had taken the blue pill instead of the red pill. But if I was honest with myself, when I let go of the fear that I might be going crazy, I was loving this magical new world I had entered when I left the Ordinary World behind.

I was fortunate to navigate this phase of my hero's journey in good company with others who had taken the red pill. I needed these people, not only to comfort me and reassure me that I wasn't crazy but also to hold me accountable to my commitment to keeping my garden hose clean. I counted on other heroes who were brave enough to push the edges of my growth, even when it was uncomfortable, people who valued truth more than coddling my old wounds, even if doing so risked the peace of the relationship. This process challenged me. It was a time of truth medicine, meltdowns, self-judgment, and tears.

When I think back on that time, I am so grateful for those who were willing to hold up a mirror so I could see how Victoria was responsible for a lot of my suffering. It was with such love that these people were offering me a chance to let Something Larger operate me so that I could finally fulfill my purpose and be free. But it was painful to examine my blind spots and stare, in the stark light of illuminations, into the truth of how I had hurt others—and myself—as a result of my own unconscious actions and choices. It's so much easier to blame others when things don't go your way, to feel like a victim of bad luck, bad circumstances, bad people, or bad genes.

But as these new mentors and friends helped me see my life through a different lens, I could see how I was creating and recreating painful patterns in my life, not because I was unlucky but because I was letting unconscious beliefs operate my life—via Victoria. While I was grateful for the insights and committed to breaking these self-sabotaging patterns, these epiphanies disrupted my stories of what kind of person I was, and these realizations were hard to face without beating myself up. I had to be very gentle with myself, and I had to be very discerning about those I let close. Some people use spiritual growth as an excuse to bully each other, and I found out quickly that this didn't work for me. There's a way to be incredibly kind and gentle while also illuminating, healing and transforming blind spots of the ego.

My whole idea of what love is changed at this point. I realized I really didn't know what love was until this point in my life. I wound up redefining love in this way.

Love is being brave enough to push the leading edge of soul growth—in oneself and another—while being kind enough to compassionately comfort the lagging edge of the ego.

In other words, we need both. Sure, it feels easy and peaceful to surround ourselves with those who affirm our self-image, who fluff up our egos and feed our ideas about who we are and how we fit into the world. And, yes, it feels comfortable to others if we buoy their egos and avoid calling them on their shadows. But we stunt our growth and the growth of those we love if we limit ourselves to those who feed our Small Selves and expect us to feed theirs. Such relationships tend to get us hooked into old patterns that usually stem from our childhoods and cause us to create and recreate unnecessary suffering in our lives. If we're willing to let relationships become part of the spiritual path, we accelerate our growth and quicken our readiness to fulfill our callings. Relationships can be the fast track on the hero's journey, if only we're courageous enough to take the medicine we are offered by those who challenge us—with love, kindness, and an open heart.

HERO'S GUIDEPOST:

Say Yes to Relationships That Grow You, But Be Sure to Nurture Yourself

Relationships can serve as a vehicle for thrusting you forward on your hero's journey. If you're interested in fast-tracking your hero's journey, say yes to those who are willing to illuminate your shadow and help you accelerate your growth. But take extra care to be kind and compassionate with yourself. Avoid the tendency to beat yourself up when you suddenly see how your ego has been running the show. Treat your Small Self like the little child that it is. Hug this part of yourself. Be gentle and loving. Promise that the larger part of you will take good care of this Small Self. Don't abuse yourself in the name of your spiritual development.

Don't let anyone else abuse you either. Spiritual bullying is not kind or effective. You can't traumatize yourself into enlightenment. Give yourself permission to request kindness, gentleness, and compassion from those who show up to serve your growth. Sure, sometimes you need a scalpel to cut yourself out of your victim story so you can align with your purpose in a pure way. But other times, we need to be tenderly met where we are in our pain. Human life is hard and sometimes life hurts, and compassion is strong medicine. So, yes, muster up the courage to attract relationships that grow you. But give yourself permission to be comforted, too. We need mentors who push us, but we also need those who hold us close and comfort us when things are moving too fast. Both are necessary to navigate the journey.

HERO'S PRACTICE:
Friends of Your Inner Pilot Light

This practice is not meant to be an exercise in judgment or spiritual self-righteousness. It's also not meant to label people in an all-or-nothing, black-and-white way. At times, people can be both a friend of your Small Self and a friend of your Inner Pilot Light. This exercise is meant to be a practice of discernment that can help you understand how to surround yourself with those who can facilitate your hero's journey. Relationships can be tricky on your hero's journey, and some people will slow your progress on the path, while others will expedite your journey. This exercise is intended to help you uncover those who will help grow and uplift you rather than feed your Small Self and weigh you down.

This practice has been modified from the Medicine for the Soul teleclass series that I teach with Rachel Naomi Remen. Find out more about this teleclass series at MedicinefortheSoulRx.com.

1. Ask yourself, "Who are the friends of my Small Self?" Who feeds your ego but doesn't help you grow your soul? Who always seems to be judging you? Who are the people who tempt you to complain or gossip? Who feeds your victim story without helping you see another possible perspective? Who criticizes you instead of being gentle and compassionate with you when you vulnerably reveal your growth edges? Who are the narcissists who make it all about them? Who blindly supports you rather than challenging your beliefs? Whose approval are you always seeking? Who makes you feel like you're not good enough or don't fit in? Who is jealous of you when good things

happen or finds glee in your failures? Who leaves you feeling depleted rather than expanded? Who is always competing with you? Who are the people who always tell you what to do and get mad at you if you don't follow their advice? Don't judge these people. Just exercise your discernment muscles and notice.

2. Ask yourself, "Who are the friends of my Inner Pilot Light?" Consider who cultivates the stillness in you and helps you feel more brave. Who helps you grow? Who challenges your victim stories? Who helps you gently illuminate your blind spots? Who is willing to examine those shadow parts of you without judgment or criticism? Who invites you to be vulnerable without shaming you? Who avoids gossip or unkindness toward others? Who loves you unconditionally while modeling unconditional love of others? Who trusts their own intuition and yours? Who cheers you on when you make brave choices based on following intuition or spiritual guidance? Who lets their own Inner Pilot Light make choices in their lives? Who offers you compassion and gentleness without coddling your Small Self? Who earns your trust and makes you feel safe enough to explore the scary, vulnerable, shadowy parts of yourself? Who lightens your mood and opens your heart? Who celebrates your triumphs without making you feel like their love depends on your triumphs? Who helps you expand your perception of what's possible and helps you believe in miracles? These are the friends of your Inner Pilot Light.

3. At certain parts of the hero's journey, you may need to cocoon yourself with friends of your Inner Pilot Light. This doesn't mean you end relationships with those who are friends of your Small Self. But it can be helpful to give yourself permission to prioritize time with those who are friends of your Inner Pilot Light. Practice discernment without judgment. When you surround yourself with friends of your Inner Pilot Light, it is easier to let this part of you take the lead in your life. As you progress on your journey, you will find it easier to be with those who are friends of your Small Self. You can hold them with deep compassion, knowing that they are entitled to their own journeys, without letting them influence your individual journey. But until you get to that point, it's okay to practice discernment and surround yourself with a bubble of true support.

CHAPTER 12

Fill Yourself First

Sometimes, when you're supposed to be on your hero's journey, fulfilling your Divine assignment, you get seduced away from your purpose and lose your way, which is what I experienced in the winter of 2011. However, when the Universe has a Divine agenda for you, you're likely to get sucked back into your hero's journey, even if you come back kicking and screaming. Your calling is always seeking you, like a soul mate, and if you stray off course and you're willing to pay attention to the signs, you'll get guided back on track.

That's what happened while I was trying to assert my new identity as a life coach. Much to my frustration, the Universe began showering me with attention, not because I was such a phenomenal life coach but because I was a *doctor*. *The Huffington Post* listed me among its "16 Health Experts to Check Out on Twitter," along with physicians like Dr. Oz. *Good Morning America* wanted me to appear on the show, not to talk about how to live an authentic life and get your mojo back but to discuss how mothers should talk to their daughters at a young age about menstruation. *Cosmopolitan* wanted to interview me about an article on PMS.

I didn't feel the least bit flattered by this. I felt pissed. I started ranting to Matt about how the world wanted to stuff me back into the white coat straitjacket. I huffed around, throwing Siena's plastic sippy cup at the wall, griping about how I wished I had never gone to medical school, how I wanted to strip myself of my MD title forever. The media was trying to position me as the next Doctor So-and-So, and I just wanted to be the first Lissa Rankin.

I was done. I mean *DONE* with medicine. Callings be damned.

I did not keep this feeling to myself. I posted it all over Facebook, Twitter, and my blog. Luckily, more magical mentors showed up just in the nick of time. Astrologer Ophira Edut of the AstroTwins reached out to me in response to what I was posting on Facebook to ask if she could do an astrological reading on me. I'd never had an astrological reading before, and Victoria thought astrology was baloney. But I had learned to ignore Victoria when the Universe sent magical mentors my way.

In order to take Ophi up on her offer, I had to track down my birth certificate to try to find my birth time, but this turned out to be no easy feat. My parents didn't own a copy of my birth certificate, so I had to special-order a copy from the state of my birth. When I finally got it, my birth certificate still didn't include the time of my birth, so I had to get my hospital records. Finally, I uncovered exactly when I was born.

I met Ophi in February to do my reading. According to the stars, I was in the midst of a potent transition time: a gestation for a new 12-year cycle when Jupiter moved into Taurus on June 4, 2011. According to Ophi, January had been a "lost at sea" time for a Taurus with a Leo moon and Leo rising. Ophi suggested that I focus my attention on "finding the baby so you don't throw it out with the bathwater."

She said that if I took a job, it would be the foundation for the next 12 years of my life and that what I needed to focus on was building the foundation for what I wanted to create come June 4. She told me Uranus was in return for me and that this only happens once in people's lives, when everything is shaken up and everything is up for questioning, especially as it relates to work and money. She cautioned me to let go of old beliefs about money, about community, about what it means to be free in the world. She told me it was a time of the counterculture; an antiestablishment, destabilizing phase; a metaphorical earthquake; a very important time not to be taken lightly or reduced to a sound bite because it would set the tone for the next phase of my life. What legacy did I want to leave?

She also suggested I take time off for a personal retreat on April 3, during which she recommended I perform a ritual in order to grieve how medicine had let me down. How had medicine broken my heart? What did I regret about it? What did I need to release in order to let go of my anger at medicine? She wanted me to create closure around the parts of medicine I would not be taking with me into the next 12 years after June 4. She told me I was destined to be a force for healing medicine. Then she said something I never forgot. "You can't make something wrong and make a difference at the same time." Where was I still making medicine wrong? What was I so righteously angry about? She recommended I use my retreat to have the best cry of my life, to steep myself in woo-woo-ville, to dance, and to, first and foremost, focus on that baby in the bathwater.

I got the message, loud and clear. But what was the baby? I decided to schedule a personal retreat at Harbin Hot Springs on April 3, as Ophi had suggested. Perhaps I would find it there.

During this time, it wasn't just Ophi who whipped me into shape. There were other magical mentors lovingly kicking my ass all at the same time. I wound up having breakfast with Regena Thomashauer, who had rallied on my behalf during the doomed New York leg of my book tour, when she relayed the news about how I needed to be "less sperm, more egg." As I told my financial sob story to Regena, explaining that I wasn't getting enough life coaching clients, she asked me to set an intention. What did I need in order to pay the bills? I told her I needed 10 regular coaching clients in order to start making a dent in my $200,000 debt. When she asked what kind of coaching I planned to offer, I ran down my list of those I could help: people in transition, those who were getting divorced, those who had lost a loved one, those on the fence about a career change, those facing an empty nest, those who were considering a major life overhaul. You know, life coaching stuff.

That's when Regena, a savvy woman with a thriving entrepreneurial business, stood up and put her hands on her hips. "Lissa, I'm going to say this because nobody else is saying it and somebody has to. We don't need you to be a life coach." She swung her purse right and left like a pendulum. "I can swing my Fendi bag and hit a life coach. What I need—what *we* need—is for you to be an effin' doctor."

I wanted to scream.

Wasn't it okay that I used to be a doctor but I didn't want to be one anymore? Can't a girl be free to switch careers without being forever burdened by her previous job? Was I going to be saddled with the straitjacket of that white coat for the rest of my life? Would my tombstone read, "Born a girl, died a physician"?

Enough already!

Soon afterward, I met Danielle LaPorte at a Ladies Who Launch conference, where we were both speaking. Over dinner, she gave me my own personal Fire Starter Session, igniting some kindling under me and encouraging me to "stop sitting on a gold mine" with my online community and start actually selling something people could buy. According to my friend Chris Guillebeau, whom I met back on my *What's Up Down There?* book tour, all I needed to do was begin with selling something small—*anything.* He thought a one-on-one coaching session with a high price tag might not be the best place to start. Instead, he suggested I start examining the e-mails my readers sent me to get a feel for what they were asking me about. According to Chris and Danielle, the easiest solution to getting out of debt was to develop an informational product I could sell online, something like an e-book or a teleclass series based on a topic my readers really cared about. I had never really thought about selling anything to my readers.

The whole idea of selling something to my precious blog readers gave me hives. I had been giving my readers tons of content at no charge for so long that I was afraid they'd all get pissed at me if I asked them to kindly fork over $149 for something that might help them. After all, wasn't what I gave my readers sort of a public service? Would it be fair to offer them something they really needed but couldn't afford? When you're helping people heal, shouldn't it be a right, not a luxury item?

By this point, I had spent around 2 years giving so generously to my online community that I was completely depleted, broke, and exhausted. I had been answering every e-mail request for support, giving away my time to help other people (with their own paid programs), writing blogs people could read at no charge, and even running programs, like a green juice cleanse, without asking participants to pay. I felt like it was my mission to serve, to help people heal, to mend their hearts, to tend their bodies. But I was devoting myself to strangers free of charge—without realizing the immense cost to my own life.

One of the biggest blessings of my life was the appearance of Michele Martin, a literary agent. I had been interviewing with literary agents for months after reaching out to my author friends and asking for referrals, but in spite of my impressive blog platform, my less-than-stellar first book sales gave people pause. Michele had a good instinct about me. She liked my writing style. But she said I was in "publishing jail."

Putting it bluntly with her thick New York accent, Michele admitted that I needed what she called "publishing rehab." I needed a radical change in order to land a big book deal, she explained. I could get my own TV show, and that would change everything. Sure! Or I could write about something exceptionally compelling—take a new spin on a revolutionary idea, remaking it as my own—that would appeal not only to my growing blog readers but also to a wider audience.

I sighed. Publishing rehab sounded exhausting. And spermy. If the Universe wanted me to publish another book, wouldn't a publisher just call and offer me a great deal for the memoir I had already written?

Leading with the disclaimer that she knew I wouldn't want to hear what she was about to tell me, Michele explained that it wasn't the right time for me to write a memoir. She said that I was a great writer. But—and she was kind as she uttered this big "but"—Michele said, "Lissa, you're a *doctor*. You need to write a revolutionary book about health, something no doctor has ever written before. That's the only way you have a chance at selling a book right now."

When Michele said that, I hung up the phone and screamed so loud that Matt came running down the stairs with wide, panicked green eyes. I seriously wanted someone to give me a gun. But the Universe had other plans for me.

I was raised in a family of doctors and missionaries, where the presiding family value was service and charity. Although I now know this wasn't true, I grew up believing that in order to be lovable to Mom and Dad, I'd have to give until I was depleted—like all good Rankins on the fast track to heaven. I wound up mistakenly thinking that the love of my parents was conditional, that my whole worth was tied up in how much I sacrificed of myself in order to be of service, even if I wound up depleted, resentful, and feeling like what my friend SARK called "the Cosmic Tit."

What nobody tells you is that most Cosmic Tits who are martyring themselves to help others have a dark side—the victim. I started blogging not only because it was a way to get my writing out there but also because I wanted to help people, to serve out my calling, to heal the world. Not long after launching my blog, I started to get pissed when readers e-mailed me asking for help. As I wound up overwhelmed by the immensity of the need, I started resenting the very people I was trying to help.

Combine my inherited savior complex with an inability to set boundaries and you have a recipe for disaster. I never learned how to set healthy boundaries as a child. I grew up believing that being all up in someone's business meant love, that codependence was the same as intimacy, and that boundaries that might protect me from getting depleted and resentful meant emotional distance, selfishness, and, ultimately, withdrawal of love.

Because of the way I showed up energetically on my blog, I wound up inadvertently inviting strangers to call upon me as if I were their trusted confidante. Strangers told me how their loved ones had just killed themselves. They confessed their sexual abuse stories, disclosed their health challenges, and shared the secrets of their traumas with me. Because they were so revealing and because I cared, I felt like it was my moral obligation to help them. Surely, no good person could just ignore such devastating need. People sent me suicide notes. I once stayed up until 3 a.m. calling 911, trying to rescue a stranger who hadn't even given me an address.

For a while, this felt good. Victoria liked being helpful. It strengthened her pride in being a generous, altruistic person who saved lives. But as my audience grew, I couldn't keep up. I was exhausted, broke, and failing to show up for the people who I really loved. Faced with the crisis of my inability to help everyone who needed it, I had to confront the part of me that was pathologically striving to save the world. What I was doing wasn't sustainable. I was going to have to either learn to set boundaries or quit blogging.

Because I grew up in a family with lots of intimacy but no modeling of healthy boundaries, I have a hard time with boundaries; boundaries feel like being rude or cold or distant. I can't stand the feeling of disappointing people, and I knew that if I started saying no, I'd disappoint people right and left. Yet my failure to erect healthy boundaries was creating all kinds of messes in my personal and professional life. It's a painful pattern to break, especially when you've already welcomed people into your virtual home and then, all of a sudden, you say, "Party's over!" It feels icky.

During this time, I had a potent dream that I was at a retreat center getting a loving ass-kicking from three powerhouse women—Regena Thomashauer, Danielle LaPorte, and Marie Forleo. In the dream, Regena, Danielle, and Marie were telling me that I could never heal the world until I first healed myself, that I had to fill myself up first. They said that if I filled myself first, then my generosity could spill over into genuine service and I could give from a healthy place of overflowing abundance rather than from a place of resentful depletion.

What these women said made me so uncomfortable that my heart was already racing when, in the midst of that dream, the fire alarm went off in my house and woke me up. Not the blaring "THERE'S A FIRE!" alarm, but the annoying little beep that happens when the fire alarm runs out of batteries.

I tried to sleep through the beep of the alarm, all the while pondering the wisdom of Regena, Danielle, and Marie, all strong, successful women. But I couldn't get back to sleep. The fire alarm kept up its beeping until I finally woke up Matt and begged him to go downstairs and get the 2-story ladder we would need in order to reach the fire alarm on the top of our pitched ceiling.

Matt, who could sleep through anything, woke up, heard the battery alarm beeping, and trotted off to get the ladder in the garage.

As soon as he left, the beeping stopped.

When Matt came back with the ladder and a new battery, he looked puzzled. "How did you fix it?"

I started humming *Twilight Zone* music.

We never did replace that battery. The fire alarm now has a green "battery works" light and has never beeped since.

Matt went right back to sleep, but I didn't sleep the rest of the night. I knew the fire alarm was a sign that I was supposed to wake up—WAKE UP!—and hear the message the magical mentors in my dream wanted me to hear.

The next morning, I was scheduled to do another Whole Body Intelligence session with Steve Sisgold. I had scheduled the appointment to help allay the nervousness I felt about an impending TEDx talk. But after the dream, I knew my session wasn't supposed to be about my TEDx talk. Instead, Steve was meant to help me deal with the limiting belief from my childhood that was sabotaging my business, my relationships, my health, and my quality of life.

I told Steve the story of my inherited family patterns and how I felt ready to finally end my savior complex once and for all. By this point, I was aware of Dr. Stephen Karpman's Rescuer/Victim/Persecutor triad, so I was aware that if I was in my savior complex, I was also at risk of becoming the victim and the persecutor. To demonstrate how this triad tends to play out, let me tell you the story of a woman I'll call Jill.

Jill had a rough childhood and grew up feeling unworthy. Her core wound was the limiting belief "I'm not good enough." So to slap a Band-Aid on her core wound and prove to herself and the world that she's valuable and worthy, she becomes the world's most helpful person. When she was young, she helped other kids with their homework, gave money to people she barely knew, volunteered at the nursing home, and doted on her best friend like she was royalty. When she got older, she started a nonprofit aimed at helping save the world.

When people wind up in trouble, they call Jill. If you've got cancer, Jill will drive you to your chemo appointment. If you're in jail, Jill will bail you out. If you need rehab, Jill will stage an intervention and help you pay for treatment. If someone broke your heart, Jill will clear her schedule so you can spend hours on the phone baring your soul while she listens. Jill brings food to those who are grieving, raises her hand at church anytime something needs to be done, and drops everything when her kids call asking for something.

Once Jill's kids left home, she took on three foster children who were crack babies, and she has started savings accounts to help pay for them to go to college. She leads a camp for kids who have cancer every summer— without getting paid for it.

Jill is a saint, right?

Well, yes. Jill is a saint. But there's a dark side to her helpfulness. Jill gives so much of herself in order to prove that she's worthy that she winds up depleted. She spends so much money helping other people that she can barely pay her own bills, much less travel the way she yearns to. She's so busy volunteering that she doesn't have time to do the things she really loves doing, like painting, skiing, and hanging out with friends who don't *need* her.

If others really appreciated all of her generosity, she would feel better. But rather than lauding her for her brilliant efforts, the people she helps tend to walk all over her. In fact, they can be downright ungrateful, and often, after Jill has given them all she's got, the needy people Jill rescues disappear, and then Jill feels used.

When she starts feeling victimized by those she tries to help, Jill can turn on you. On her good days, she can be so saintly that you feel like you're looking into the eyes of Jesus. And then, because she's pissed off that nobody appreciates her, Jill lashes out, and you're suddenly shocked because Jesus just slapped you.

It's not just that. Lying very shallowly beneath the surface of her desire to rescue you lies Jill's desire to control you. When you're in need—you've just lost a loved one, you're in the middle of a divorce, you just declared bankruptcy, you have a new baby—you may be feeling overwhelmed, and you're more than happy to let Jill come in and "fix" you. This is when Jill rises to the occasion and feels good about herself. On one level, this "fixing" Jill offers looks helpful. Jill will clean out your cupboard, throw away all of your unhealthy food, and fill your kitchen with fresh produce and unprocessed foods. She'll give you advice about your marriage and teach you everything she's learned about relationships. She'll help you breastfeed your baby, buy you baby clothes, and offer you parenting advice. She'll insist you come to her church because the people are so helpful and nice. She'll try to fix your business by offering up her creative ideas.

Before you know it, Jill is steamrolling right over your life, trying to control every aspect of it in the name of "helping." When you're not so needy and start to feel stronger and more empowered, you may resist Jill's efforts to fix your life by setting boundaries and doing things your own way. But then Jill gets pissed off. Now you're the ungrateful person who doesn't appreciate all Jill did to save you.

You just got slapped again. In these instances, Jill functions as the persecutor.

Many of us spend our whole lives cycling through this dysfunctional Rescuer/Victim/Persecutor triad. We may not even be aware of it. I've certainly been there myself.

Recognizing this dysfunctional triad was a real eye-opener for me. Sure, pure service is part of why we're here. It's tied into our life's purpose, our calling. It's how we express the divinity within, as love for others, for nature, for the planet. But there can be a dark side to service when it's driven by the ego and not the soul.

I realized before I went to see Steve that the only way out of the Rescuer/Victim/Persecutor triad was to gain insight, accept responsibility for the fact that I create my own reality, and heal the core ego wounds and beliefs that motivate me to fall into these patterns. Knowing what I did about Steve's work, I also knew that while I could heal the limiting beliefs in my mind, unless I also cleared them from my body, they were likely to keep enacting themselves.

I told Steve I was ready to be free. I also told him about the dream I'd had.

Steve invited me to state my limiting belief. I said, "I have to give until I'm depleted so I can be a good, worthy person." Then Steve led me through a whole session to cleanse my body of that limiting belief.

We started by turning the limiting belief into an affirmation. "I fill myself first so I can heal the world."

We focused on my pelvis, and Steve asked me to repeat after him, "I accept myself as I fill myself up first so I can heal the world." I repeated the mantra, and I breathed.

We focused on my throat. "I express myself as I fill myself up first so I can heal the world."

I felt all sorts of resistance. My mind was on board, but my body was struggling.

My eyes filled with tears. I felt uncomfortable sensations in my body. Memories of hurt little Lissa sacrificing her own needs in order to try to please Mommy surfaced.

Then the Gremlin appeared. "You're selfish and narcissistic if you take care of yourself first. You have no value unless you're helping others. Your blog audience won't love you anymore unless you give until you're depleted. Your mother won't love you anymore, either."

Steve asked me what my body was feeling. I said, "My body feels freezing cold." My hands and feet were icicles.

Steve said, "I'm wearing short sleeves and shorts and you're wearing sweats, but I can bring you a blanket and turn up the heat. But let's investigate that feeling."

I said, "Only cold people fill themselves first. Warm people give until they're depleted."

Steve said, "Bingo."

We breathed and worked through some more emotions, and I moved my body in strange ways that it wanted to move. When it was over, my body felt at peace, and I was able to stand out on Steve's balcony and stare at the bay while repeating, "I love, accept, and express that I fill myself first so I can heal the world."

My body was done fighting me, and my nervous system felt relaxed.

Steve said, "You know you can help more people if you fill yourself up instead of letting people deplete you. You can help a lot of people leading by example. Fill yourself first and give other people permission to do the same."

I knew Steve was right. I knew *in my body* he was right, that I could no longer deplete myself, that I had to protect my own hard-earned life force, and I couldn't keep selling myself out because of my childhood patterns.

Steve pointed out what I was doing with my hands. My arms were outstretched, palms out. I was setting a boundary, making a declaration.

I fill myself first so I can heal the world.

I was claiming my life force as my own. I worked hard to earn it—with meditation, personal and spiritual growth work, green juice, daily hikes in nature, prayer, connecting with people who lifted me up, regular orgasms, engaging in work I love, healing old traumas, and making a commitment to living as fully and vitally as I could. If I was overflowing with abundant life force, instead of giving until I was depleted, surely I'd have plenty left over to give to others. I was done sacrificing my own energy in order to save someone else.

The Gremlin started prattling, "If you fill yourself first, nobody will love you. They'll all stop reading your blog. They only read what you write because you're willing to help anyone who reaches out. You'll wind up all alone. The only reason anyone loves you is because you're a sucker who will help anyone. If you fill yourself first, everyone will think you're selfish. You'll lose everything. Don't do it."

My Inner Pilot Light knew better. She said, "Go ahead, darling. You can set a boundary with your readers and still be loving."

So I did. And it felt like a deep exhale.

This session with Steve was a critical turning point for me. Prior to 2011, much of my service in the world was what you might call "Small Self service." This doesn't mean we shouldn't help others. In fact, that's what those of us on a hero's journey are here to do. But there's another way to serve, which I'll call "pure service." Pure service can be differentiated from Small Self service because pure service leaves you with a feeling of gratitude. You're grateful to have your gifts fully expressed in service to a Divine mission, and you use resentment as your cue that you're giving too much and need to pull back and practice self-care. When you're in a place of pure spiritual service, it's not about self-sacrifice—though the more you walk the spiritual path, the less and less "self" there is to sacrifice as you begin to really inhabit the interconnectedness of all things. Over time, you become less self-focused, so there is a way to serve that is incredibly generous but always leaves you with a grateful, rather than a begrudging or resentful, heart. In this way, perhaps even Jesus offered his service with gratitude. Even as his body was suffering, he was grateful for the opportunity to serve in the way that he did.

When I think of my own service, I know ease and joy can be my metrics. I shouldn't have to sacrifice being with my daughter too much, because being with her brings me such bliss. I shouldn't have to sacrifice sleep or eating well, because self-care supplies the vessel of service that allows Something Larger to come through and serve. I shouldn't have to sacrifice happiness and fulfillment in the name of service, because we are here on this earth, living in these bodies, to experience vital aliveness. That doesn't mean we won't sometimes be physically uncomfortable or emotionally heartbroken when we offer our service. Sometimes we are asked to do hard things in the name of service, but as long as we are offering ourselves with a grateful heart, we can avoid the pitfalls of Small Self service and the resentment and burnout that accompany it.

How do you tell the difference? Small Self service stems from Small Self agendas—fear of disappointing someone, feelings of unworthiness if you're not overly giving, being motivated by feelings of pity rather than empathy, or the desire to impress someone. Pure service arises from love itself. It's the natural impulse to cultivate and nurture life—which propels you out of your chair with gratitude and joy and a burst-open heart—and to help another by allowing yourself to be a vessel for that which wants to be born through you. It feels magnificent to serve in this way. There isn't an ounce of feeling like you're giving until you're depleted. Even if you're exhausted, you're energized by the service. A certain grace accompanies you when you're serving in this way, and you may even find that you are superhuman in ways you never imagined.

So, yes, your service may sometimes look like self-sacrifice to others. You may be shivering in the trenches or putting yourself at risk to save another. You may have hunger in your belly at times. But you will do so with gratitude, feeling deeply fulfilled and smack-dab in the center of your purpose, even if, like Martin Luther King Jr., you die in the process of fulfilling your purpose.

I asked Rachel Naomi Remen what she thought about all of these musings on service. She said, "It is such a deep, spiritually central, and confusing issue. Maybe we are just meant to rassle with it for our whole lives."

I felt so expansive by the time I returned from my session with Steve, like everything was about to turn around, like anything was possible. But then I came home and bumped right into Matt's fear. While I was struggling to manage my own anxiety around the financial uncertainty of our life, Matt had hit the wall of his tolerance. I was in love with where we lived, where the redwoods and mountains meet the ocean in Marin County. But this part of the country was expensive, and I had put Matt in the difficult position of expecting him to manage our finances without involving me in the details. I was trying so hard to stay safe within my "fearless" bubble that I forgot how anxiety-provoking my perpetual risk-taking was for Matt.

Because we were flat broke and maxed out on our credit cards, Matt wanted us to move to a 700-square-foot cabin in Julian, California, the little gold mine vacation town in the mountains of Southern California where he had cut his fingers with the table saw several years earlier. Since Siena was about to finish her school year, Matt wanted to move immediately to staunch the hemorrhage of our financial life.

But I was dead set on staying put. Not only did I love Marin County more than any place I'd ever lived, but in my astrology session with Ophi, she had insisted I not make any big decisions until after June 4. She said everything would change on June 4, and I should simply wait to make any big decisions, if at all possible. Matt said he was absolutely not making decisions about whether or not to move based on an astrologer's prediction. I pushed back, knowing full well that my argument sounded crazy and his plan made much more sense than mine.

Matt was adamant. We simply couldn't afford to stay. Either I needed to go back to a stable hospital job or we needed to move someplace *way* cheaper than where we were living. So we compromised. I told him he could move forward with plans to move, but I wasn't willing to actually pack the moving truck until after June 4.

We had a big storage unit filled with old art of mine that hadn't sold in galleries and had been shipped back to us. Because I was so prolific back in my San Diego days, hundreds of unsold paintings were stacked to the ceiling in this storage unit. Not wanting to move all of those paintings to a tiny house in Southern California, we decided to have a moving sale at Siena's school and sell all the art at rock-bottom prices. I was really scared this whole time, but I was calmed by a growing sense of irrational faith that I was being nurtured and, in spite of all evidence to the contrary, everything would turn out okay. Maybe I was a reckless optimist, lacking good judgment. Maybe I was confident when I should have been more humble. Maybe I was secretly psychic, somehow intuiting that everything was going to be okay. Or maybe I had just lost my mind. It was really hard to tell in those days. I couldn't muster up much of a cohesive argument when Matt told me it was time to get realistic and just cut my losses. But somewhere, underneath the doubts, blind faith was sprouting. I still believed I would one day land butter-side up, though the likelihood that this would happen was looking undeniably grim.

If you're in this phase of your Road of Trials, you may find yourself with competing doubts and reckless optimism, too. You may question your sanity, and others might, too. You may need to reach out to magical mentors who can help you. But most importantly, you'll need to learn to discern the wisdom of your Inner Pilot Light and trust its voice, even when there's no evidence that this part of you is trustworthy. This is a time for confidence, but it's also a time for humility. Be willing to be wrong. Be open to guidance from those who are there to support you, even if their support sounds like criticism. Challenge everything you think you know. And trust that you will be guided to whatever is most right, even if it's not what you think you want.

HERO'S GUIDEPOST:
Heal the World from a Place of Overflowing Abundance

When you're motivated by the soul's yearnings rather than the ego's "not enoughness," giving to others feeds you. Service can be like breathing. You give on the exhale, but the giving itself breathes life into you and you are nourished by the giving. But if you're giving until you're depleted, you're probably motivated by outdated childhood patterns that no longer serve you. How can you tell the difference between a noble motivation to serve (pure service) and an ego-driven motivation to please (Small Self service)? Take a tip from equine therapy. When you enter a ring with a horse, the horse will only "join up" with you if the horse wants to. Horses don't do favors. They only join up if they want to bump their life force up against yours. If they're not in the mood to join up, they simply won't, no matter how much you wish they would.

Does your ego drive you to seek approval or avoid disappointing people through the vehicle of service? Or is your motivation to join up with those you might serve clean, like a horse? Go ahead and help someone if you genuinely feel called to serve and are motivated by the impulse of love. If you feel grateful for the opportunity to serve, let this be your compass. But give yourself permission to say no if it will deplete you and leave you feeling resentful. You'll need all the energy you've got to make it through what comes next.

HERO'S PRACTICE:

Check Your Motives

The next time you consider being helpful or saying yes to service, pause. Get quiet and ask yourself, "Why am I doing this?" Are you afraid of disappointing someone if you say no? Are you motivated by pity or fear? Will you feel like "not enough" if you don't do it? Are you trying to impress someone? Does it exhaust you to even think about saying yes? If any of these feel true, graciously say no to the opportunity to serve, knowing that you are not just filling yourself first but also protecting yourself from getting caught in a Rescuer/Victim/Persecutor triad, which will lead you to inadvertently hurt yourself and others.

If, however, you are motivated by surges of love—which generate the impulse to leap out of your chair and say yes, free of any hidden baggage—go for it! If you're so far down the spiritual path that there is little "self" to self-sacrifice and you are full to the brim with the desire for pure service, knowing how fulfilling it is to serve in a clean way, say yes.

Practice this exercise every time you are inclined to serve. This will help you learn to be very discerning about your relationship to service and those you serve, and as a result, you will not only avoid depleting yourself but also expand in your capacity for fulfillment and joy.

CHAPTER 13

The Only Way Out Is Through

As astrologer Ophi had instructed, I scheduled my personal retreat at Harbin Hot Springs for April 3. I packed my bags and said good-bye to Matt, and he wished me luck. He knew I was nervous about what I had been assigned to accomplish during this retreat. I was supposed to release the traumas of my relationship with medicine and distill down my next steps—to find the baby in the bathwater. As I drove north, I was burdened with a strong intuition that this wasn't going to be a holiday.

What I didn't quite realize at the time was that I was approaching the Innermost Cave on my hero's journey. Once the hero approaches the Innermost Cave, things start to get really scary. If the hero is the star of a movie, this is when the audience sits in suspense, holding their breath, uncertain whether the hero will survive. Because I was living my life on such a public stage at this point, my blog audience was holding their breath, too. Things were not looking good.

The Innermost Cave is that place the hero can only go alone, where the forces of darkness face off against the light within every hero. Magical mentors can give you tools to assist you on your Road of Trials, and you may be escorted right up to the mouth of the Innermost Cave. But once you step inside, you are on your own; you don't really know what lies ahead, and nobody can prepare you.

You wind up in what Rachel Naomi Remen calls "the narrow place," where you feel like you're getting squished from all sides, like an infant about to be born. When you're in the Ordinary World, you swim around comfortably in the fetal home of the womb until your hero's journey begins, when things start to feel tight and uncomfortable as labor ensues. You find yourself getting squished down into the birth canal. The entry into the pelvis isn't so bad. You can still move your head from side to side and kick your legs around during labor, until you reach a certain point. Then, suddenly, you find yourself in the narrowest part, the part that you must get beyond if you're going to make it to the other side and begin your new life, the part where the walls around you feel so tight you can barely move.

When you're in this narrow, squished place of the Innermost Cave, you may be tempted to retreat in the opposite direction, back into the comfort of the Ordinary World. But doing so would be counterproductive. Babies can't go back into the womb once labor has begun. Fetuses who go too far past their due date outgrow the life expectancy of the placenta, and the blood vessels that feed them shrivel up. Ultimately, if the baby isn't born, it dies. The only way out is through.

At some point, the inevitability that you are being called forward becomes obvious. You have two choices: Surrender to the narrow place and let yourself be drawn into the Innermost Cave without resistance or get forever stuck in the small part, thwarting your destiny and dying a slow soul death. Too many people get stuck in the narrow place, too afraid to let go, too resistant to surrender to what wants to be born.

Allowing yourself to do what you must to surrender to the narrow place requires serious ovaries, but it takes real balls to make it to the other side. You have to knowingly go someplace that hurts. Your cornered ego, feeling threatened like a wounded, caged animal, will thrash around, pulling out all the stops to backpedal out of the Innermost Cave. But your soul, now in charge, bravely steps into the great unknown, all alone in the human world, with only your spiritual cheerleaders egging it on. With no promises of what lies on the other side, it is a defining moment. Are you in, or are you out? This is the climax of the journey. This is where the real gold lies, if you're brave enough to mine it. The path is a courageous one. Only real heroes survive.

How do you survive the Innermost Cave? You boil things down to their purest dilution, and when you do, you find the thread that pulls you through, that essence of who you are and why you're here once you remove everything that isn't your soul. In other words, you find the baby in the bathwater.

That was my mission when I arrived at Harbin Hot Springs. On the drive up, I had been given instructions by a spirit guide I had come to call "Sebastian."

Sebastian showed up in my life in a very playful way. My assistant Joy, who I'd met during my first visit to Esalen, had been studying the law of attraction and felt that I was getting quite skilled at what she called "manifesting." She called me on the phone one day and challenged me to name something I wanted to create.

She said, "Say purple kangaroo!"

I laughed and repeated, "Purple kangaroo."

Joy said, "Did it work? Is there a purple kangaroo standing in your living room?"

Right at that moment, a deer approached my window and stared right at me with big doe eyes.

I said, "No, but there's a deer staring at me from the other side of my window."

Joy said, "But he's eating purple flowers! He's wearing a purple bow around his neck. He's got purple eyes."

I giggled.

Later that day, Joy and I shared this story with Dana, who worked with Joy and me as part of my blog team, and Dana said, "You're not going to believe what I just got as a gag gift. It's a calendar of toilets. And guess what September is?"

No kidding. September was a purple kangaroo toilet. We named him Sebastian Murphy, and he became my unlikely spirit guide.

The voice of Sebastian was similar to the voice of my Inner Pilot Light—loving and tender but more direct, more masculine, almost bossy. My Inner Pilot Light's voice was more feminine, maternal, nurturing, comforting. Sebastian's voice, while not harsh like the Gremlin's, was more of a scalpel of truth. I didn't quite know what to make of these inner voices, all vying to give me guidance. I wasn't sure which voices to trust. I wondered sometimes whether I was simply going crazy, except that when I followed the guidance of voices like my Inner Pilot Light and Sebastian, my life seemed to get better. I was collecting more and more evidence that it might be safe to trust the guidance I received.

On my drive up to Harbin, Sebastian was clear and specific. I was supposed to do a Watsu session, which is a form of shiatsu massage performed while you're floating in warm water. I balked at this suggestion. I first tried Watsu 5 years earlier, right in the midst of my Perfect Storm. I was newly postpartum with a freshly healed C-section scar. Dad had just passed away, and on a lark, without a clue what I was signing up for, I decided to go to a spa and try Watsu.

I wound up vomiting.

I have a tendency to get motion sickness, and because Watsu is a lot of swirling and twirling and spinning in warm water with your eyes closed, I got nauseated. So when Sebastian told me to do Watsu at Harbin, the birthplace of Watsu, I argued. Couldn't I just get a regular massage instead?

No. Sebastian was adamant. I was supposed to get a Watsu session with a man named Nico.

Sure enough, Nico was there when I arrived.

To say that this was *way* out of my comfort zone is an understatement. First of all, Watsu at Harbin is done in the nude. A naked stranger holds you in a way that even your lover probably doesn't hold you, cradling you like a baby while your legs stay buoyant with little floaties strapped on your ankles. The Watsu practitioner twists and turns you in the water, your bodies so close that you start breathing in synchrony. As you can imagine, emotional issues surface.

As if that wasn't uncomfortable enough, even though I grew up in Florida and California, I've always had an irrational resistance to the water. I live by the ocean, but I rarely swim in it, and when I do, I almost never go underwater. I love pools and hot springs, though, where the environment is controlled and I don't have to worry about getting swept under by a riptide.

Yet, as an option in his Watsu sessions, Nico offered Waterdance, which required going underwater and letting someone else be responsible for when you could take your next breath. I would definitely have skipped that part, except that Ophi had said I should dance while on my retreat.

I trembled as I took my clothes off and slipped into the 98-degree Watsu pool. Nico was a middle-aged man with gentle eyes. In a calming voice, he explained what he was going to do, and I admitted to being uncomfortable and afraid. Nico reassured me that everything would turn out fine. He asked if we could get started. Reluctantly, I nodded.

As Nico rocked me, I tried to breathe. His coarse chest hair prickled against my breasts. I noticed that my rising panic got better as I breathed. I tried to slow my breathing. In . . . out . . . in . . . out. Slowly, my muscles began to let go as Nico held me close. I was able to stay relatively relaxed until it was time to dance. Nico signaled to me that he was about to push me underwater, and when he did, the Gremlin took over.

What are you doing? Why are you naked with this stranger? Don't you know it's not safe to go underwater like this? Don't you know it's not safe to LIVE like you're living? You were an idiot to quit your job in San Diego. You had a great life until you went and blew it. You had to keep upping the ante so you could be a writer. Now you have no agent, no publisher, no money. Your husband would be totally justified if he bailed on you at this point, not only because you're in the arms of a naked stranger but also because you're a total failure.

I was underwater, gasping for breath and reeling from the crushing words of the Gremlin. I couldn't find the surface so I could catch my breath. Where was the surface?

Nico pulled me up just as I started to panic.

The next time I went under, Nico held me by my feet so my head swayed around underwater like the arm of an octopus. As I tried to release the resistance in my muscles, my body floated, but the Gremlin prattled on.

Everyone is going to know what a failure you are. It's going to be so lame when you crawl back to the hospital after all these years. You should have listened to me when I told you not to leave San Diego.

Nico had wrapped my body into a fetal ball, dunked me underwater, and spun me like a pair of socks in the rinse cycle. I felt disoriented, and I tried to open my eyes so I could see which way was up, but that just made me feel more lost, so I squeezed my eyes closed again as I felt my heart race. I had felt this way before, as a young child riding the waves in the ocean, when my boogie board flew out from under me. I had been bounced around by the waves and breathed in salt water through my nose until my whole face stung. When I finally washed up on shore, sputtering and gasping, my mother held me close and told me it would all be okay. But it didn't feel okay. I stayed away from the ocean for a year after that.

When he finally brought me up for air, Nico held me like my mother had.

The next time I went under, my breath ran out in the middle of the arc my body was cutting through the warm water. My lungs ached. I didn't think I had 1 second of air left. I panicked. What was happening? Where was the surface? I started to struggle, flailing around, trying to escape from Nico's arms, kicking out my arms and legs, and trying to push myself up so I could find solid ground. But Nico lifted me up before my feet hit the ground.

I gasped again, and Nico cradled me while I cried. My rapid, shallow breathing slowed back down. The Gremlin kept up its tirade.

See, you can't trust anyone. You have to take care of yourself, because if you put your trust in someone else, they'll keep you down too long. They'll drown you. Nobody is looking out for you but you, so you'd better come up with a plan to get yourself out of the mess you've made.

I was back underwater again, but this time, something deep and brave and true within me rose up and told the Gremlin to shut his piehole and leave me alone. I remembered the words of Gandhi, "I will not let anyone walk through my mind with their dirty feet." I cursed the dirty feet. For just a split second, I felt the freedom of surrender in the Waterdance as the water played me like a harp made of kelp, with the lapping waves strumming the strings of me. I closed my eyes underwater so I could feel the seeds of my faith in the maelstrom of my fear. As Nico spun me upside down, I breathed water into my lungs and then felt the sting in my nose and throat. I desperately grabbed Nico's ankle until he lifted me to the surface in both arms.

I sputtered, coughing and sneezing, and Nico held me like that until my breathing slowed down. He asked if I was up for going under one more time.

The Gremlin screamed, "Get out! It's not safe here!"

Victoria said, "You need to let me get you out of this mess. I know better than you how to protect you."

My Inner Pilot Light said, "You're safe, darling."

Sebastian said, "Honey, it's time to let go and turn it all over to God."

God said, "I've got this. You can trust me."

The poet and metaphysician Charles Upton once said, "When God has become the conscious center of one's life, then, as in a time of civil war, the various citizens of the psyche are forced to take sides."

In that moment, something miraculous happened and my faith beat the crap out of my fear. I nodded to Nico that I was ready to go under.

And that's when it happened.

I was swept underwater and my body fell limp and became a wave itself, cresting, falling, churning, as if I was dissolving, becoming water myself. My cells became porous, opening, closing, breathing with the water. I was sea-weed and Nico and the blue sky I could see from under the water, all at once. The Gremlin and Victoria were silent and my chest overflowed with butterflies, beating their wings and lifting me up to where my face surfaced and I could drink in the sweet nectar of air and honey and hope. Nico smiled at me, and then his face dissolved into the face of Jesus, and Sebastian said, "All is well."

The rest of the Waterdance was a symphony, with Nico as the conductor and me as the instrument. The melody was an underwater waltz. The harmony was the ebb and flow of back and forth, with my arms a solo violin, my fingertips a piccolo. With no resistance, my breath rose and fell in response to the taps of Nico's finger on my rib cage or my shoulder. Our wordless pas de deux was a dance and a meditation.

No longer constricted with fear, the movements liquefied and length-ened, my body sweeping the length of the warm pool from side to side, the dance at once measured and limitless. A sense of time disappeared, as did my own understanding of form or separation. I was not only water and Nico and sky but also redwoods and bees and soil. My heart—the heart of the collective Consciousness—expanded, opening, awakening, encompassing All That Is. And the fear was just gone, as if it never existed, and all that remained was love and faith.

It sounds so trite trying to explain the experience in words. How does one explain a particle of a rainbow and the entirety of the rainbow with its pot of gold in a sentence? All I can say is that I touched heaven, and it felt like bliss, and I knew in those moments, in my cells, that there was nothing to fear and that it was safe to surrender to the warm, loving embrace that holds us all.

That's what I felt when the dance was over—warm, loving arms around me, rocking me, my body wrapped in a ball like a caterpillar in the cocoon, a scratchy beard pressed against my cheek. Then one hand touched my heart and another held me from beneath until I was floating on the surface. Then, with the floaties on my ankles removed, my feet touched the floor of the pool, and my back was up against the pool wall. I rested. From behind, dark hands covered my cheeks, then my eyes, and the sunlight that had been streaming through my closed eyelids went dark. Everything was still and quiet. And then Jesus lifted His hands off my face, until only His fingertips were left.

And I was alone.

Only I wasn't. The voice of God said, "You are never alone. Abide in me."

And then the pool was still and silent, and when I finally opened my eyes, I noticed that the surface of the water was still as glass, as if nobody had ever been there at all.

A while later, as I was quietly digesting what had just happened, Nico appeared and whispered, "Do you need to talk about what just happened?"

I looked him in the eye and could tell that *he just knew.*

He said, "I know I left you under a little too long a few times there. But you know that was all part of The Plan."

His words rung in my ears long after he left. *That was all part of The Plan.*

Maybe that's what the Ordeal in the Innermost Cave of my hero's journey was all about. Maybe the Universe had intentionally left me gasping, scared, afraid I'd run out of air. Maybe the failure of my book; the loss of my agent, my publisher, and my medical practice; the financial devastation; my husband's anxiety; my crisis of faith—maybe I was being kept underwater a little too long because it was all part of The Plan. Maybe what I needed was a dose of humility, a test of the limits of my faith, a taste of death that would leave me no choice but to surrender into the narrow place and allow myself to be reborn. Maybe my faith needed to beat the crap out of my fear only to realize it's not a battle anyway, that the way to survive the Ordeal isn't to fight but to let go.

My whole body felt electric as I recovered in that warm Watsu pool, where I spent the next hour by myself with my eyes closed in silence. When I finally opened my eyes, everything appeared in Technicolor. The forest was dense green and filled with the heady scent of pine and sage, and when I tried to focus on the trees, they shimmered. When I tried to make out the edge of a flower that grew near the pool, its borders dissolved into the blue sky behind it. When I saw a woman appear out of another Watsu pool, her body was surrounded by a hazy ring of pink, and when the woman who accompanied her exited the pool, I noticed a glow of yellowish green around her.

For the rest of the day, the natural world that surrounded me at Harbin never quite came into focus, as if I had taken off my contacts and the borders of matter grew fuzzy, like the solid edges were pixelating. Everything appeared unusually beautiful. A hawk was a sunbeam. A pinecone was starlight. The water as it crested over the rocks in the stream spoke to me. I felt like I had been transported into the movie *Avatar.*

That night, my sleep was alive with dreams that slipped through my fingers before I could interpret them. And when I woke up, the world had gone back to normal. The borders of matter had returned, and try as I might, I couldn't see rings of color around the people in the morning yoga class. But the peace I had felt the day before stayed with me.

As I soaked in the hot springs after a yoga class, I had a flash of insight. Why did I have a little temper tantrum when the media came looking for *Doctor* Lissa? Why was I annoyed at getting lumped together with other MDs on *The Huffington Post*? I had made medicine "wrong," hanging onto my righteous indignation as a way of distancing myself from the profession that hurt me.

But this was just a defense mechanism. It's not what was true for me. The truth is that I *am* a doctor. I love medicine. And even though medicine broke my heart, I long ago made an agreement with the Universe about my calling. When we've accepted a Divine assignment, the Universe doesn't let us turn our backs on such an assignment lightly. I knew that I needed to let go of my victim story and release the built-up resentment I felt toward medicine so I didn't take that with me into the next 12-year cycle of my life.

I suddenly felt in every cell of my body that I was here on this planet not to reject medicine but to help heal it. My mission was to start a revolution in health care, to work with empowered patients and conscious health care providers who were committed to redefining health and reclaiming the heart of medicine. I couldn't fall into Victoria's old savior-complex patterns. I needed those I sought to help to find their healing within, where they could replenish their vitality and life force at will rather than expecting me to resuscitate them. When I gave people my life force, it was only a Band-Aid. I couldn't save anyone. But I could model for people how to generate their own healing life force, so they could transfuse themselves whenever necessary.

I had this grounded feeling of truth around my destiny to be a force for healing health care. I knew that I might one day teach other health care professionals what I had learned in my integrative medicine practice and in my study of spontaneous remissions and that I would bestow upon them my understanding of health as something infinitely more expansive than pills or surgeries, or even nutrition and exercise. I knew it was my mission to teach people through example that being wholly healthy also meant expressing yourself creatively; letting go of ego attachments; connecting in loving relationships with others; finding work that resonates with your soul; tapping into your sensual, erotic self; and, of course, nourishing and tending to your body. Perhaps my calling was leading me not to practice medicine in a clinical sense but to teach others about what I had learned.

The resistance that arose when I thought about all of this showed up as a feeling of helplessness and hopelessness. How could I change a system that was as rooted in dogma as any fundamentalist religion? Medicine struck me as brimming with the toxic vibe of "scientists" who were actually high priests in The Church of What Most Intellectuals Believe Right Now. The whole system smacked of dogma. I was starting to question everything I had learned in the church of medicine, and I knew that if I went public with what I was learning, there would be backlash. When you threaten someone's religion, that person's hackles go up.

How could we evolve as a profession if we weren't willing to explore things we didn't understand, like energy medicine or shamanism or the intersection of health and spirituality? As a scientist, I didn't understand these woo-woo ideas. I couldn't explain what happened to April. But I was curious enough to call my shaman friend and read a book about energy medicine. If you look back at the history of science, most radical breakthroughs flew in the face of scientific dogma, and those on the cutting edge were initially dismissed by the scientific community as quacks and crazies. But science must remain objective. The minute we start censoring anything that threatens the dominant scientific worldview, we fall into dogma and lose the opportunity to be real scientists who seek only truth and are happy to be proven wrong. As a doctor, I just wanted to illuminate universal truths. The truth can never be discredited, because it's just true.

The faith-filled part of me was willing to accept that there are things we experience that science simply can't explain yet. Sometimes science just hasn't developed the technology to prove the existence of the phenomena we are actually experiencing as "real." Those who theorize something are often proven right years later, but during the messy in-between, these people sometimes get burned at the stake. Until their ideas can be verified by science, these kinds of visionaries must cling to something intangible. Call it faith. Call it intuition. It was radical for me to even conceive of the idea that healing might involve factors we simply can't explain with science yet. But my mind had already been dismantled with question marks, and I simply couldn't unlearn what I was learning.

Was this my baby in the bathwater, this impulse to seek truth in medicine? As I drove home from Harbin, I still wasn't sure. Part of me felt excited and hopeful, but then cynicism and doubt slipped in. How in the world could I possibly help heal medicine? What could one person possibly do when the system was so broken? The place where my passion to be of pure service and my cynicism and hopelessness intersected was a hurting place.

This tendency to get cynical right when we're at the edge of a breakthrough is common for heroes on a journey. In *The More Beautiful World Our Hearts Know Is Possible,* Charles Eisenstein writes, "The derision of the cynic comes from a wound of crushed idealism and betrayed hopes. We received it on a cultural level when the Age of Aquarius morphed into the age of Ronald Reagan, and on an individual level as well when our youthful idealism that knew a more beautiful world is possible, that believed in our own individual destiny to contribute something meaningful to the world, that would never sell out under any circumstances and would never become like our parents gave way to an adulthood of deferred dreams and lowered expectations. Anything that exposes this wound will trigger us to protect it. One such protection is cynicism, which rejects and derides as foolish, naive, or irrational all of the expressions of reunion. The cynic mistakes his cynicism for realism. He wants us to discard the hopeful things that touch his wound, to settle for what is consistent with his lowered expectations. This, he says, is realistic. Ironically, it is in fact cynicism that is impractical. The naive person attempts what the cynic says is impossible, and sometimes succeeds."

Maybe I needed to return to the naive idealism of the Squirrel Girl. Maybe it was safe to hope.

For the first time in many years, I realized that the anger aimed at my profession had melted. Instead, I was awash with a wave of compassion for every doctor on the planet who had been traumatized by medicine the way I had. I was also overcome with love for every patient, nurse, hospital worker, and alternative medicine practitioner who had been traumatized by the doctors, most of whom suffered from post-traumatic stress disorder like I did. Something had shifted in me during my retreat, and now I felt called to lean into medicine rather than run away from it.

But how? I didn't know the answer, but I had a new, abiding faith that the way would be shown to me.

The day after I returned from my personal retreat, I was hiking on the North Coast trail right off Highway 1 on the way up to the Pantoll ranger station on Mount Tamalpais, when, suddenly, it appeared to me—the baby Ophi had charged me with finding in the bathwater. A vision appeared right in front of me: ten stones in a balanced pile, like those little rock sculptures you see marking beaches, hiking trails, and sacred landmarks. Each stone had writing on it. The words were all the categories that the writers on my blog wrote articles about—relationships, work/life purpose, creativity, spirituality, sexuality, money, the environment, mental health, and physical health. The largest stone, the foundation stone upon which all the others were balanced, was the Inner Pilot Light.

This was the wellness model—the Whole Health Cairn—that would be the subject of my next book and featured in a 2011 TEDx talk titled "The Shocking Truth about Your Health." Suddenly, everything synthesized. I had found my holy grail.

Breathless with excitement and heady with ideas, I raced down the hiking trail back to my house, where I pulled out a Sharpie and a piece of watercolor paper and drew the pile of stones. I scanned it and sent it to Michele, the agent who still hadn't signed me. I told her I had figured out how to write a revolutionary health book. The Whole Health Cairn offered an integrated visual representation of what I had been blogging about for years. Frustrated with the narrow definition of health that was limited only to the biochemical view of the body, I had been trying to push the limits of the "health box," expanding my own definition of health to include more than just modern medical treatments or even diet and exercise. I would make the health box so expansive that everything that interested me, everything I knew was related to true, whole health, would fit within it. I could climb back into the "doctor box," but I wouldn't be selling out in a white coat straitjacket. I would make the white coat so expansive that there would be room for me to dance within its boundaries without feeling constricted. I wouldn't have to limit myself.

I suspected that, if I went looking, I would find scientific proof that every stone in the Whole Health Cairn affects the health of the body as much as, if not more than, pills and surgeries. I would track down the evidence to demonstrate this. I would write about what I had learned from my patients in Marin County, about how spontaneous remissions began to happen when my patients intuitively uncovered what their bodies needed in order to heal and were brave enough to put those self-guided prescriptions into action. I'd research the spontaneous remissions I had uncovered in the medical literature to find out whether these were just flukes or if they involved proactive steps that made our bodies more likely to experience spontaneous remissions.

I wouldn't stop there. I'd dig deep into the literature to try to get to the bottom of what so many in the new age community were talking about regarding mind-body medicine. A lot of it sounded like mumbo jumbo to me—how the mind could heal the body with nothing more than thoughts, feelings, and beliefs, that all you had to do was say affirmations to make your cancer go away. But what if there was actual science to back up such statements? If that kind of data could be reviewed and annotated using legitimate scientific methodology, now that would be a book I'd want to read!

I could hear a cautious optimism beneath Michele's cynical New Yorker demeanor. She said, "Write me a book proposal for *that* book, and then we'll talk."

And so I did.

The baby I found in the dirty bathwater of medicine became the thread that helped me through the Ordeal of the narrow place, that thread you can use to inch yourself, oh so gently, out of the Innermost Cave of the bony birth canal. I now realize that I would not have found the holy grail had I not been willing to stay in the discomfort of the narrow place until it was time to pass to the other side. Only in retrospect did I realize what a blessing the initiation of the narrow place really was.

Perhaps you're there right now, in the midst of your own Ordeal, in the discomfort of your own narrow place, where you're searching for the baby in the bathwater you're ready to dump, trying, in vain, to find the thread that will inch you to freedom. If that's how you feel, I encourage you to do what you must to just make peace with where you are, to resist the temptation to run backward into the comfort of the Ordinary World.

Why should you suffer this way? Why not ease your fear and anxiety by comforting yourself with the Ordinary World once more?

You can. It's your journey, and you have free will. Don't beat yourself up if you choose to do so. Be extra gentle and loving with yourself if the Gremlin leads you back to the Ordinary World. Every hero's journey happens in its own perfect timing, and it's not cowardly to feel the need to comfort yourself when you're scared and broke and have no energy to stay on your Road of Trials.

But know that if you do go back, your calling will not stop ringing, and because you've come as far as you have on your hero's journey, the Ordinary World will be less tolerable than it once was. You can use it as a bridge if you must. But I'll warn you now. You won't ever be the same in the Ordinary World, because you have tasted the sweet nectar of the freedom of the Special World, and you'll never again be able to tolerate being in chains.

Why should you move forward? Why endure the terror of going into the belly of the beast? Because the rewards are infinitely sweet and there are many others you can help back in the Ordinary World once you survive your journey. Within the narrow place lies a gift, a gift you may not recognize when you're in that space. When you're stuck in the narrow place, everything gets boiled down to its essence, and if you pay close attention, this is where you discover the thread of who you really are and what really matters to you.

When people face death, they often talk about seeing their lives flash before their eyes, and in that moment, many see the thread of what their lives are all about. If they make it through the narrow place and avert death in that moment, they emerge reborn. Only now they hold the precious gift of the thread that guided them through.

HERO'S GUIDEPOST:

Say Yes to the Ordeal in the Innermost Cave

There comes a time on your hero's journey when your ego gets cornered and starts to panic. You feel busted. The jig is up. There's no place to hide anymore. Your ego and your soul will battle it out to see who gets to control the wheel of YOU, and it won't be pretty. When it's time for your Ordeal in the

Innermost Cave, you're going to be tempted to run screaming in the other direction. Fear will rear up like a Tyrannosaurus rex. This is your initiation, the test of your mettle.

To find the holy grail, you must be willing to lean in and let go. If you traverse the narrow place and survive the near death of your Ordeal, you're certain to be rewarded, for on the other side lies a whole new life. To become who you must, you must let go of who you've been. What you will lose will be worth sacrificing because of what you will gain. You will have rescued the baby but thrown out the dirty bathwater. You will be reborn, but you will now hold the holy grail in your heart.

This is your graduation, the day you really become a hero. Your courage to say yes will inspire all who have witnessed your journey and watched you make brave choices. You will become a beacon of light for those who journey with you.

HERO'S PRACTICE:
Find the Baby in the Bathwater

When you're in the midst of your own Ordeal, try asking yourself a few defining questions.

- Who are you and why are you here?
- What is the unchanging essence that runs through you and your life?
- What is your soul here on this earth to heal, learn, and teach?
- What do you keep escaping, only to have it keep coming back?
- Who will you be if you are no longer afraid?
- What might you do if you could not fail?

Imagine if you never again felt lonely or disconnected from the Divine. Imagine being *that* expansive. Imagine waking up to the perfection of you and the perfection of every other Divine spark on this planet. This is what your soul craves. It's what every soul craves. You are being called to say yes.

CHAPTER 14

The Road Back

While I was battling dragons in the Innermost Cave, Matt had forged full steam ahead to move us to Julian. The moving sale he had planned in order to cleanse our storage unit of art was all scheduled, and he was packing boxes to get us ready to leave Marin County. The day of the sale dawned, and Matt had laid out literally hundreds of paintings. To the shock of both of us, paintings flew off the walls. People bought 10 or 20 at a time.

By the end of the day, Matt was counting checks, and his voice shook when he announced that we had sold more than $40,000 worth of paintings. That's when my eyes landed on the date written on one of the checks.

It was June 4, the day Ophi had told me everything would turn around.

The money we earned paid the rent for the rest of the year, allowing us to stay in our home in Marin County and keep Siena at the Waldorf school she loved.

Mom had planned what she called "Nana Camp" for her four grandchildren, and so Siena and I spent that summer at my mother's lake house in Ohio. The kids spent the summer Slip 'N Sliding, riding roller coasters, boating, kayaking, and making art while I took a deep dive into the medical literature, searching for evidence that the Whole Health Cairn was a scientifically verifiable wellness model. What I uncovered in the medical literature blew Victoria to smithereens. She simply didn't know how to live with the paradox of decades of deeply entrenched beliefs about health and medicine that conflicted with evidence I was finding in the conventional medical data proving, without a doubt, that there was a whole other body of data out there about what makes the body healthy, things like positive thoughts, beliefs, and feelings; the love of a supportive community; healthy communication; engaging in meaningful work; falling in love; being optimistic; and communing with other spiritual seekers.

To have found copious evidence that the mind has the power to heal the body without a doctor's intervention, at least a percentage of the time, was an impossible truth that Victoria simply couldn't accept. I endured the trauma of medical school and residency ostensibly so I would understand the human body better than my patients did. Yet, the more I researched, the more I found evidence that patients may know what's best for their bodies, because nobody else can really know what happens in a patient's mind, and the mind may be the best medicine of all. When the mind heals from loneliness, anxiety, fear, depression, resentment, anger, and negative beliefs about health and life, at least a percentage of the time, the health of the body follows suit.

After researching the placebo effect, I realized that the medical establishment had been proving that the mind can heal the body since the 1950s, when it became evident that approximately one-third of patients in clinical trials got better, even if they were only treated with a sugar pill, saline injection, or fake surgery. But as doctors, what were we supposed to *do* with this information? Were we supposed to be doling out sugar pills to our patients? Was there some biochemical mechanism that explained the placebo effect, and if so, was there any way to activate this mechanism without the need for sugar pills and deception?

That's where the Whole Health Cairn came in. The vision I had been given as what my spiritual friends called a "download" provided me with a visual framework that I could use to translate all the data I collected, proving that loneliness is a greater risk factor for your health than smoking or not exercising, that totally healthy young people can literally die from overwork (in Japan, they even have a name for it—*karoshi*), that people who attend spiritual services live up to 14 years longer than those who don't, that happy people live 7 to 10 years longer than unhappy people, that optimists have a 77 percent lower risk of heart disease than pessimists. These and other shocking statistics I found provided evidence that every stone in the Whole Health Cairn not only affects your health but also *dramatically* affects your health.

At this point, I knew I still had a lot to learn and my research would be ongoing, but I had enough concrete evidence to move forward with writing the book proposal Michele had challenged me to write. I got the sense that she was right when she had said *Broken* wasn't the right book to publish at this point in my career. My calling wasn't to complain about what was wrong with medicine by telling my victim story. My calling was to help heal it from a place of empowered but hopeful acceptance of what was true.

I hadn't realized when I wrote *Broken* that my soul chose perfectly the path I needed to take to bring me to my rightful place in the Divine orchestra. Something had shifted in me since then. Now I felt so much compassion for medicine, so much love for medicine at its pure essence, such a strong impulse to be a force for healing it. I had reconnected with the lineage of healing, a lineage that recognizes that medicine is a spiritual practice, that you practice medicine like you practice meditation or yoga, as if you'll never quite get it right. It's the same lineage that calls not only doctors but also medicine women, shamans, and every other type of healer that has ever lived. By tapping back into that archetypal lineage, I was able to reclaim my calling rather than make medicine wrong.

As Ophi said, you can't change something by making it wrong. Like the dream I had where the people were shoulder to shoulder, lining the mountains, facing north and illuminated by the light, you can only love those who are facing south and hope that, if it is their path to do so, they choose to turn around and face the light with you. We have to stay compassionate with the cynics and doubters, realizing that there is a hurting thing lying at the root of their cynicism, a shattered idealism we can all understand. We have to love the persecutors within these broken industries, knowing what they must have endured in order to become the persecutors, knowing, perhaps, that if we were in their shoes, we might wind up the same.

When we stop forgetting that we are all interconnected, equal players in a conscious, intelligent Universe, we can come back to the heart, and from this place of compassion, we remember who we really are.

Michele decided to pitch my new book proposal to publishers in September 2011. I trusted that if getting a big deal for this book was in Divine alignment, it would happen, and if it didn't happen, it was because the Universe was guiding me in a different direction. But knowing this and actually feeling peaceful about it were two different beasts! My belly was full of butterflies and I couldn't eat. I was meditating for literally 2 hours at 4 a.m. every day just to try to make it through the day while we waited to hear back from publishers. As if my own anxiety wasn't running high enough, I felt a lot of pressure from Matt. This was a make-it-or-break-it moment, he insisted. If this didn't work, I would simply have to put my tail between my legs, admit defeat, and go get a job at the hospital.

The day of the deadline arrived. I waited for the phone to ring. But when it finally did, it was Michele telling me we hadn't gotten a single offer. I was devastated. The Gremlin started to have a heyday, but Michele sent out a reminder notice, and much to my relief, almost all the editors wrote right back. They were interested but hadn't had a chance to fully review the book and wanted more time.

Phew! At least they weren't rejecting the book. But then the sleepless nights of waiting lingered on for several more weeks, which gave me a lot of practice with what my cousin and therapist Rebecca Bass Ching called "bench-pressing" my discomfort with uncertainty. In other words, I couldn't make what I wanted happen, so there was nothing for me to do other than to practice being with the fear and anxiety of not knowing what the outcome would be, much like you would practice lifting weights to get stronger muscles.

In retrospect, these were great muscles to bench-press, because something wonderful happened after years of bench-pressing fear, anxiety, and uncertainty. Around this time, a critical shift happened within me. Instead of focusing on the fear of uncertainty, I started identifying with the excitement of possibility. They're two sides of the same coin, really. When you don't know what the future holds, something bad could happen, or something wonderful could happen. I started waking up every morning excited for my day, because if anything was possible, then some fortuitous surprise might await me. Oprah could call! I might receive a windfall of unexpected cash like I did at the art sale! I might bump into someone awesome on a hike! I might get a book deal!

It took me another year to really make the next part of that shift, when I was able to start releasing judgment about whether a particular outcome was good or bad, when I was able to see all outcomes as part of my hero's journey, even if they weren't the outcomes my ego desired. I definitely wasn't there yet as I waited to hear back from those editors. Hours of meditation ensued as I bench-pressed anxiety. I wanted to be so Zen about it, but the stakes were high, and I honestly didn't know what I was going to do if Michele couldn't sell this book.

One morning, when I was in San Diego visiting old friends, I took a hike in a canyon in Rancho Santa Fe at sunrise after a 2-hour meditation. The trail I was hiking ended at a park, and in the park was a white gazebo that beckoned to me. I approached the gazebo, and when I stepped inside it, the voice of Sebastian said, "Dance like you just got the book deal."

So I did just that. I turned up the volume on my iPod and danced with my eyes closed for nearly an hour until I was drenched in sweat and feeling a lightness of being that made me giddy.

While I was dancing, Michele called. One of the interested publishers was Hay House, which just so happened to have its headquarters in Carlsbad, about a 5-minute drive from where I was staying. The acquisitions editor and the president of Hay House were both in Carlsbad to celebrate Hay House founder Louise Hay's 85th birthday, and they both wanted to meet me.

When Reid Tracy, the president and CEO of Hay House, asked me how my book was different from all the other books out there about mind-body medicine, I fumbled my answer, muttering some unintelligible gibberish.

"No," he said. "What makes this book different is that yours is the first book written by a mainstream medical doctor making a solid case that there is scientific proof that you can heal yourself, complete with documentation from the mainstream medical literature. In fact, that should be the subtitle of your book."

We renamed the book right then and there—*Mind Over Medicine: Scientific Proof That You Can Heal Yourself*. The president told me his plan. If they published my book, he was interested in producing a public television special about my work that would air on PBS stations around the country.

I was in shock.

My cell phone rang right after I finished my meeting. It was Michele. Hay House had just offered me a six-figure book deal.

You'd think I would have been elated with this wonderful news. I had worked so hard to hear these words. Yet, when I heard them, the Gremlin went nuts, shouting things like "What fools they are! You'll never live up to what they're offering you. You've just pulled the wool over their eyes, but they'll find out soon enough that it's all hype, that you'll never deliver on what they think is possible, that you're just a fraud who talks a good game. This is just temporary."

The Gremlin can be a total buzzkill.

I tried to allow myself to feel the glee of hearing Michele tell me that Hay House wasn't the only publisher that wanted to buy my book. Four other publishing houses were interested, so they would have an auction. I tried to get excited, especially when I was invited to Louise Hay's blowout birthday party, where I would meet Louise and all the other Hay House authors who were gathering to celebrate her.

This is when I had to start bench-pressing my receiving muscles. I hadn't realized those muscles had gotten *way* out of shape during the past few years of struggle. I tried to bench-press a few sets before heading out to Louise's party.

When I got there, I felt like a fish out of water. I was totally starstruck when I was introduced to all the spiritual self-help celebrities whose books I worshipped. The Gremlin told me I had no right being there, that I was an imposter, that I'd better run quickly before everyone discovered that they'd made a mistake by including me in these inner ranks.

Victoria, on the other hand, had a field day. I watched her schmooze and preen and show off, all glammed up in her party dress, when I knew she was just overcompensating because she felt insecure. Try as I might, though, I couldn't keep her in check. She was on the loose, name-dropping and bragging about how many people read her blog. As I sat there next to well-known self-help authors like Louise Hay, SARK, Cheryl Richardson, and Suze Orman, I thanked Victoria for all that she had done to get me to this moment, acknowledging that if she needed to be in the driver's seat to get through this party, it was okay. No need to beat her up. If Victoria wasn't there, the Gremlin might have kept me hiding in a corner. Shaming Victoria wouldn't help. It would just make her more defensive. My Inner Pilot Light was able to see the sweet beauty of how it was all unfolding.

Soon after Louise's party, I signed a book deal with Hay House, and although I still heard the Gremlin telling me I didn't belong and wouldn't measure up, another wiser part of me felt like I had come home. I was awash in gratitude.

You'd think this would be the time for popping champagne corks and party music, but instead of the smooth sailing I expected at this celebratory time on my hero's journey, I faced yet another obstacle. Matt and I had both been anxious while we waited to see if *Mind Over Medicine* would sell, and after it sold, I felt awash with profound relief. Phew! We could finally pay the bills!

But for reasons neither of us understood at the time, Matt's anxiety skyrocketed. It was a wake up call for us both. Prior to that moment, both of us were under the illusion that it was within my power to make Matt happy, that if only I could fill up our bank account again, he could relax and begin to enjoy the many passions he was exploring as an artist, writer, and stay-at-home father. But that's not what happened. After I got the book deal, the locus of Matt's anxiety just shifted to something else, rather than disappearing, as we both expected it would. We realized we were facing a problem bigger than money issues, one that would require deep inner work for us both.

As I examined our relationship, I realized that we had made an unconscious agreement back when we first met. I had met Matt only three months after leaving a relationship that didn't feel safe, and all I desired at that point in my life was safety. I craved someone gentle, loving, trustworthy, and incapable of hurting me, someone who would turn my home into a nest and let me rest in it, someone who would support me in following my career passions without feeling threatened by my success or expecting me to be a stay-at-home mother, someone who would let me grow without holding me back. Matt had gifted me with nine beautiful years of this, and I was incredibly grateful for the gift. The safety Matt offered me allowed me to take brave risks I might not have taken if Matt hadn't been grounding me in the solidity of his love.

In return for his gift of unconditional love, safety, and companionship, I had agreed to support Matt, emotionally and financially, to stand in for the mother who had abandoned him as a child, to create a cocoon for his growth and development, to help him heal from the wounds of his childhood, to take care of him so he didn't have to return to the traumas of his corporate job, and to shield him from the expectations our culture puts on men. Taking on this role granted me a sense of purpose, made me feel like I was doing something good for someone I loved, and, unbeknownst to me at the time, fed my Savior Complex and created the perfect conditions for co-dependence.

As many couples do, we had hooked into each other's wounds, not realizing at the time that we had agreed to baby each other's "owies," when we might have been better off digging into those wounds in order to heal them at their roots. Our agreement had worked seamlessly as long as I was working in the hospital. I had upheld my end of the agreement until I quit my job and we ran out of money. At that point, we started sticking needles in each other's wounds, as our dance of co-dependence intensified. We both wound up feeling abandoned by the other.

All I wanted during those painful months of financial crisis was for my husband to help me feel safe, to hold me in his arms and say, "I'm with you in this. Let me help." All he wanted was for me to restore the security I had promised him and remove from his shoulders any pressure to perform. Whatever had been alive between us began to die during this part of my hero's journey, and it frightened us both.

I was in this vulnerable, exposed place when I read Martha Beck's *Finding Your Way in a Wild New World*, a guidebook for heroes on a journey to heal the world. I had already read all of Martha's other books after I was introduced to her work during that first trip to Esalen (which I had gobbled up like candy corn), but this book resonated even more than all the others.

The book was an almost impossible read for me at such a fragile time in my life. One of my friends, Momastery blogger Glennon Doyle Melton, described her feelings about Martha's work better than I could. She wrote on her blog, "She's really bright. Like ouch-hurts-my-eyes bright. It's easier, so much easier, to just sort of stumble around in a little darkness, isn't it? To pretend that the problem is that there's just not enough light to see what the hell I'm supposed to do instead of admitting that, actually, the problem is that I'm not sure I'm ready to see what I'll see in the light. I'm also afraid to admit that it hurts a little to see folks living big in the light when I've been a little too scared to step into it myself. Does that make any sense? Reading Martha's books just requires so much *feeling* and *living* and *courage,* and these three things are scary. It's like sometimes I switch off a song before the words start when I know the words are Too Good and True. And sometimes I only watch the very beginning of a movie—just long enough to meet and fall in love with the characters. Then I switch it off before I have to witness all their uncomfortable pain and glory when the inevitable conflict and solution arise."

That pretty much summed up perfectly how I felt when I read Martha's book. Victoria wanted to turn away from Martha. She was just too bright, and Victoria was afraid that she would simply dissolve in Martha's light. But my Inner Pilot Light was magnetized by Martha. I had a strong sense that she was a key magical mentor who would help me at the crucial part of my hero's journey that lay ahead. I instinctively knew I would need Martha in order to bring the holy grail back to the Ordinary World. Martha and I had never met, but that was about to change. My journey would begin to accelerate, which is what commonly happens once you find the holy grail.

Let me first tell you a little bit about Martha, in case you don't already know her. In a world ruled by fear, Martha is one of the bravest women I've ever met. First, she chose to keep her pregnancy after finding out she was carrying a baby with Down syndrome while studying for her PhD at Harvard, where she felt pressured to terminate the pregnancy. Then she moved with her husband back to Utah, where she grew up, because the Mormon community holds children with Down syndrome in high regard. She thought her son Adam would be well served in the religious community.

After taking a job at Brigham Young University and realizing that the university was so ruled by the Mormon Church that it was trying to squelch data generated by the scientific community, she went public about this breach of science. And after years of keeping the dark secret that her Mormon-royalty father had sexually molested her, she wrote a tell-all memoir called *Leaving the Saints* that not only exposed the shadow side of the Mormon religion but also revealed the truth about her father.

As if that wasn't enough bravery for one lifetime, she and her husband subsequently divorced because he came out of the closet about his homosexuality. And much to her surprise, Martha then fell in love with a woman, who she has loved and lived with ever since.

Martha and I first met on the telephone, where we were leading a teleclass about finding your calling for 10,000 listeners. (Listen to Martha Beck, Amy Ahlers, and me lead a free teleclass about finding your calling at FindYourCallingNow.com.) The energy of the people who participated in the call vibrated at such a high level that we literally fried the phone lines. When Martha and I were debriefing on the phone afterward, my whole body felt electric with the knowledge that something big was about to happen. I felt like Martha was about to change my life and this teleclass had been just a baby step in the marathon we were about to run together.

When I met her, Martha had just taken a leap of faith of her own: She had used her entire life savings to buy a horse ranch in Central California.

Why? Because she had been called to do so. She had no clue why. But there was a very good reason. She was sure of it. The way would be made known to her. That's how much she trusted.

Having that kind of faith doesn't mean you don't still get moments of panic. And it doesn't mean you don't question your sanity. During one of our phone calls, Martha was confiding in me how anxious she felt about the horse ranch she had just purchased. All the signs from the Universe had aligned for her to buy it. But once she spent her life's fortune on it, the signs slowed down. She wasn't sure what to do next, and she was in the uncomfortable phase of gestation that requires awaiting further instructions.

Around this same time, I was in the midst of a strange flurry of signs from the Universe that I was having trouble interpreting. Confusion had now become a signal to me that it was time to get away and get quiet so guidance could come through. I reached out to my assistant Melanie (who had replaced Joy when Joy became a life coach) to ask her when I could get away to Esalen. She said I was booked. It would have to wait until December. Then, right when I was about to fly to New York to speak at a Hay House conference with Wayne Dyer, Louise Hay, and many other Hay House luminaries, Hurricane Sandy blasted through New York, and the conference was canceled.

Melanie called me and said, "It's a sign! Go to Esalen!"

So I hightailed it down to Big Sur. As soon as I got in my car, my spirit guide Sebastian started talking to me. As I was driving, Sebastian was transmitting messages to me so fast I could barely keep up. I got information about my marriage, my business, and my book. I was so distracted with all that was coming through that I missed my exit and drove an hour out of my way before I realized I was going the wrong way.

When I arrived at Esalen, Sebastian instructed me to sit down at my computer and proceeded to dictate an e-mail titled "Calling All Visionary Physicians."

When I was done taking dictation, I asked Sebastian what I was supposed to do with this e-mail. The maddening answer I received was, "Do nothing. Await further instructions."

What? You tell me to write an e-mail but I'm not supposed to send it?

Fast-forward 6 days. Martha and I were chatting on the phone after one of our teleclasses. In spite of the fact that I thought she might call the men with the white coats, I confessed to Martha that I had a spirit guide named Sebastian and that Sebastian had just downloaded a bunch of instructions to me.

Martha said, "Tell me more."

I explained that I had gone to Esalen and Sebastian had dictated an e-mail, but when I asked what I was supposed to do with it, Sebastian told me to await further instructions.

Martha asked me to send her my e-mail. She read it while we were on the phone. The minute she finished reading, Martha's voice got even higher and she said, "Oh my God, you're supposed to bring the doctors to my ranch. I've known I was supposed to use this land to heal the people who will heal the planet, but I hadn't realized I should start with the doctors. Of course we start with doctors!" Suddenly, Martha was spouting off details about dates and curriculum and where these doctors would sleep and how much we'd charge and how she'd bring in her horse-whisperer friend Koelle Simpson and how all these doctors would go out and amplify our collective visions, like threads of a web covering the earth.

By this point, I was weeping. Martha wanted to teach doctors with me. Holy crap. I thought back to the voice that had instructed me to go to Esalen that first time. When I had arrived there, Martha's had been one of the names I had been given when I told people I was supposed to meet someone at Esalen. I was humbled and in awe. Somehow, Someone had known. Somewhere, Someone was orchestrating this whole thing.

When you survive the Ordeal and find the holy grail on your hero's journey, it's tempting to hold the grail close to your heart, to protect it. But that's not what heroes do. The holy grail cannot be reserved only for selfish gain. So the hero isn't out of the woods yet. This is the real test of the hero. To complete the hero's journey, the holy grail must be taken back to the Ordinary World, where it can be used for the highest good of the collective.

I was on The Road Back in my own hero's journey, where the hero has to deal with the consequences of having battled the dark forces of the Ordeal. This is when the darkness, which was slayed in the Ordeal, will come raging back, trying to make sure the hero doesn't get to keep the holy grail. In the movies, this would be when the chase scene ensues, as the hero is pursued on The Road Back by the vengeful forces that were shaken up when the holy grail was acquired by the hero. The Road Back also marks the hero's commitment to returning to the Ordinary World, accepting that the Special World must be left behind in order to play a healing role in the Ordinary World.

I wasn't fully aware of the fact that I was on The Road Back. But Martha said she knew right away that I was destined to be a force for healing our broken health care system and that the holy grail I was given held the key to healing the Ordinary World of medicine.

Martha said, "I know you're scared, kiddo. I know you think you can't do this. But I can see it already. In some other dimension, they're already here. I'm looking out my window right now, and the doctors are here at the ranch, over by the stables. This is what wants to happen. It's what's best for the highest good. You can do this because *the Universe wants this.*"

She went on to explain that she would "hold the plane" for me.

"You know how sometimes you're late for your plane, and you're running through the airport, with your luggage flying around as you bump into people? But then you realize that your friend is already on the plane, so you call your friend and say, 'Tell the pilot to hold the plane! I'm coming!' That's what I'll do for you. I'm already on the plane. I know you're destined to do this, and I'll hold the plane for you until you get here. Sometimes I'll need you to hold the plane for me, too."

I agreed to support her if I could, though I wasn't sure I was far enough ahead of Martha to hold any planes for her. Martha had spent years studying and practicing what she calls "the four technologies of magic." In her workshops and books, Martha teaches how to manipulate energy in order to bend spoons, call in the whales, lift heavy men with your pinky finger, and bring into form what wants to become, when your desires are in alignment with what the Universe wants. She promised me that anybody could do these things and that she would teach me. I believed that Martha had done those things, but the Gremlin and Victoria *did not* believe I would be practicing magic anytime soon.

Martha had already told me unbelievable stories about bending steel rebar like it was putty in her hands in front of a bunch of shocked construction workers who couldn't do it when they tried to use their very big muscles. She led workshops in Africa at Londolozi Game Reserve, where she taught people how to become One with the safari wildlife so that the animals would walk right up to them.

The first technology of magic, "Wordlessness," requires moving from your thinking, word-forming, "we're all separate so every man for himself" left brain into your intuitive, feeling, "we're all connected" healer's right brain. In other words, you can't think or plan or write or "sperm" your way to making magic happen. Essentially, the techniques Martha teaches are ways to manipulate energy on what she describes as the "energy Internet," which connects us all.

She compares the four technologies of magic to our use of computers. If we're all connected and we're nothing more than interdependent vibrations of energy, as quantum physics scientists suggest, then, essentially, we live in The Matrix, which is one construct of form, but not the only one. Martha suggests that we can manipulate The Matrix to bring into form something that begins only as an idea and then drop into Wordlessness to log onto the energy Internet. Most of the techniques for moving from your limited left to your unlimited right brain are forms of meditation practice. For example, one of my favorites Martha calls "sense-drenching."

Close your eyes and picture yourself looking at something beautiful without using words to describe it to yourself. Then add in your favorite taste, your favorite smell, your favorite soft thing to feel, your favorite sound. Try holding all five sensations in your mind without using words. If you're able to do this, you'll be operating primarily from the right side of your brain, and you'll be automatically Wordless.

The second technology of magic, my personal favorite, is "Oneness." Oneness practices are built upon the idea that we are not independent, separate beings but part of a collective consciousness that vibrates together energetically, that what affects one of us affects all of us, and, therefore, that we can communicate with and influence each other without using words.

If dropping into Wordlessness allows you to access the energy Internet, then tapping into Oneness allows you to send e-mails. With the practices Martha teaches, you can learn to "become one" with a fork and bend it, allow the veggies at the farmers' market to tell you which ones your body craves, call in the animals as Martha did during a workshop where they called in hundreds of whales and made international news, and send telepathic messages to other humans.

Once you've got Wordlessness and Oneness down pat, you can start practicing the third technology of magic, "Imagining." Imagining is about tapping into and intuitively seeing what wants to happen according to Divine Will. For example, Martha and I were Imagining when I wrote that e-mail to the visionary doctors and she saw a vision of the doctors already walking on her ranch. The vision I had received about the healing ritual I did with April is another example of Imagining.

Imagining is not some law of attraction practice whereby you imagine a Ferrari and a Ferrari appears. It's not about practicing magic for the purpose of personal gain. It takes the idea of visualizing further than the law of attraction by separating the ego's desires from the visualization. It's not about fantasizing or conjuring up a vision based on what your ego wants. It's about feeling into what wants to become based on that which is truly in the highest good for all beings.

Martha teaches that when you Imagine what wants to become, the Universe kicks The Matrix into high gear to deliver on a silver platter anything you need in order to bring this vision into reality. If that doesn't happen, you probably were Imagining something from your ego rather than something that's in alignment with Divine Will.

The fourth technology of magic, "Forming," is about bringing into being, without forcing, exactly what you Imagined. Forming requires following two rules.

1. Play until you feel like resting.

2. Rest until you feel like playing.

Martha says that if your work doesn't feel like play, it's probably not aligned with what she calls "the Everywhen," and it may be a sign pointing you in another direction. Because play and rest come in cycles, there will be times of busy play during the Forming process, followed by times of stillness, during which your only job is to await further instructions for how you're destined to play next.

I had been practicing the four technologies of magic, with varying results, for almost a year by this point, but I really started practicing the technologies after Martha and I decided to teach the doctors together. After practicing the Wordlessness techniques during my meditation practice, I moved on to Oneness. On one of my hikes, I sat on the trail, closed my eyes, got Wordless, and became one with an image of a coyote in my mind's eye. I practiced becoming the coyote, so there was no difference between the coyote and me. I asked the coyote telepathically if he wanted to play—no pressure, no attachment, just an invitation, in case he thought it would be fun. (The minute you start attaching to a certain outcome, Martha says it can't happen.)

When I opened my eyes, lo and behold, there was a coyote in front of me. Moments later, hundreds of coyotes started howling.

My whole body erupted into goose bumps. Victoria freaked out. But my Inner Pilot Light felt giddy and lit up.

When I got home, I ran into April, the client I had the healing session vision about. I had also Imagined a second vision regarding April. After the healing work that led to her spontaneous remission from the weird blood disorder, I had been hiking by the ocean when I saw a vision of April moving into my guest house, and when I asked Sebastian if I was supposed to invite April to live with me, Sebastian said yes. April had been living with me as a personal assistant and nanny ever since.

April, whose phobias were much less intense than when I had first met her, looked unusually panicked. Both April's cat Emmy and my puppy Bezoar had gotten out and were missing.

April said, "Did you hear that pack of coyotes howling?" She had heard them and was terrified that they had eaten Emmy and Bezoar.

While April looked at me with raised eyebrows, I explained that these were good coyotes and that I had called them in. April said, "Well, if you can call in the coyotes, will you please call in Emmy and Bezoar?"

With no confidence that I could actually reproduce what I had just done, I agreed to try. I started with Emmy. I went down to April's guesthouse, sat inside the room I wanted Emmy to return to, and practiced calling her in. Within a minute, two coyotes showed up right at the guesthouse door, which we had left open so Emmy could come in.

Clearly, I hadn't mastered my magician skills yet.

Telepathically, I told the coyotes that I loved them and appreciated their visitation but that we'd have to play another time. I asked them if they wouldn't mind leaving so Emmy wouldn't be frightened to come home.

Wouldn't you know they just pivoted around and walked away, just like that!

I tried calling in Emmy for a while after the coyotes left, but it wasn't working. April said, "I know my cat. No way she's coming home when there were just two coyotes at the door."

So we walked up the hill. I figured I could call Emmy from up there instead, and while I was at it, I called in Bezoar. Within moments, Emmy trotted up, and when we went back down to the house, Bezoar was perched on the back of the sofa, looking at us as if she didn't understand why we were all worked up.

April looked at me, wide-eyed, and said, "It's official. You're a witch."

I had told my mother, who was staying with us for the month in California, the story of what had happened. Delighted by my story, Mom had an idea. As a huge whale fan, she spent many hours sitting on cliffs in coastal California trying to spot whales. But she hadn't seen any this year. After hearing about the coyotes, Emmy, and Bezoar, Mom asked if I might be willing to do her a favor and call in some whales. We were in Monterey at Point Lobos State Natural Reserve, and I said I'd hike ahead and try to call in the whales, and she could catch up with me. Hopefully, there would be a whole show waiting for her by the time she got there.

The ocean was still when I arrived, but I asked the whales if they wanted to play. By the time Mom arrived about 30 minutes later, there were dozens of whales, breaching, smacking their big tails against the water, and blowing water through their spouts. It was quite the spectacle.

Mom was in awe. She marveled at the sea of whales putting on a show. But I wanted to keep hiking, so I told Mom to sit and enjoy the show. As I hiked along the coastline, the whales were everywhere I looked. There seemed to be at least a hundred whales. My heart was bursting. It was a sight of such inexplicable beauty, but underlying the physical beauty of nature, a feeling welled up in the deepest part of my soul and left me in tears. If this is possible, even predictable, then this was concrete proof that we really are all One.

I was raised to believe that everything in the Universe is separate. There's me and there's you. There are animals and plants, but they can't communicate with us unless you teach an animal to respond to body language. None of us are actually connected, and we certainly can't communicate telepathically. Plants certainly don't have consciousness, and, Lord knows, spoons and steel rebar aren't conscious. How could they be? Consciousness exists in the brain, and trees and spoons don't have brains.

But what I was experiencing after practicing Martha's four technologies of magic violated everything I had grown up believing. These magical, mystical, almost miraculous experiences felt like evidence that life was far more wonderful than I had ever dreamed possible. What if it was true that we are all interconnected beings in a conscious, intelligent, purposeful Universe? And what if these various forms of consciousness could communicate with one another? How thrilling! What if the idea of Oneness was not just some spiritual fairy tale? What if what I experienced after my Ordeal in the Watsu pool was real, that feeling of being simultaneously me and the trees and the birds and the water? What if this was concrete evidence that I am the spoon, the coyote, the cat, the dog, and the whales?

Maybe it was all one big coincidence. Or maybe I was just going crazy. I certainly felt that way sometimes. But what if I wasn't crazy? What if this was evidence that we are all Consciousness engaging with Consciousness itself, able to communicate and influence each other through forces we don't fully understand and can't completely prove with science.

It was shocking and confronting and exciting, and in my heart, it felt like love. My heart kept bursting. I became embarrassingly sensitive. I found myself crying with joy when a stranger let me cut into traffic. So I could barely contain myself when the whales were dancing all around me during my hike.

When I got back to where Mom was, she looked at me with a sad face. Apparently, she had been sitting there bored since I had left. The whales had disappeared as soon as I left her spot.

Was it possible that they had followed me on my hike?

Words fail me when I try to describe what my heart was feeling during these experiences, so let me use Martha's words. On her blog, Martha wrote about the magic that was happening at the ranch she had just bought.

Several tribe members gathered with a Shaman to dedicate the land to the objective of "Restoring Eden"—healing animals, ecosystems, and humans, in any way possible. At one point the Shaman took me aside and said, "Martha. Stop trying." Without words, she helped me find an incredibly deep flow wave of movement in my lower torso. "There," she said, "that anchors you and you can let others anchor there as well. Then, let it heal them."

She didn't say what "it" was, because on one hand, it is inexpressible, and on the other hand, once you've felt it, there is no need to describe it. It is the TAO. It is Love. It is saturating the air you breathe as you read this. Be still until you can let it find you. That is your only job. And then, what the hell, call some whales. Because that's AWESOME.

Maybe it was all a series of coincidences. But maybe that's just part of how the Universe dances with us.

Notice whether any part of you feels cynical or skeptical after what you just read. Do you believe me? Do you think I might be exaggerating? Or delusional? Or lying? Or flat-out crazy? If so, I've wondered all of those things about myself. As a recovering skeptic, I too questioned such things, in myself and others. Like members of the Skeptics Society, a group of rationalists devoted to debunking just such stories, I respected those who upheld scientific materialism and provided scientific explanations for why mystical and paranormal phenomena couldn't be real. For many years, I was an avid appreciator of the discernment and scientific orthodoxy promoted by this organization, which publishes its findings in *Skeptic* magazine.

But at some point, I stopped paying attention to all the naysayers because, even though their debunkings made sense to my mind, something else felt more true in my heart. When you experience such mystical phenomena personally, it feels more real than anything you can read in even the most intellectual magazines.

So it provoked a huge smile when, years after such mystical experiences began to happen to me, I read an article written by Michael Shermer, founder of the Skeptics Society and editor-in-chief of *Skeptic* magazine. The article, published in September 2014 in *Scientific American*, was titled "Anomalous Events That Can Shake One's Skepticism to the Core." In the article, Shermer tells the story of what happened on his wedding day on June 25, 2014. His soon-to-be-wife Jennifer had been very close to her grandfather, who had served as her father figure. But he died when she was 16. Jennifer was from Germany, and before the wedding, Jennifer shipped her belongings to Shermer's house, where the wedding was to take place, but many of the items were damaged in shipping. Among these items was a 1978 Philips 070 transistor radio, which had been owned by her grandfather and wouldn't play music.

As an offering of love, Shermer set about trying to bring the radio back to life so Jennifer would have a piece of her grandfather with her. But after trying everything, including "percussive maintenance" (smacking it against something hard), the radio simply would not play.

Three months later, they were married in Shermer's home. Jennifer was feeling lonely, wishing her grandfather could have been there to give her away at her wedding. She whispered to Shermer that she wanted to tell him something in private, so they escaped to the bedroom, where they heard music playing. With no sound system, iPhones, or laptops around to play music, they searched for open windows, thinking the music must be coming from outside. They even checked the printer/fax machine, thinking perhaps it had a hidden radio.

They found nothing.

The article describes best what happened next.

"At that moment Jennifer shot me a look I haven't seen since the supernatural thriller The Exorcist *startled audiences. 'That can't be what I think it is, can it?' she said. She opened the desk drawer and pulled out her grandfather's transistor radio, out of which a romantic love song wafted. We sat in stunned silence for minutes. 'My grandfather is here with us,' Jennifer said, tearfully. 'I'm not alone.'"*

The radio stopped working the next day.

The article goes on.

"Jennifer is as skeptical as I am when it comes to paranormal and supernatural phenomena. Yet the eerie conjunction of these deeply evocative events gave her the distinct feeling that her grandfather was there and that the music was his gift of approval. I have to admit, it rocked me back on my heels and shook my skepticism to its core as well. I savored the experience more than the explanation. The emotional interpretations of such anomalous events grant them significance regardless of their causal account. And if we are to take seriously the scientific credo to keep an open mind and remain agnostic when the evidence is indecisive or the riddle unsolved, we should not shut the doors of perception when they may be opened to us to marvel in the mysterious."

Maybe it was a coincidence that the coyotes started howling right when I called them in. Maybe coyotes can't really telepathically communicate with humans. Maybe humans can't really become One with steel rebar until it wants to "play."

Maybe it didn't mean anything that the radio started playing on Jennifer's wedding day. Maybe it's impossible for the dead to communicate with us through inanimate objects. Or perhaps the Universe is simply more mysterious and marvelous than we can yet explain with scientific rationalism. Maybe science will one day catch up.

Or maybe some things are meant to stay a mystery.

As Martha says, "The miracle is always a coincidence in which God chooses to remain anonymous."

But don't trust me. Try it for yourself.

HERO'S GUIDEPOST:
Be Open to Magic

As long as you're stuck in a cynical worldview that dismisses magic and miracles as nonsense, you'll limit your access to real-life miracles. But even if you're awash in doubt, you just might get surprised. Miracles aren't reserved for mystics and monks. Sometimes they show up to break through the cynicism of even the most skeptical among us. *Because that's how loved we are.* The Universe wants you to believe in magic so much that

Consciousness will pull out all the stops to remind you that we are all connected and everything is purposeful. Especially if you're a hero on a journey with an important mission to fulfill.

While not widely discussed in mainstream culture, such miracles are a commonly experienced but poorly understood phenomena among meditators; in ashrams, monasteries, and spiritual retreat centers; and on the yogic path. The Sanskrit name for these miracles, *siddhis*, refers to a variety of spiritual superpowers that may be side effects of the spiritual path. Siddhis are reported to include such things as psychic powers; the ability to perform healings; the capacity to influence outcomes; the ability to remember past lives; unusual tolerance of heat, cold, and hunger; the ability to choose the timing of one's death; and teleportation and levitation (advanced siddhis). Spiritual teachers recommend caution around siddhis like these, which can degrade into sorcery, be used to manipulate others, and become a hook for the ego, a spiritual cul-de-sac distracting you from the true path. But when practiced from a place of pure integrity, perhaps such siddhis can be used to help heal the world. Are you curious? Would you be open to such things being real? If you're willing to be humble, stay open to miracles, and allow yourself to be used as a pure vessel in service to one of God's holy ideas, you just might become a practitioner of white magic.

HERO'S PRACTICE:
Become One with Synchronicity

When synchronicities happen, they feel like miracles, and this helps us feel connected to All That Is. But most of us tend to see the synchronicity as "other," as if it's happening outside of us, a miraculous gift from beyond. Such synchronicities feel haphazard. We can't predict when they'll come, and yet we crave more of them once we've tasted a few. But what if, rather than waiting for synchronicity to visit us, we can *become* synchronicity? Rather than simply hoping for more synchronicities, transpersonal psychologist Ted Esser, PhD, invites us to merge with synchronicity itself and allow ourselves to be synchronicity, not only for ourselves but also for others. The first day I practiced this, I was just walking around, living my everyday life without doing anything special, and three separate people told me that I was a "sign from the Universe," delivering much-needed messages that guided their paths. It felt like the Universe was winking at me.

So try this. Instead of waiting for synchronicity to find you, let yourself become synchronicity for someone else. When you let the Universe use you, you just might become someone else's miracle without even lifting a finger.

1. Each morning, take a moment to close your eyes and quiet your mind.

2. Set the intention to merge with synchronicity.

3. Feel yourself becoming One with synchronicity.

4. Invite synchronicity to guide you in your daily life, and if it resonates with you, ask that synchronicity use you to be someone else's miracle.

5. Heighten your awareness as you navigate your daily life. If you're not paying attention, you might miss synchronicities that arrive to guide your path. Notice whether other people comment that your presence is a synchronicity for them. The more you practice this, the more you're likely to become aware of the synchronicities that are all around you.

CHAPTER 15

Commit to Illuminating the Truth

Melanie and I had been counting down the days until we went to Martha's ranch, and when the day of our trip finally arrived, we were both too excited to eat breakfast. We drove down to San Luis Obispo from San Francisco, and as we got off Highway 101 and started driving east, out into the boonies, the fog hung low over a lake. Melanie said, "It feels like the Mists of Avalon, like we're leaving the real world and pulling back the veil."

She was exactly right. Birds stopped singing. Time seemed suspended. It was clear we were opening the wardrobe to enter Narnia. Then—voila! We were driving into Martha's ranch, right up to the butterfly gates (of course there were butterfly gates!). What proceeded to unfold was so magical I'm still pretty Wordless about the whole experience.

Martha invited Melanie and me into the ring with the horses, along with equine therapist Koelle Simpson. Koelle brought me into a pen with a new horse who had been brought in just for this exercise. I was instructed to simply set an intention of what I wanted to learn from the horse and then observe what showed up. I set the intention to examine my leadership skills, both strengths and weaknesses, in preparation for this training program for doctors all of us were co-creating. I wasn't feeling confident in my leadership skills, so I wanted the horses to teach me where my growth edges might be.

Feeling shy and a bit awkward, under the microscopic gaze of Martha, Martha's CEO and master coach Bridgette Boudreau, Koelle, and Melanie, I went into the covered ring, alone with the horse, and started walking around to see what the horse would do. The horse followed me around the ring, sniffing at me as we walked.

I got more daring. I spun in a circle. So did the horse.

I switched directions. The horse spun the opposite way.

Then I picked up my speed, running around the pen. The horse ran, too.

I got more frisky. I did a cartwheel. And the horse backed away from me, looking at me with a sideways glance.

Martha and Bridgette laughed, pretending to give voice to what the horse was thinking. "Ooh, bitch got all upside down on me."

I noticed that when I started getting attached to the horse doing what I wanted, when I got graspy or panicky or anxious or fuzzy in my intention, the horse looked at me like I had two heads.

Note to self about my leadership skills: Tap in, get clear on intentions, don't attach to particular outcomes.

I loved the feeling of joining up with the horse. It felt like having hundreds of whales dancing, so I spent a lot of time buddying up with the horse, getting all up in her face and hugging her. The horse cuddled back. Koelle said, "You seem a little timid around the horse. Try making your energy bigger."

I said, "I don't want to scare her."

Koelle handed me a rope I could throw around. She assured me it wouldn't hurt the horse and suggested I try playing with it. I didn't know what to do with it, so I curled it up and just threw it at the horse. She jumped—startled—and backed away. I ran right up to her and apologized for scaring her.

That's when Martha called me on it. "Hmm. Lissa, you set a boundary, asked the horse to move back a bit, and then when she respected your boundary, you apologized. Why?"

Gulp. I did do that. But I didn't mean to set a boundary. I was just throwing the rope around. I loved snuggling the horse. I didn't want her to go away. I approached her and joined up with her again.

Martha pointed out what I had just done. "Why are you afraid of setting boundaries with the horse?"

"Because I'm afraid she won't like me."

"But she's eating your hair right now, Lissa. She's slobbering all over your pretty sweater. Do you want her that close?"

I petted the horse. "Sure, it's fine."

"Don't you ever feel like you just want a little space, like maybe the horse is too much all up in your business?"

I asked myself honestly how I felt. Yes, the horse was a little too close for comfort. But she was sweet. And I wasn't scared of her. Sure, my sweater was getting a little slobbery, but it was washable.

Martha asked, "What are you afraid will happen if you set a boundary?"

I felt silly admitting that I felt like the horse wouldn't like me and wouldn't want to join up again if I set too many boundaries. I didn't want the horse to get the wrong idea. I was afraid if I created space, the horse wouldn't come back.

That's when I saw it. There it was again, glaring right back at me through this horse. My desire for intimacy was so frickin' grasping, so needy. I needed to be needed in order to feel good about myself, so I energetically invited people to snuggle up so close to me that I let myself become the Cosmic Tit. I failed to set boundaries, then I would give until I was depleted, and then I'd get royally pissed because people were too close and demanding. They'd start eating my hair, and I'd start feeling like a depleted doormat. Yet it was nobody's fault but my own! I was literally inviting this dynamic, which had become a pattern all over my life. Others were just reading my energy, just like the horse was, and it was saying, "Come on in. I'll be your best friend, even though I don't know you at all." I thought I had broken this pattern, but it was so ingrained that it still snuck out.

Koelle suggested I try throwing the lead at the horse again. I did, and the horse backed away.

Martha said, "See, she respected your boundary, and she's not mad at you. Try joining up again."

The horse joined up right away and started spinning when I spun in circles.

Martha said, "Did she reject you? Did it ruin your connection?"

Nope.

Note to self: Boundaries are healthy. Cosmic Tit = depletion. If I was going to train doctors, I needed to join up at appropriate times, but I needed to keep a clear boundary so I didn't make it my mission to personally save every single doctor in the program.

For the next exercise, Bridgette, Melanie, and I were invited into a fenced-in area that had one inner ring with a small entry that opened into an outer ring. Three frisky horses awaited us inside the outer ring. Martha explained that the purpose of this exercise was to demonstrate that, while one-on-one join-ups with a horse feel good and come easily to me, they weren't scalable. If I was really destined to heal health care on a grand scale, I would need to learn what she called "herding energy," which was a way to use energy so that you could lead many horses (or people) at once without depleting yourself.

The goal, we were instructed, was for us to work as a team to take all the horses on one lap around the outer ring before peeling off one horse into the inner ring—and keeping him there. Then we were to get the other two horses to go around the outer ring again before peeling off the second horse into the inner ring. Then we were to have a final lap with the one remaining horse, and after the last lap, the third horse was to join the others.

To make things harder, we weren't supposed to talk, but we could freely use elaborate charades to try to communicate what we wanted to do.

Our first attempt was, well, a total cluster fuck. The horses galloped, out of control, cruising right past the entry to the inner ring. At one point, I was inclined to just go up to one horse, join up, and lead him into the ring. But Martha noticed my inclination and stopped me. That was my pattern, but that would have been cheating. This was a herding exercise. No one-on-one join-ups were allowed.

So we regrouped. We modulated our energy. Brought it down. Waaaaay down. We got Wordless. We tapped into Oneness. We communicated non-verbally with the horses and asked if they'd be willing to play our little game. We stopped grasping and let go of attachment to outcomes. Then, with nothing but very subtle hand motions, the first horse trotted into the center ring, then the second, then the third.

It felt like magic.

Note to self: Be careful what you communicate without words. Make sure your energy is in alignment with your intentions. Avoid the tendency to solve problems with one-on-one join-ups, which aren't scalable.

———————————————

After we finished the equine therapy, Martha and Bridgette led Melanie and me through a fork-bending exercise. Martha brought out special forks she had bought just for this purpose, since she had become silverware's nemesis after learning to bend flatware and had been forbidden from bending any more silverware in her home by her partner, Karen.

So how do you bend very thick metal you couldn't bend with sheer might? Martha recommends getting Wordless, then becoming One with the fork and asking it if it feels like "playing."

Easier said than done.

I was so frustrated from 6 months of trying to bend my fork that I was tempted to utter "Bugger off, Martha" when she picked up her fork and effortlessly folded it in half with her tiny hands. Bridgette followed suit.

Melanie and I asked our forks if they wanted to play. I thought mine said, "Sure!" But then I realized I'm not very fluent in fork. Clearly, I misinterpreted what my fork was saying because that fork was not budging. *No fork for you, Lissa.* Using the exact same forks Bridgette and Martha were using, Melanie and I could not, either with sheer might or energetic cooperation with forkness, bend those damn forks. Martha told us to take the forks home with us, to keep practicing, to keep the faith in Oneness and magic, and to wait until the forks told us they wanted to play. I pocketed my fork with a bruised ego and a bit of a chip on my shoulder.

When I thought about why I could easily call in the animals but I could not, for the life of me, bend my fork, I realized that my failure to bend the fork might revolve around a limiting belief. While I still had my doubts, I had no problem with the idea that animals and people have brains and, therefore, consciousness and that, perhaps, on an energetic level, we can communicate telepathically. But I did have trouble buying that people can communicate energetically with inanimate objects. I believe that a whale has consciousness. But a fork? I get that everything is made of energy and that a metal fork is just as much made of energy as a human or a dolphin. But to me, inanimate objects—not to dis forks—are less *alive* than an animal or a human. When I got honest with myself, I realized I didn't truly believe I could become One with a piece of metal.

As long as I believed bending my fork wasn't possible, it simply wasn't possible. Surely, Martha and Bridgette were just special: Watching them bend their forks didn't convince me it was possible. Shortly after we returned from Martha's ranch, Melanie texted me a photo. It was her fork—folded all the way in half like a sweet little yoga forward bend. When Melanie did it, I realized I'd be able to also. Suddenly, my belief shifted.

I was at a Christmas party when I got the text, but as soon as I returned home, I approached my altar, got Wordless, and asked the fork whether it wanted to play. The fork said, "I thought you'd never ask." Then I picked it up, closed my eyes, and bent that fork in half effortlessly. It was like cutting into softened butter.

I then went on a rampage around the house, finding increasingly thicker and thicker silverware. All of them wanted to play, and I was bending forks and spoons willy-nilly until Matt banned me from the silverware drawer because some of the flatware wouldn't bend back without a funny little kink.

The time Melanie and I spent at Martha's ranch had been an experiment. Martha and her team used us as guinea pigs to see how a doctor would respond when taken to what they jokingly called "Magic Camp." The experiment gave us confidence that it was aligned to move forward with launching the Whole Health Medicine Institute, which was birthed in the spring of 2013, just before the launch of my book *Mind Over Medicine.*

Both launches were a lesson in surrender. The old Lissa, the Victoria-driven Lissa, would have clung to certain outcomes, such as attaching to whether or not we filled the program at the Whole Health Medicine Institute, whether my book hit the bestseller list, or whether the PBS special came through. I said a little prayer as I rang in New Year's 2013. I lit candles and burned incense on my home altar, and I asked that Divine Will be done, regardless of what I hoped to achieve. I turned over my desires in service to the highest good of all beings, trying to let go of attachments to particular outcomes. I realized that, if you're always striving to get "there," you never really enjoy being HERE. Having befriended many ambitious celebrities by this point, and potentially being on the threshold of becoming one of those ambitious celebrities myself, I realized there was a trap that would be easy to fall into. I discovered that many of these celebrities were always striving for the next big achievement, no matter how rich, famous, successful, and helpful they were. There was always something more to achieve: More people to serve, more awards to win, more external validation to gain. Martha and Rachel had influenced me greatly, helping me to recognize that there was no "there" there. There was only right here, right now, and we were all "enough" in the present moment.

I realized that if I was always grasping at the next big shiny achievement, my life and my work would become a black hole of dissatisfaction and unmet longing. I didn't want to become one of those people who, the minute she got what she desired, leaped straight into desiring the next sparkly accomplishment. I realized that the constant striving to get "there" was a real joy killer. Although Victoria cared deeply about achievement, I had distanced myself from her during the past few months, and my Inner Pilot Light cared more about being happy than about being rich, famous, or even succeeding in fulfilling my calling. I wanted to be able to savor my achievements and rest in the gratitude for how far I'd come on my hero's journey, even if I never made it any further than I had. As the clock struck midnight, I declared myself "there," regardless of what happened in my career.

I was left with a great sense of inner peace and fulfillment that New Year's Day. I realized I was good enough, just as I was. I had nothing to prove. I was worthy. I was valuable. And I didn't need external achievements to fill the hungry ghost within me, because I wasn't empty anymore. The flame of my Inner Pilot Light had expanded to fill me internally. I felt genuinely whole, perhaps for the first time in my life.

This realization of fulfillment and wholeness was its own sort of holy grail, but I was still caught up in the holy grail I was teaching about in *Mind Over Medicine*. The wellness model I had downloaded on my hike, which I had written the book about, offered a radically different way for patients and doctors to partner in the approach to illness and health. And, of course, once the hero finds the holy grail, the next step is to bring it back to the Ordinary World.

Launching the Whole Health Medicine Institute and publishing my book was part of my journey on The Road Back. But one last phase of the journey awaits before the hero returns with the holy grail: The Resurrection. The hero has to be metaphorically purified before returning to the Ordinary World with the proverbial bloody hands of the journey. Having been to the realm of the dead in the Innermost Cave and having been cleansed in the Ordeal, a final Resurrection is necessary before bringing the holy grail to the Ordinary World. The forces of darkness get one more shot at the hero, so The Resurrection is a sort of final exam. If The Resurrection is a success, the hero can return to the Ordinary World reborn as a new being with new insights.

If the hero doesn't "die" and get resurrected before returning to the Ordinary World, those she left behind can't receive what the hero will bring home. You may have experienced this in your own journey. Sometimes you break from the Ordinary World, you visit the Special World on your hero's journey and gain new wisdom and insights, and you try to share what you've learned with those you left at home. Yet, they can't hear you yet. To those in the Ordinary World, you're still the Squirrel Girl, the kid who used to rescue baby animals in hopes of winning her parents' approval. They still view you as one of them, even though you've changed. Because they don't realize you've evolved on your hero's journey, they can't yet receive you as someone who can help.

Not to compare myself to Jesus, but apparently even Jesus—the quintessential hero—struggled in this way. In *Jesus: What He Really Said and Did,* scholar Stephen Mitchell writes, "Jesus's townspeople, like his mother and brothers, couldn't accept him as a genuine teacher and healer. They saw him only as he had been: a poor carpenter, with a rumor of illegitimacy about his birth. They didn't see the magnificent human being he had become after his awakening." This is why the final "death" and resurrection is an essential part of the hero's journey. Once the Ordinary World has witnessed this miracle, the hero is transformed into someone those at home can trust to serve them, though perhaps we will always have trouble being perceived as heroes in our own literal or metaphorical hometowns.

After *Mind Over Medicine* launched in May 2013, I felt a quickening in both my professional development and my spiritual growth. For a while, I had been feeling the pulse of something big that was going to happen in the future. But now there was no more waiting for some elusive "someday." The time of grooming was behind me. The big thing was happening at warp speed in present time, and I just had to trust the process, strap on my seat belt, and go for the ride. I was about to arrive home with the holy grail, and then my real service would begin.

———————————————

Along with that feeling came the burden of a heavy responsibility. I sensed the gravity of what I had been called to do, and I knew I had to tread carefully in order to step into the role I was called to play in healing our broken health care system. I was brooding about this responsibility on a plane ride to Fargo, North Dakota, where I planned to give a TEDx talk. Just as we were about to touch down, right before the wheels hit the ground, the pilot gunned the engine, and the plane took off again into the wild blue yonder.

This had never happened to me on a plane before, and most of my fellow passengers acted as surprised as I was. Everyone on the plane exchanged worried looks. My first heart-stopping thought was "Terrorists have hijacked our plane!"

My phone was still in airplane mode or I would have called my daughter while we were low to the ground. What ever happened to those satellite phones docked in the seat in front of you above your tray table? While the plane flew back up into the skies, I rehearsed what I would say if I could pick up the phone and call the people I love most.

I would call Siena and thank her profusely for choosing me as her mother. She would tell me she used to be a fairy and then she fell in love with me, and because she was a fairy, I couldn't see her, and it made her sad. So one day she flew into my vagina and deposited her fairy wings into my heart so I'd always have fairy magic in my heart, and then, wingless, she hobbled over to my belly and grew into a baby so she and I could kiss and hug in person. I'd thank her for giving up her wings so we could spend whatever time we had in this life together. And I'd remind her that she is here on a Divine assignment and that her only job is to be the most Siena she can possibly be.

I would call my mother and thank her for being the best mother a girl could ever have. I would apologize for being the worst version of myself whenever she was around and bow at her feet for loving me unconditionally. I would call Matt and remind him that it has been an honor to be his wife and that I have never felt as loved by anyone as I've felt since I met him 11 years ago. I would thank him for sticking with me, even after I quit my job and threw our lives into turmoil.

I'd call all of my friends and family, one by one, and thank them for being in my life, for helping me grow, for making me a better person, for challenging me, for celebrating with me, for shaping me, for loving me in spite of, even because of, all of my imperfections, and for being patient with me on my hero's journey. I'd cry over how much I love them and promise to come back if there's an afterlife. My heart would burst open. Maybe I could play them love songs through broken radios, and they would know I was still with them.

If I could only find a phone, I would ensure that no love was left unexpressed by the time I died in the plane crash. Nobody would ever doubt that they mattered to me. I would feel complete.

This is what went through my mind as the plane soared east for at least a half hour.

Then, slowly, as my heart burst with love, the plane turned around. A while later, the plane circled back to the airport, and we finally landed. I remembered in that moment that we must all do this, we must all remember to express our love and open our hearts, not only when tragedy strikes but also every day.

I barely made it to my connecting flight, but when I did, I had a whole new perspective on everything. During the flight, I e-mailed one of my magic mentors, a psychologist who gave a TED talk that, at the time of this writing, has garnered over 18 million views. I expressed my fear that my TEDx talk would wind up alienating the very people I was trying to help. When I arrived in Fargo, I received her reply, and after reading her response, I realized what I needed to do with my speech.

———————————————

There's a whole polarity in medicine between two often vehemently aggressive camps. The closed-minded Western medical camp believes that it's all bunk unless you can prove it in a randomized, controlled clinical trial. These are the mind-body skeptics for whom I wrote *Mind Over Medicine*. For years, I was firmly in this camp, as was my father. Then there's the alternative/holistic/antimedicine camp, which believes that doctors are evil and that Western medicine is out to get us and that we should skip all drugs and surgeries.

Many wonderful healers lie in the middle, joining neither camp while accepting the best of what both camps have to offer. Like them, I am not in either camp. I am Switzerland, and when I sought counsel from my magic mentor, she reinforced the need for me to stay this way, that as long as I refused to be baited into picking sides, I could be of great service, that as long as I stayed smack-dab in the middle, I was dangerous because neither camp could write me off. As long as I was free from agenda or ego-driven motives, as long as I stayed pure in my open, unattached, curious seeking of the truth, nobody could make me wrong, because the truth is never wrong. Open, humble curiosity in search of the truth makes you bulletproof.

In an article about medical education published in the journal *Family Medicine*, Dr. Catherine McKegney compared the medical hierarchy to a neglectful, abusive, dysfunctional family.[1] In her model, the "grandparents"

————————————

1 McKegney, C. P., "Medical Education: A Neglectful and Abusive Family System," *Family Medicine* 21, no. 6 (November–December 1989): 452–57.

are the department chiefs and senior faculty at university programs. The "parents" are the attending physicians, the junior faculty at universities, and science teachers in medical schools. The nonphysician faculty are the "in-laws," with the gift of perspective but the stigma of being an outsider. Senior residents are the "older adolescents," worried about their impending independence as they're about to fly from the nest. Interns are the "school-age children," yearning to be competent but not really having a clue what they're doing. Medical students are the "babies," and they're the most vulnerable to the abuse.

We know that abused or traumatized children go on to have a predictable set of characteristics, and, often, abused children go on to become abusers. But the general public doesn't realize that our medical education system is fraught with ritualized abuse that functions very much like an abusive family dynamic. In order to heal health care and awaken the industry, reclaiming the lineage of the healer, we have to stop the cycle of abuse. This means that if my calling is to help heal this dysfunctional system, it's imperative that I stay Switzerland and be very careful not to pick sides. My role as a force for healing health care is to be the dysfunctional family's therapist and to mediate from the heart. Like postapartheid's Truth and Reconciliation Commission, all parties need a chance to be heard, honored, and acknowledged. Apologies and forgiveness will be required. Amends must be made. We would all have to open our hearts to find the compassion for one another that would allow healing. That's what I needed to convey when I got up on stage in Fargo.

I did my best to relay this message, all the while feeling the gravity of my mission. I almost cried up there on that stage. The day after my speech, I led the first of many community conversations on my book tour among doctors, nurses, alternative health care providers, and patients. As we all spoke, I had a breakthrough. As doctors, we are traumatized by our training, the limitations of the health care system, and the very nature of what it means to be a doctor, which is to be on the front line of a lot of suffering: death, disease, disability, despair. We've had to come to work sick, we've skipped our postpartum leaves and left our babies, we've had bloody scalpels thrown at us by physician professors who cursed at us, and we've stayed awake to help others when we should have been sleeping. We've witnessed children dying, dismemberment, and those who die when we did everything we could to save them. We've gone through a hazing worse than any fraternity, something similar to what soldiers experience. Yet people expect soldiers to have post-traumatic stress disorder (PTSD). They don't expect doctors to suffer from this.

Having gone through all of this trauma, it's easy to get frustrated with the entitlement of patients and the disrespect of alternative health care providers who dismiss the often life-saving work we do as doctors. Sometimes it feels like they don't appreciate the sacrifices we make in order to do this work. Doctors feel unappreciated, devalued, and disenfranchised. They feel helpless and victimized by the system. They've forgotten that we are not helpless, that our profession belongs to us, that the lineage is on our side, and it's not only our right but also our *responsibility* to take back our calling.

Rather than feeling victimized by forces that may seem corrupt—managed care insurance companies, the pharmaceutical industry, and political lobbies—perhaps we can feel grateful for these organizations, for all they have taught us about how *not* to practice medicine, for helping us recognize what is out of alignment with the integrity of the true healer. Rather than judging those who participate in these organizations, shaming them and making them wrong, maybe we can thank them for helping us remember who we really are as healers. Maybe we can even find it in our hearts to feel compassion for the perpetrators of abuse within our system. What must have happened to make them capable of committing such acts of emotional and physical violence against those they have vowed to serve? What untended wounds are eating away at their souls? Is it possible that if we soften our judgments, we can meet them at the level of the heart and appeal to the humanity we all share? I believe that, at our core, we are all in service to the same thing. Some have just lost their way. They don't need our judgment; they need our love. Love is exactly what we need in order to reclaim our profession and bring the "care" back to health care. And it's not just medicine that has lost its way. All of our systems are at risk: politics, the law, banking, education, and corporate America.

Bringing "care" back to health care is easier said than done, though. There are many forces threatening to sabotage reform. It's not easy to mobilize doctors and other health care providers to reclaim our profession when so many are gripped with PTSD. Health care providers need to help themselves before they can participate in healing our system, otherwise they just infect the system with their own wounds. The problem is that most don't even know they have PTSD. We tend to normalize the trauma. Every health care provider has been through the fire in some way, so we've come to think it's an unavoidable part of the job. We've been brainwashed to believe that it's our job to just buck up and keep going, not realizing that by failing to acknowledge the trauma and heal from it, by shutting down and closing our hearts, we are losing the very part of us that makes us exceptional healers.

Some health care providers have done a great deal of difficult personal and spiritual growth work to heal from the trauma of our profession. But most are blind to the fact that they have experienced profound trauma. They don't even realize they may be perpetuating the cycle of abuse because of their own unhealed trauma.

It's not just doctors who are traumatized. Nurses, nurse practitioners, physician assistants, midwives, and other health care providers who report to doctors are often traumatized by the doctors, who are so exhausted and abused and overworked that those who help them care for patients often bear the brunt of their misplaced anger. Psychologists call it sublimation, a defense mechanism whereby you suppress a socially inappropriate impulse and replace it with a substitute you deem to be more socially acceptable. (Your boss yells at you, and you're not allowed to yell back, so you come home and kick the dog.)

But nurses are not dogs paid to get kicked by traumatized doctors who haven't healed themselves. Nurses and physician extenders are healers in their own right, and when it comes to the art of true healing, they often practice it better than doctors. Doctors can learn much from those who take orders from them.

The trauma is systemic. Complementary and alternative medicine practitioners—the acupuncturists, chiropractors, naturopaths, energy healers, Reiki masters, and homeopaths—often suffer the disrespect of doctors, who tend to dismiss them as quacks. These practitioners practice their healing arts and get real results with patients; sometimes their patients even experience spontaneous remissions. Then when the patient shares what's happening with the doctor, the doctor may tell the patient that the treatment is a waste of money or it's dangerous. The doctor may even scoff at a spontaneous remission or write it off as a misdiagnosis. In doing so, the doctor is disrespecting both the alternative medicine practitioner and the patient who has chosen to see that healer. The doctor is questioning the patient's intuition and undermining the authority of a fellow healer. Such behavior eats away at the patient's self-trust, disempowering the patient's own self-healing abilities.

Patients are also traumatized by the doctors who don't acknowledge the body's inner healer. They're hurt by the physicians who get pissed off if a patient questions them or asks for a second opinion. They're harmed by the doctor who walks in, makes no eye contact, and then delivers bad news without a lick of compassion or any healing touch. They're traumatized by having their autonomy disrespected when the doctor walks in and starts performing a procedure without fully explaining what is happening. Patients are taught to respect doctors and follow their orders, so it's hard for them to speak up and ask for what they need, and when they do, they're often met with resistance on the part of the doctor, so they wind up learning helplessness and feeling victimized by the system. It makes it that much harder for the patient to be proactive.

Like others within the system who have given away their power, patients wind up playing the victim role, blaming their doctors or getting angry at the system. Like the limp, shocked rats in the study on learned helplessness, patients feel powerless to change their circumstances. And, as I explained in *Mind Over Medicine,* this learned helplessness has been scientifically proven to weaken the immune system and inhibit the body's ability to heal. Just as healers must stand up and reclaim the lineage of their professions, patients must reclaim their own power, standing up with their autonomy, their intuition, their willingness to question and participate in changing the system from within, and their vote. It all starts with change at the level of the healer-patient relationship. When patients and healers participate in this call to action, not from a place of blame or judgment, not as angry activists out to shame the "bad guys" in politics or the legal system or health-related industries but as a call to the hearts of the human beings who participate in these systems, we just might be able to perform white magic in health care.

This too is easier said than done. The temptation to lash out with anger and judgment or to allow the aftermath of trauma to paralyze us into inaction seems almost unavoidable. But after what I've experienced on my hero's journey, I now believe in miracles. In fact, I'm not even so sure they're miracles anymore. Perhaps they are the new normal.

I finally understand part of my role. I am a bridge, a translator. I find myself apologizing to patients on behalf of doctors who have hurt them. I apologize to doctors for the fact that they've been harmed by other doctors, and I apologize on behalf of patients who don't appreciate their service and sacrifice. I apologize to alternative health care providers who feel dismissed and disrespected by doctors who don't understand what they do. And at the same time, I'm standing for all of us to move beyond our victim stories into a place of sacred activism. If we can stop feeling helpless and at the mercy of forces we believe are beyond our control, if we can forgive each other and ourselves, if we can claim our true power, free of ego, and if we call in white magic instead, maybe real healing within the system can happen.

As a bridge, I attempt to stand with one foot in science and one foot in the spiritual realm, and I help people cross between the two. Most of all, I am a healer who supports empowered patients and conscious healers as they navigate their own hero's journey so we can all heal not only our health care system but also this planet that longs for us to wake up.

We can't keep fragmenting into "us" versus "them." The only way our health care system will heal is for all of us—healers and patients alike—to hold hands, united by a common intention, fueled by that which is in the highest good. Maybe then, by tapping into our compassion for those who participate in the system in a way that feels greedy, closed-minded, or self-interested, we can activate a revolution of love that recruits our fellow human beings—the doctors who may have lost their way, the politicians who have compromised their integrity in order to get reelected, the hospital administrators who prioritize the bottom line over patient care, the malpractice attorneys who are just out to make a buck, and those who work for pharmaceutical companies and the insurance industry. These human beings are all patients, too. They have families and bodies that need care. They all have hearts. It's their health care system, too.

Regarding sacred activism, Charles Eisenstein writes, "What do we really want? Is it to triumph over the bad guys and be the winners? Or is it to fundamentally change the system? You might think that these two goals may not be contradictory. I think they are: first, because the pattern of 'fighting evil' comes from the same mentality as our competitive, dominator system; second, because in demonizing those we perceive as other, we drive them toward the very behaviors that justify our demonization; third, because we are unlikely to win at the power elite's own game; fourth, because even if we do win, we will have become better at being them than they are; fifth, because if we enlist allies based on the motivation of triumphing over those greedy folks, they will abandon us once we have achieved that goal, even if the deeper systems remain unchanged. This is what happens nearly every time a dictator is toppled. Thinking they have won, the people go home; someone else steps into the power vacuum, and soon everything more or less goes back to the way it was."

In other words, as astrologer Ophi Edut said to me just before my Ordeal in the Innermost Cave, you can't make something wrong and make a difference at the same time.

I now realize that we can't change health care—or reform the education system or affect climate change or feed the hungry, for that matter—by shaming people into doing the "right" thing.

So how do we affect real, systemic change when we feel helpless and hopeless? Whether it's healing health care or making change in whatever way your hero's journey might call you to participate, real change requires a combination of Being and Doing. Being, which represents the path of the spiritual seeker, stems from ending our inner wars, freeing ourselves from the judgments and limitations of the ego, radiating love, and being the change we wish to see in the world. It's about ending the story of separation and inviting those who participate in the system to make kind, compassionate choices, trusting that real change starts with accepting the world as it is, seeing the perfection in it, and then practicing love as an invitation to others to step into their higher selves.

But Being without Doing risks keeping love in a theoretical realm, a safe realm where it isn't tested and developed by encounters with the world. Moreover, we are not separate beings. To exist is to relate. Sooner or later, this state of peaceful Being naturally leads to Doing, stemming not from righteousness or moral outrage but from love. When you stop judging, accept the world as it is, and shift your consciousness, love inspires you to participate in spiritual service, to make yourself an instrument of change, simply because you care about your fellow human beings.

Activists who advocate for more Doing think it's not enough to just sit around on meditation pillows or pray for peace or Be love. Such activities seem to them a bit "airy-fairy"—a waste of time when there is so much urgent work to be done. They think it's naive to assume that evil will just evaporate because enough of us start Being love, and they assert that sometimes force is necessary in order to protect the innocent and the planet. But unless we combine Doing with Being, Doing risks reinforcing what isn't working, repeating ineffective actions that are determined by our own hang-ups, wounds, and blind spots. We are not separate beings. What we encounter outside ourselves mirrors something within. Sooner or later, the Doer moves naturally toward the inner work that marks the pursuit of Being.

Whether you're on a mission to heal health care or affect change in the world in the hundreds of other ways your hero's journey may lead you, the questions are the same. How must we Be? What must we Do? Sometimes, when we don't have clear answers, we're being called to simply stop, to pause, to regroup and reflect, to allow ourselves to rest in the space between stories and see what inspired action emerges when the time is right.

For me, the inner journey of Being came first and led me to the outer action of Doing. I chose to bring the holy grail home by teaching doctors and other health care providers at the Whole Health Medicine Institute, along with guest faculty like Martha Beck, Rachel Naomi Remen, Larry Dossey, Bernie Siegel, Bruce Lipton, Martín Prechtel, SARK, Jon Rasmussen, and other pioneers in the disciplines of mind-body medicine, shamanism, and spirituality. I'm facilitating community conversations to help heal the rifts in our system by spreading the word in *Mind Over Medicine, The Fear Cure,* and *The Anatomy of a Calling.* I'm broadcasting this revolution of love on two public television specials. I'm getting up onstage to speak about what I've learned. I'm teaching teleclasses like Medicine for the Soul, Finding Your Calling, Coming Home to Your Spirit, and Visionary Ignition Switch. I'm blogging my heart out and posting daily on Facebook.

Periods of Doing are still regularly interspersed with the call to pause and just Be. In the midst of all of this, in the flurry of a business that threatens to turn successful authors into megalomaniacs if we're not attentive to our inner work, I'm still committed to my daily meditation practice, as well as other spiritual practices that keep me grounded and centered in the core of my Beingness. Prioritizing the time to Be has required me to define success on my own terms.

In this very book, I am writing the definition of what success means to me.

Success is not defined by how famous I get, how much money I earn, or even how many people I serve with my work. Success is, first and foremost, making myself an offering to the Divine, allowing myself to be fully expressed, being an instrument of pure service, willingly participating with Something Larger that uses me in order to bring that which wants to be born into the world. I can't always know what the Divine has in store for me, so I can't even attach to a definition like "Success is putting the 'care' back in health care," though I sincerely hope that happens, if that is what is aligned with the highest good for us all.

Success is loving well, practicing kindness and compassion, and making sure those in my inner circle know they are my first priority, even more so than the fulfillment of my calling, though I believe the two are intertwined in a way that doesn't require me to choose between them. Every act of love—love for a child or a grandparent or a lover or a patient or a stranger— uplifts the revolution of love. Success is trusting my intuition and letting my heart lead, even when what I am being asked to do feels scary. Success is good health, abundant energy, moving my body often, and using a body compass that says "Hell yeah!" whenever possible. Success means lots of playtime, stillness, snuggles, music, laughter, roller coasters, dancing, skipping on the beach, time communing with nature, and intimate connections with my soul community. Success requires running a conscious business, such that every team member has an equally crucial role and is supported in all ways to serve out his or her purpose within the business impeccably.

While I don't define success by how much money the business earns, I do include in my definition of success a financial abundance that allows me to live comfortably and to be generous with my staff and my loved ones. I don't require much excess beyond that. Part of success is to recycle back any financial surplus in ways that serve the interconnectedness of all beings. Money is a side effect of my calling rather than a goal itself. If my business isn't a direct by-product of living smack-dab in the center of my purpose, I'm willing to release it. Most importantly, success is the deep, nourishing soul fulfillment that comes with being brave enough to choose love and make daily choices that keep you impeccably aligned with your purpose. Success is the buoyant joy that accompanies knowing your soul is leading the way. Success is freedom.

By this definition, I am grateful to feel very successful these days. It's been a long messy journey, but I feel incredibly blessed that I dared to say yes when that phone first rang. Mine is a big calling, not that anyone's calling is any more important than anyone else's. We are all bees in the hive serving out our equally crucial roles. But my journey continues to require a lot of courage. Sometimes it feels daunting. I finally stand before my calling— ready, willing, humbled—allowing myself to be used by the Universe. As Dr. Larry Dossey said to me when I was feeling discouraged, "The time is now. Welcome to the dance."

I know I am not in this alone. There are hundreds of thousands, millions even, who share this calling. We've all been on our own little ships feeling adrift at sea. But the time has come for us to find one another so we can create a powerful collective ship, one we will all steer, with no particular individual at the helm. This ship will amplify our individual intentions, and what is most right will prevail.

These days, I often find myself thinking back to the dream I had many years earlier, the one with all the people standing on the magnificent mountains, dressed in brilliant colors and tribal garb from all over the world. The people were standing shoulder to shoulder, covering the mountainsides like a great quilt, and all of them were facing due north, where a bright light was shining on their faces, illuminating them. That's what I see when I think of healing health care—or getting involved in environmentalism or humanitarian causes, or reforming education or politics or the economic system, or engaging in whatever greater purpose calls you forth. I see all of us standing shoulder to shoulder, each of us healing one another, facing north and being the light, united in Oneness as part of this revolution of love.

It all starts with you on your own hero's journey. This is how we change the world.

Once you've found the holy grail and you're on The Road Back, the forces of darkness will threaten to sabotage you. It's a constant practice to keep choosing faith over fear, to reach out to your magical mentors for help when you need them, and to get up on that metaphorical stage, speak your truth, and deliver the message you're here to deliver. The hero's journey is not just about finding a great job. It's about love. It's about enlightenment. It's about the evolution of consciousness of our planet, commanding us all to take this journey for ourselves.

Wherever you are in your hero's journey, keep the faith. The Cosmic Forces that dialed up that phone and called you to service will never abandon you. When you feel most adrift, you will be sent help in the form of magical mentors and synchronicities that feel like miracles. You may feel lost at sea, but you will *never* be alone, and you cannot fail if you are brave enough to follow the guidance that is with you always.

As Theodore Roosevelt expressed best in a quote that inspired the title of Brené Brown's book *Daring Greatly*, "It is not the critic who counts; not the man who points out how the strong man stumbles, or where the doer of deeds could have done them better. The credit belongs to the man who is actually in the arena, whose face is marred by dust and sweat and blood; who strives valiantly; who errs, who comes short again and again, because there is no effort without error and shortcoming; but who does actually strive to do the deeds; who knows great enthusiasms, the great devotions; who spends himself in a worthy cause; who at the best knows in the end the triumph of high achievement, and who at the worst, if he fails, at least fails while daring greatly, so that his place shall never be with those cold and timid souls who neither know victory nor defeat."

It's time to get in the arena. Claim your place in the mysterious unfolding of all that calls you forth.

HERO'S GUIDEPOST:

Gather with Your Soul Community to Expedite Your Hero's Journey

In *Cat's Cradle*, Kurt Vonnegut writes about how God organizes the world into units called a "karass." A karass is a group of incarnated beings whose job it is to bring into existence one of God's holy ideas. Members of a karass all further the collective purpose seamlessly, though many never even know they are part of this karass. Even if they never meet, they work together in harmony, in impeccable service to God's holy idea. Everything about their lives furthers the purpose perfectly, even though they may be furthering the purpose unconsciously. When you meet someone who is a member of your karass, even though it may make no sense to you on a human level, you will recognize them as a family member instantly. Your souls will resonate, even if you appear to have nothing in common on the human level. This is how the Divine gets important things done in the world. Your karass is like a peaceful army that activates to bring light into the world.

Vonnegut compares the karass to its polar opposite, which he calls a "granfalloon." A granfalloon is a group of people who think they are connected to each other in some way but have no spiritual connection whatsoever, like the Harvard class of 1986 or the Republican party or Mets fans. The people in these groups are completely unrelated to each other when it comes to their soul purpose. They may think they belong to the same tribe, but the bond is shallow, whereas the bond between members of a karass runs deep and pure. Members of the same karass are held to their purpose like electrons around a nucleus. Some live very close to the purpose. Some are further out. But all are held to the purpose by a spiritual magnetism. They may have never met each other, or they may be married to each other. They may work in the same field, or they may have very different careers. But their lives fit together in service to this shared spiritual purpose.

We are all here for an unknown purpose, and serving this purpose makes us feel fulfilled and enriched. But if we get seduced off purpose by ambition, fame, money, or the ego's grasping at comfort, our vitality gets stolen from us. When we commit to the purpose we're here to serve, when we give ourselves to serving it with great impeccability, everything begins to fall into place.

HERO'S PRACTICE:
Find Your Karass

Your karass is out there. You are already a part of it. Your life has great meaning, and if you become conscious of it, it speeds up the process. When the members of a karass know that others exist, something activates and the karass gets organized and can operate more efficiently. You may not know yet which karass you're in, but if you do, consider whether you know who's in your karass. See if you can find even one person who is serving the same purpose you are. Reach out to these people. Make a connection. Acknowledge your shared vision. These people are not your competition. They are your allies. If we all do this, perhaps we can serve our purpose more effectively.

If this idea resonates with you and you're interested in trying to find other sacred activists in your karass, sign up at Karass.org. As I write, this website is currently just a landing page, but if the Universe smiles on it, Karass.org will become a collaborative Open Source social media platform, co-created by generous spiritual software engineers who are trying to use internet technology to help sacred activists participate in movements that will uplift our world. If you want to be the first to participate in such a platform, just register your e-mail, and you'll be the first to be notified of ways you might find your karass, offer your gifts, and receive support for your visionary ideas.

Still need help sensing into whether you're part of the larger karass that is here to uplift humanity and save the planet? Then listen up. Shamans from indigenous cultures often use storytelling as a form of spiritual initiation and activation.

Shamans from indigenous cultures often use storytelling as a form of spiritual initiation and activation. If you're ready to be activated, download the MP3 of "The Gathering of the Tribe," a story written by Charles Eisenstein and published in *The More Beautiful World Our Hearts Know Is Possible*. Visit TheAnatomyofaCalling.com for the free download.

EPILOGUE

I thought this was the end of the story. Girl gets called to adventure. Girl takes a journey. Girl battles the forces of darkness. Girl finds the holy grail. Girl brings it home. End of story.

But I was wrong. I was humbled to realize that what I taught in *Mind Over Medicine* and shared as curriculum with other healers in the Whole Health Medicine Institute was not, in fact, the only holy grail I was meant to find. There was a whole other grail, one I was about to receive as a sacred transmission from Tosha Silver, the author of *Outrageous Openness*. The way Tosha and I met is no less magical than many of the other stories in this book, a cosmic dance of synchronicities that made it hysterically obvious that we were supposed to meet. When I met the Yale-educated, spiky-haired, tattooed, ex-astrology-reading, Hindu goddess–worshipping, Jew-who-loves-Jesus, wisdom-keeping, spiritual-teaching Tosha, she took one look at me and said, "We should hike. I think we have karma together." I giggled and thought, "Only in Berkeley."

The holy grail Tosha gave me was a scalpel, slicing through the layers of my Small Self and laying bare my soul. Until I met Tosha, I had been trying to learn the art of spiritual surrender, or rather, I should say that Victoria had taken over the wheel of my spiritual quest and was grasping at enlightenment the same way she clung to overachieving in medicine and writing. There's nothing more sneaky than the spiritualized ego! Yet, as Tosha taught me, letting the ego grasp at enlightenment is just another form of "Doership," another spermy way the ego tries to push its own agenda and make things happen. Before meeting Tosha, my relationship with surrender was one of resignation. Just like I surrendered the book that never got published as an offering of burnt ashes to the ocean, surrender was always a last resort. As Rachel Naomi Remen wrote, "Anything I had ever let go of had claw marks on it."

But Tosha taught me to surrender *first*. The process is simple. You acknowledge, without judgment, all of those things the ego grasps at—the problems you think are yours to solve, the desires you think you have to manifest, the unmet longings that weigh heavy on your heart, the disappointments you can't seem to release. Then you simply make them an offering to the Divine. You turn them over to Love Itself and trust that it's all handled. You ask for guidance and support, but you stop trying to control your life. It's not about handing a shopping list to God, filled with specifics about exactly what you want and what you don't want. Tosha says, "God is not your Costco."

The process is about truly letting go of grasping for what you want and resisting what you don't want. If you can't stop grasping or resisting, you can say a "change me" prayer. "Change me into someone who can let this go. Change me into someone who can accept what is." If you're trying to make a decision and feeling stuck, try this prayer: "If I'm meant to do this, show me a sign. If not, stop me." All the pressure to make the right decision falls away. The heart is unburdened almost instantly.

The art of spiritual surrender can be easily misunderstood as passivity, but there's nothing passive about it. It's just that in the wake of letting go, actions arise not from the grasping or resisting Small Self but from the inspired actions of the soul. You can tell the difference between enlightened action and ego-driven striving based on how you feel in your body. Is it inspired energy that leaps you to your feet and makes you say, with a full-body YES, "I'm doing this!" Or are you exhausted just thinking about what it will take to force what you desire into being? Say yes to inspired action because it's a Divine yes. Say no to dread because it's an ego trap.

After twelve years together and four difficult years of trying to repair our marriage, Matt and I finally decided to divorce. For years, we had been clinging to the happily-ever-after fantasy that we would still be together when we were 85 in our rocking chairs, but in spite of how we grasped at this fantasy, our marriage was tearing apart at the seams. We tried marriage therapy, read books about marriage, and worked on our patterns individually and jointly through psychologists, spiritual counselors, life coaches, and personal growth workshops. Matt and I loved each other. We parented Siena well together. We were peaceful domestic partners. But all of our efforts to save the marriage failed to feed the parts of our souls that yearned to be fed. As our individual soul paths diverged, we clung together. He tried to lure me down the path he was traveling, and I did my best to drag him along my path. But the distance between our respective hero's journeys grew increasingly obvious, as one crystal clear sign after another pointed towards the end of our marriage.

As anyone who has ever clung to a dissolving relationship can understand, it's no small feat to stop grasping at someone you love. It sounds noble and spiritual to try to let go of attachment to outcomes and trust that you'll be steered in the direction of the highest good, even if it means accepting the Cosmic No. But when that someone is your husband, the father of your child, your best friend, and your business partner, letting go feels like dying. It triggers all of your core survival fears and stirs up anything unhealed deep within—all your childhood traumas, your doubts about your worthiness, your vulnerability, your inner critics, your sense of not belonging, your worries about security, your concerns about what other will think, and the fear of growing old alone. As the end drew near, our fears got the best of us, rearing up like vicious beasts and taking us over as if we were possessed.

Making the decision to separate was hard enough, but neither of us could bring ourselves to say the word "divorce." For almost two years, Matt, Siena, and I still lived in the same house, with Matt living in the guest room and me staying in the bedroom we had shared. Denial can be a powerful delay tactic, but in our case, it was a life saver. If we had been forced to face the pain of divorce from the beginning, I'm not sure we would have had the coping tools to separate with kindness. Co-habitating as a separated couple worked for a while, until the ragged way people fall out of love started to take a toll on us, and we grew bitter and resentful. When we finally admitted to each other that it was time to move on, my heart hurt so much that I could feel it contracting, as if I was in labor. The pain would grip me for a minute or two, and just like during childbirth, the only way I could survive it was to breathe through it until the pain subsided. Then another contraction would wrack me until it too passed.

Matt was hurting too, and because we were in so much pain, the divorce mediation process started to get contentious. Worried about how I would continue to provide security for my daughter and myself and fearful that I would have to work even harder to provide for Matt as well, I stopped thinking about what was best for Matt, forgetting, in my self-absorbed fear and grief, that this is a man I love, someone who has been an extraordinary father to Siena, someone who I wish well. With my sense of security threatened, I armored up and started to defend myself, and Matt did the same. This led us both to lock into our singular points of view as we demanded what we believed we deserved. Things started getting ugly. We both knew this wasn't how we wanted to end our marriage, but we felt powerless to break out of the spiral of blame, defensiveness, fear, judgment, and jockeying for security.

That's when Tosha stepped in. Seeing how I had gotten caught in a struggle for survival, clinging to what I felt was rightfully "mine," Tosha said, "You think this is *your* money, *your* books, *your* house, *your* business. But Lissa, you wouldn't have *shit* if it weren't for God's largess."

Her words cut through the arrogance of my narrow, self-oriented perception like a scalpel.

"Remember, 100 percent of the money belongs to God, and God has the perfect solution." Tosha went on. "Ask to be shown the perfect settlement, as the steward of but NOT the owner of the money. Once you remember that all of it belongs to God, the right actions become clear. Let God take over. Give the whole divorce to God. This is your holy moment. You are ready, Lissa. You can do this."

I whispered an earnest prayer in the "change me prayer" format Tosha teaches. "Change me into someone who can surrender this to Divine Will without defending or grasping." The minute I said it, I felt my heart burst open to this man I had loved for so long, this man who gifted me with the most beautiful daughter, who is the best father I've ever met, whose happiness means the world to me. I felt an upwelling of compassion for him as I saw how his fears had been triggered, just like mine. When I told him about the epiphany Tosha had inspired, we were able to look into each other's eyes for the first time in months.

The next divorce mediation meeting became our last. The positioning and defending and angry energy dissipated, and we hammered out a settlement that felt generous to us both in less than an hour. A couple of weeks later, I got a very large and unexpected check in the mail, made out to me for exactly the amount of money I had agreed to pay Matt in the divorce settlement. Two years later, Matt and I now live next door to each other, where we share meals together from time to time, enjoy a genuine friendship, and happily co-parent Siena. The whole thing feels like one giant miracle. At the beginning of separation, Matt and I promised each other that love never ends; it simply changes form. For a long time, it seemed like love was getting lost, replaced by fear, anger, and judgment. But by remembering who we are and where all blessings come from, we are able to realize our dream of letting love change form in a way that nourishes us all.

Having lived this way for the past several years now, my life has become a vast, mystical experience of awe. Unexplainable miracles are an everyday occurrence, and they no longer surprise me. In fact, they have become my new normal. When I was telling spiritual teacher Byron Katie about some of the synchronicities that felt like miracles, she said, "Lissa, these things have been happening all along. It's just that you now have the eyes to see and the ears to hear."

I sense that she's right. There are miracles happening all around you, too. Do you see them? Do you hear them? Such miracles have increased my faith that it's safe to turn my life over to the Divine, to make myself an instrument and let the Universe play me. I trust that Divine Will is infinitely more intelligent than the will of my Small Self, and I no longer trust my Small Self to know what's best for me. I'm more interested in wading into the mystery every day, curious how the Divine will use me today, pregnant with possibilities.

It has been quite the emotional journey to navigate all of this. To expose my wounds to the people I care about—the ego stuff, the fear stuff, the personal growth edges that I haven't quite mastered—takes courage. Letting others see what my friend and colleague Amy Ahlers calls our "big ugly tails" tends to trigger all of our core fears of rejection and abandonment, of withdrawal of love. But to bear witness to someone's big ugly tail is a privilege and an opportunity to deepen the relationship beyond the idealistic views we might have of each other into the real truth of both our light and our shadows.

In a perfect world, maybe Victoria would be safely strapped into the backseat of the car of Lissa forever, with my Inner Pilot Light always at the wheel. But that's not what happens. Sometimes Victoria still inhabits the driver's seat and runs amok with me. The Gremlin still prattles on from time to time. I now realize that instead of judging or shaming these parts of my psyche, I'm better off just loving them, like gorgeous and treasured but sometimes naughty little children that I adore and accept. I now spend a lot of time practicing various versions of an Inner Child Meditation when Victoria or the Gremlin act up. Rather than judging or resisting the meltdowns of my Small Self, I finally realized she calms down much more quickly if I just treat her like a beloved child who needs my help. I ask her what she needs, listen patiently to what she wants me to hear, and promise her that she doesn't have to worry about any of it anymore, reassuring her that I am an adult and can handle it for her, so she can relax and go play. I let her express whatever emotions she might feel—sadness, fear, anger—and I sit with her emotions without belittling her or making her wrong for feeling what she feels. Then I comfort her until she feels better, holding her in my arms like I would my own daughter. (Download the free Inner Child Meditation I created at TheAnatomyofaCalling.com.)

When we can find compassion for how our egos and fears try to rule us, we can be gentler with ourselves and each other.

Another big epiphany came when I realized that the Universe doesn't just guide us with synchronicities that affirm we're in the flow and on the right path. We're also lovingly guided with doors that close. I used to think that if you couldn't open a closed door, you were a failure. But I now know that closed doors are not failures. They're merely redirects guiding us to the right path of our own hero's journey. We must be as grateful for the Cosmic No (or the Cosmic Not Yet) as we are for the Cosmic Yes.

When you're on a hero's journey, sometimes you'll get that inner nudge that insists that it's time to leave, as I did with leaving medicine and divorcing Matt. But keep in mind that a hero's journey doesn't always require leaving. Sometimes the most subversive, revolutionary act is to stay with something when it's hard. Staying when it would be easier to leave can be the ultimate spiritual practice. Sometimes staying requires the greatest feats of courage. If you're on the fence about staying or leaving, how can you tell the difference? This is when you'll want to turn your decision over to the Divine and follow the signs. Try this prayer: "If I'm meant to stay, guide me. If I'm meant to leave, make it clear."

There is within each of us a hero's journey waiting to happen. You may still be in the Ordinary World, feeling frustrated and waiting for the phone to ring with instructions for your Divine assignment. Or you may have received the call, but what was being asked of you is just too disruptive, too scary, so you're still refusing the call. Perhaps you accepted the call with the enthusiasm of a hero ready for the journey, only now you're on the Road of Trials, and things aren't going quite as you planned. You may even be in the Innermost Cave, battling the demons of darkness in your Ordeal. You may have found the holy grail, or you may not yet know what you are seeking. If you've found it, you may, like me, question whether it's the right grail. Once found, you may struggle on The Road Back as you return the holy grail to the Ordinary World. Wherever you are in your journey, may you trust the process and find your peace.

It wasn't until recently that I had a revelation about my hero's journey. Part of my journey was my own transition from a traditional hero's journey, as exemplified by the Star Wars–type heroes of Joseph Campbell's teachings, to a *heroine's* journey. As I walked the spiritual path and shifted from the head to the heart, I transformed from masculine operating principles to those of the Divine Feminine. How are a hero's journey and a heroine's journey different? Depth psychologist Anne Davin, PhD, who directs the Whole Health Medicine Institute with me, makes the following differentiations. Although the hero in Joseph Campbell's model goes into the Innermost Cave alone, ever the rugged individualist, the heroine is interdependent on others for her survival. The hero views humans and the Divine as separate. For the heroine, there is no separation between spirit and matter. All are One. The hero is self-sacrificing; the heroine receives from others. The hero survives against all odds; the heroine's ego dies to the perfection of whatever is happening, coming into agreement with what is, rather than forcing her will. The hero dominates; the heroine surrenders. The hero competes; the heroine collaborates. The hero revels in his victory, filled with pride; the heroine wears her humility as a jeweled crown. The hero never questions his value or direction; the heroine lives her life as an open question. The hero fights death, living in perpetual fight or flight; the heroine dives willingly into the still point of Beingness. The hero asks, "What can I get for myself?" The heroine asks, "How can I serve the dream?"

Like many heroines, my journey was initiated by a rupture in the form of my Perfect Storm. Anne Davin describes this rupture as an activating event that creates the perception of loss or disappointment, which leads the heroine to descend into a swamp of what can almost be described as delicious grief. During the rupture, she refuses to play the victim, instead embracing the tragedy with grace and sensual surrender. She then moves into a phase of transparency, using the action and power of her vulnerability to embody her wholeness in every moment. She courageously embraces all the many faces of her feminine self, including what may be judged by the culture as repulsive or frightening. This leads to a phase of receiving, during which the heroine remains open, exposed, and vulnerable while she receives the soothing contact and assistance from others who tend to her. She recognizes this as essential and compassionately allows herself to be nurtured through her crisis, which leads her to a final phase of action, during which she experiences a profound emotional and spiritual restoration that energizes new attitudes, perspectives, and outward movement.

The heroine's journey isn't about being male or female. As the consciousness of the planet shifts, more and more men are incorporating elements of the Sacred Masculine into their own journeys in ways that uplift the feminine, healing and empowering us all. Regardless of our gender, as we come into our wholeness and regain the balance between the Divine Feminine and the Sacred Masculine, we raise the vibration of the planet and bring more light into the world.

When it comes to finding and fulfilling your calling, you'll discover that you don't conjure up a calling; callings shape and remake you. Once upon a time, when I was the Squirrel Girl, I thought that my calling was to practice medicine. Then I thought my mission was to heal our broken health care system. Now I think our health care system is just a microcosm of many other systems that are ready to wake up. It's not just medicine that has been corrupted by out-of-balance masculine forces. It's not just medicine that is now yearning for an infusion and reclaiming of the Divine Feminine within the industry. Many others have been called to their professions the way I was called to medicine, only to find themselves feeling thwarted in their missions. Whether you're a healer, a teacher, a lawyer, a politician, or working in the corporate world, you may have found yourself in situations that threaten your integrity. You may feel like others in your industry are more fueled by greed than a true sense of purpose. You may feel helpless and victimized by the system.

But you are not a victim. You are heroic. If you have a calling, it's your responsibility to claim the calling. No matter how bad things have gotten within your industry, you are not helpless. You have the power to make a difference. As Margaret Mead said, "Never doubt that a small group of thoughtful, committed citizens can change the world; indeed, it's the only thing that ever has." Think one person can't make a difference? Try telling that to Nelson Mandela. Or Martin Luther King Jr. Or Mother Teresa. Or Gandhi.

I once had a more narrow view of what it means to be a healer. I thought it required me to go to medical school. In my case, given the grand scheme of things, I think I did the right thing by following that path. But I now realize that even though I don't work in hospitals anymore, I am still a healer. And you too are a healer if you are a force for Love in a hurting world. But practicing love doesn't require grandiose measures. You can be a force for love no matter what you do. You can be love in line at the coffee shop or while waiting to pick up your child from school. You can be a healer by volunteering at a soup kitchen or simply being kind to those who may not often receive kindness: the persecutors, the disenfranchised, the wounded. If you find yourself judging or blaming or shaming someone, ask yourself, "What would love do?" You can practice love by being gentle with yourself. You can choose love all day, every day, regardless of what you do for a living. In doing so, you claim your place in the revolution of love this world will require in order to become the more beautiful world our hearts know is possible.

To let love lead requires that you make peace with your ego so your Inner Pilot Light takes the driver's seat of your life. Doing so opens you to a vast world of mystery, awe, and wonder, where inner peace and freedom lie. Once you find this peace that transcends comprehension by the cognitive mind, once you turn your life over to be used by Divine Will, you will be given everything you need in order to fulfill your life's purpose. Your role may not be grand or sexy. It might be your calling to clean toilets with love or stock shelves with purpose. But your role will be every bit as important as the calling of the president. Each one of us has equal value. We are all part of the wholeness of things. All the parts of the whole have the same value in terms of the spiritual significance of things. I figure that if we can crack hearts open in the world of medicine, if we can help doctors and other health care providers get in touch with their hearts and their intuition, anything is possible.

This afternoon, after I finish writing this book, I am giving Grand Rounds to several hundred doctors about how to be the kind of doctor who practices love, with a little medicine on the side. It's the first time I've been invited back into the hallowed halls of the mainstream medical establishment, and instead of being scared, I'm brimming with excitement and gratitude. I used to be pissed at doctors. I was traumatized by doctors in the past when I felt like it was their job not only to avoid harming me but also to protect me. I felt victimized by doctors. But I now realize that those who hurt me were just as traumatized as I was and that they were passing along their wounds to me. We need not judge those who are hurting, those who are blind to their wounds and perpetuating the cycle of trauma. They are doing the best they can, and if we had endured what they did, we might do the same in their shoes. Instead, we have to break open our hearts to each other and heal the wounds from their source so we can reclaim what belongs to us: the ability to love, and with that love, the ability to heal.

I feel very purposeful in my desire to share the holy grails I have found. It's been a long, scary, beautiful journey, but by going back to the hospital, I am tapping into the lineage of the healer that predates antibiotics, scalpels, and chemotherapy by millennia. The hospital was where the biggest traumas of my life happened. At one point, I thought I'd never go back.

But the hospital is where I belong. I'm finally coming home.

This journey isn't so much about your job, though a professional mission can certainly be part of your life's purpose. It's bigger than that. This journey requires a lot of personal and spiritual growth work. Once you've done the heavy lifting, it requires a lot of maintenance. This is the meaning of your life, to become a clear channel so the Divine can flow through you and allow you to serve out this mysterious unknown purpose only you can fulfill. Your path won't be easy, because your ego will attach to what it desires, and you will be frightened of not getting what you want.

When you clear your channel of the residues of ego, when you truly trust that living in Divine alignment will bring you peace and magic, when you commit to letting yourself get used in service to this higher purpose, the fear dissipates, the ego takes its rightful place in the backseat of your life, and the majesty of your Inner Pilot Light can ignite this planet on fire. In the wake of this transformation, you will be left with nothing but gratitude. You will sit in awe, overflowing with wonder at the mystery that unfolds like a rainbow-colored rose, every petal more splendid than the last.

This morning, I noticed that my heart felt—open. That's not quite the right word, but it's the closest word I can find. It feels raw, vulnerable, fragile, tender—but, really, it's more like open. "Open" almost feels like a wound. But this opening doesn't exactly hurt. To quote Brené Brown, "I feel like a turtle without a shell in a briar patch." As uncomfortable as it feels at times, I wouldn't avoid it, because I choose this opening. It's more like feeling unguarded in a world filled with people who walk around with armor. To walk around this way feels supremely risky. I wonder what will become of me. Surely, it's foolish and naive to stand before a guarded person and lay down your armor. And yet, I keep laying my heart bare, in spite of the risk. I question whether this is the wisest practice. Maybe I should guard my heart more. Yet deep down, I sense that the open heart is not a weakness; it's the strongest thing in the Universe. Maybe we don't need to protect the heart in order to stay safe. Maybe it's where our ultimate safety lies. Or maybe we can simply trust ourselves to discern when we can lay our hearts bare and when it is most loving to tend to the delicacy of the heart with the self-nurturing of gentle protection, the way a daffodil bulb might get sheltered so that it can flourish into a blossom.

I don't really know. After all of this, I realize that the more I experience, the less I know. All I know is that we are here to love and to be loved, to open our hearts all the way and to let the impulse of love spawn a revolution that helps us remember Why We Are Really Here. Each of us will participate in this revolution of love in our own unique way as we navigate our own heroic journey. As we journey together, we will all wake up to the truth of what is real and why our souls chose to incarnate at this special time on Planet Earth.

This is why you are here, so we can co-create a more beautiful world together, one little miracle at a time.

If the phone is ringing for you, trust your heart if it tells you to take the call. Your instructions await you. The time is now.

ACKNOWLEDGMENTS

When you have been twice born in one lifetime, you start by thanking the ones who birthed you into the world the first time. Thank you, Mom, for all the ways in which you made it possible to be who I must be. I remember you telling me when I was a child, "All I want is for you to be happy." Thank you for supporting me as I followed my heart. I also remember you telling me, "The relationship is more important than being right," and you have lived that spiritual teaching with absolute impeccability. When people hear the story of my hero's journey, they often ask me how I had the courage to take the leaps of faith that I have, and I always tell them I somehow knew I would always land butter side up. I have you to thank for that. Thank you for all the love, sacrifices, and nurturing you have blessed me with my entire life. No daughter could possibly feel more loved.

Even though you're not with us in human form anymore, thank you, Dad. I miss you more than words can express, but I know from a thousand signs that you are with me always. I would never have walked this path without your influence. Sometimes I wonder whether you left us on purpose in order to help me make this journey from the head to the heart. Maybe, at least on a soul level, even the most rational fathers do such things in order to help their daughters become who they must be. I will be forever grateful for the blessing of being born your daughter.

I am grateful to all my ancestors for their influence in my life, especially my grandparents, Pearl Katherine and Victor Rankin, and Sara and Ed Wirick.

Thank you also Larry and Trudy Rankin for introducing me early on to many of the spiritual ideas that once seemed shocking but now feel mainstream. Thank you also to the whole Wirick clan for always helping me feel like part of a happy tribe.

For those who helped birth me the second time around, I have no words to express my gratitude, and there are so many of you who touched me in countless ways. Thank you Rachel Naomi Remen for allowing me to rest in your nest so love could hatch me. When a woman at Esalen told me, "You need to meet Rachel Naomi Remen," I wonder if she had any idea what a gift she was giving me. (Thank you, naked Esalen woman, whoever you are!) It is a rare blessing in our culture for a young woman to be adopted and initiated by an elder shamaness. I sometimes pinch myself, wondering what I did to get lucky enough to sit at your kitchen table. I love you like my second mother.

So many thank you's to you, Martha Beck. You had already been where you saw me going, and you normalized the experience for me in a way that allowed me to stay on course without freaking out too much or letting my ego run amok. Thank you for calming my shocked and scared mind. Thank you for believing in me, for supporting my path, for taking me to the mat countless times, for sharing with me all your magic stories and listening to mine, and for loving me, even when I had a hard time loving myself. I will always be grateful.

Oh my, thank you Tosha Silver. As I have said in this book, I thought I had found the holy grail until I found you and experienced your message. I'm so grateful for the reframe you gave me around surrendering first. This has changed everything for me, both in my personal life and in the journey of my life purpose. Learning to make everything in my life an offering to the Divine has radically altered my relationship to the world, and every day is a miracle unfolding. Bless you for showing me how to have a Bhakti love affair with the Divine. And even more so, thank you for your deep and sustaining friendship.

Thank you, Matt, for giving me permission to change the course of our lives over and over again, even when it felt scary and uncomfortable. Your trust in my journey, even when my heart chose to take us in directions that felt crazy, meant the world to me. Thank you for being the world's most amazing father to Siena and for always saying yes when I wanted to do something that sounded insane. I know it was hard on you, and I know how hard you worked to bring my dream into being. I see you. I get you. I recognize and appreciate all that you did to make this journey possible. I will always love you.

Thank you to my daughter, Siena, for being the wisest spiritual teacher among us. Your embodiment of what it means to live an authentic, unencumbered spiritual life has been an enormous inspiration to me. If all children on our planet were as kind-hearted and pure of spirit as you, I would know that Mother Earth is in good hands.

Extra special thanks to April Sweazy, who asked if she could be my family one day, and thank Goddess, I said yes. As my house partner, soul sister, and chosen family, you are one of the greatest blessings in my daily life. I could not have done any of this without you. Not only did you teach me to believe in real, live miracles, you have been the miracle I needed in order to ground my life. I am infinitely grateful for all that you bring to my life and this planet.

Thank you also to Dennis Couwenberg, my twin-flame-unibeing-sky-love-spiritual BFF. In those moments when I almost didn't come out of the closet with my whole story, you gave me courage. When I needed my mind to be silent, you took me there. When my Small Self threatened to grab the wheel of Lissa, you loved me back to consciousness. I could write a whole sequel about the mystical rollercoaster we've experienced since we met, though I wonder whether anyone would believe the things we've experienced. I might have to write it as fiction! Suffice it to say I now have proof that it is a friendly Universe because God gave me YOU.

Much gratitude goes to Brandy Gillmore. You looked at me with your leopard eyes and peered right into my soul. Thank you for all the guidance, for being brave enough to speak truth, and for helping me unblock everything that keeps me from stepping fully into my calling. When you find a spiritual teacher who is also a friend, who can sing at the top of her lungs with the top down in a convertible while dashing around curves on windy roads in Maui, you know you've got a winner. I love you and appreciate you, sunshine.

Thank you Issac Trotts for choosing the red pill when I offered you the choice, "Red pill or blue pill?" May there be many more condors with halos and hummingbirds alighting in the palm of your hand as you navigate your hero's journey.

Enormous thanks to Jon Rasmussen, the shaman who started this whole journey on my wedding day in Big Sur. Your influence on me has been profound, not only in the spark in me you ignited and your support of my mystical experiences, but in your ongoing guidance around my exploration of Sacred Medicine. You are clearly an angel, sent to me to wake me up, and I am grateful.

Thank you Amy Ahlers for always having my back in a thousand ways. Without you, my Inner Mean Girl might have thwarted my journey even more than it already did! Your steady support and tireless presence in my life has been a rock of love for me. Your kindness touches my heart and inspires me to be my best self. I am so, so grateful.

Thank you Sarah Drew for being my guardian angel along this journey. If it is more than fiction that the Priestesses of Astara have been guarding and gathering in order to prepare for this time we are living right now, then count me in to hold your hand and dance in circles by the firelight of an awakening planet.

Deep thanks to Steve Sisgold, not only for many therapy sessions that helped my body keep up with the awakening of my spirit, but for the pure and loving friendship. I am so grateful to have you and Amanda among my chosen family. Thank you for standing for my soul while also being patient enough to comfort and tend my Small Self with so much gentleness. What a teacher you have been for me. I am so grateful.

Thank you Cari Hernandez for being with me during this whole journey, when so many others couldn't stay. It gives me so much comfort to be with you and realize what we've endured together, growing stronger all the while in our love and support of one another. You have taught me what true friendship can be. Thank you for navigating all of our Narcissus/Echo story rewrites, as we both wake up together and stand for each others souls. You give me hope about how people can grow and change while staying together instead of growing apart. Through it all, we have endured, and there is such joy and comfort in the history we share.

Thank you Chris Guillebeau for all these years of sweet connection since we met on our first book tours ages ago. As I told you many of the stories in this book in real time, as they were happening, I know you must have thought I was losing my mind. Yet, here we are, growing together, inspiring each other, uplifting each other's hero's journeys, knowing deep in our hearts that yes, we were born for this.

Thank you Tricia Barrett for dealing with Victoria Rochester for all those years and loving me still. Your influence on me was profound in its almost surgical incision though all that wasn't the highest part of Lissa. I am grateful for how much you grew me and how intimately we shared our lives.

Thank you Charles and Stella Eisenstein, for introducing me to the more beautiful world our hearts know is possible and for breaking me open more than I thought I could possibly open. I carry you both in my heart.

Thank you Rose Levenberg for dancing with me, seeing through me, calling me on my shit, and remaking me. What a bright spark of light you are in my life!

Thank you Elisabeth Manning for being the first one to truly show me what it means to turn your life over to the Divine and let Spirit lead you. You have been such a high vibration influence on me, and I love and appreciate you so much.

On the Road of Trials, I met many allies who appear like magic, at just the right time, with just the right gift. These allies made it possible for me to continue on my journey, and they deserve my undying thanks. Thank you to the many sisters who have uplifted me: Rachel Carlton Abrams, Nancy Aronie, Christine Arylo, Debbie Baker, Sera Beak, Caroline Bobart, Joan Borysenko, Bridgette Boudeau, Brené Brown, Kris Carr, Jacqueline Chan, Rebecca Bass Ching, Sonia Choquette, Karen Drucker, Ophi Edut, Stella Eisenstein, Monique Feil, Patty Gift, Brandy Gillmore, Janell Gottesman, Christine Hassler, Louise Hay, Immaculee Ilibagiza, Katsy Johnson, Byron Katie, Susan Ariel Rainbow Kennedy, Tama Kieves, Danielle LaPorte, Scarlett Lewis, Tracy Moon, Anita Moorjani, Christiane Northrup, Rachael O'Meara, Joanne Perron, Barbara Poelle, Keli Rankin, Kim Rankin, Betsy Rapaport, Aviva Romm, Neha Sangwan, Wendy Sax, Marci Shimoff, Kira Siebert, Koelle Simpson, Vera Sparre, Barbara Stanny, Regena Thomashauer, Jane Thompson, Eckhart Tolle, Kelly Turner, Maggie Varadhan, Danielle Vieth, Doreen Virtue, Stephanie Walker, Lakenda Wallace, Claire Zammit, and Diane Zeps. I could not have lived this life or written this book if you all hadn't granted me the gift of your presence at a crucial time in my journey.

Thank you also to the brothers who have been the sacred masculine support I so desperately craved during my hero's journey: Doug Carlton Abrams, Adyashanti, Ben Ahrens, Rafael Bejarano, James Clear, Scott Dinsmore, Joe Dispenza, Larry Dossey, Jonathan Fields, Jay Fiset, Chris Grosso, Craig Hamilton, Robert Holden, Lewis Howes, Ken Jaques, Fred Kraziese, Bruce Lipton, Augie Maddox, Stephen Mitchell, Bharat Mitra, Nick Ortner, Nick Polizzi, Dean Radin, Chris Rankin, Scott Richards, Mike Robbins, Bernie Siegel, Mark Thornton, Reid Tracy, Jason Wachob, Paolo Wakham, Brian Weiss, Edward West, and Nicholas Wilton.

Infinite thanks to my team, friends, and second family: Bruce Cryer (aka

Brucie Baby star person), I'm so grateful for your Divine masculine presence in a business surrounded by women. But even more so, it's awesome to have dance parties at work. Thank you for all the ways in which you uplift me and touch my heart. Anne Davin, when I got that intuitive hit that you and I would be working together, I never realized how brilliantly I was being guided. I adore working with you and am so grateful that you bring your gifts to my calling. Beth Elliott, you really are the human dolphin. It's such a blessing to have you surfing your joy among us. Pearl Roth, thank you for being April's bestie and my right hand. I know you work tirelessly to bring my message into the world seamlessly. Jeri Brady, you have become the Mama Bear of Owning Pink and the pixie dust sprinkler of the Daily Flame, and I am so grateful for your radiance! Melanie Bates, I miss you in our business but am so proud of all you have become in your shamaness-writer-coach-genius self. Thank you for being with me during some of the most challenging parts of my hero's journey. I really truly could not have done it without you, Mel. The same is true for Megan Monique Lewis, Joy Mazzola. and Dana Theus. It really does take a village to bring a calling into being, and I couldn't have done it without the vision, wisdom, expertise, nurturing, love, and support of each one of you. I love and appreciate you all.

Finally, because I really do save the best for last, infinite thanks goes to my publishing team. Thank you, Michele Martin, my literary agent, career-rescuer, discernment filter, and beloved friend. You knew this was the book I always wanted to write, but you also knew when the timing was right. Thank you for keeping me sane, herding me on track when I fell out of impeccable alignment, cheering me on when I was ready to walk away, reminding me who I am and why I'm here, and saying "yes" when I asked you to do crazy things. I feel so lucky that I was introduced to you (thank you Gabrielle Bernstein for that enormous blessing!). I love you. And I bow to you. Namaste.

Thank you to the entire team at Rodale Books, especially Maria Rodale, Mary Ann Naples, Ursula Cary, and Isabelle Hughes. Rodale was this book's perfect home, and you have demonstrated that in a thousand ways. With each step, you have made it clear to me that you truly understand that this is the book my soul has always yearned to write and you have helped me birth something that feels so deeply authentic.

It's not only people who have supported my journey. There have been many unseen forces that have uplifted me and helped me navigate this journey from the head to the heart. Call these forces God, Goddess, spirit guides, angels, animal totems, plant, mountain, and ocean spirits, or Pachamama. For me, they're all tangled up into Consciousness Itself, and they're all Divine. Thank you, Universe, for loving us all so much and making me truly believe.

I think every one of us should write acknowledgments at least once a year, whether we write books or not. Such a process asks you to spend hours in a state of deep appreciation. What if we could all walk around like that, just appreciating each other? Let it be an invitation for us all to drop our petty grievances so we can just open our hearts and love one another.

ABOUT THE AUTHOR

Lissa Rankin, MD, attended Duke University, the University of South Florida, and Northwestern University during her twelve years of medical education before practicing as an OB/GYN physician in a conventional medical practice for eight years in San Diego. In 2007, she left her practice and spent two years realizing that you can quit your job, but you can't quit your calling. She wound up working at an integrative medicine practice before starting her own spirituality-based medical practice, where she became fascinated with spontaneous remissions and began a sincere study of mind-body medicine. Since 2010 she has dedicated her life to writing, teaching, and speaking full time.

Lissa is the author of four other books, *Encaustic Art*, *What's Up Down There?*, the *New York Times* bestseller *Mind Over Medicine*, and, most recently, *The Fear Cure*. She is currently researching another book, *Sacred Medicine*, meeting with shamans in Peru, Qigong masters from China, energy healers from Hawaii, electric healers in Bali, and John of God in Brazil to study "anomalous" healing. Lissa's work is the focus of two National Public Television pledge specials—*Heal Yourself: Mind Over Medicine*, which explores the critical role our thoughts, feelings, and beliefs play in our health and well-being, and *The Fear Cure*, about how you can let fear cure *you* by coming into right relationship with uncertainty and loss. She is on a grassroots mission to put the "care" back in health care, to reunite healing and spirituality, and to inspire sacred activists to participate in the

267

transformation of consciousness that is revolutionizing the world with acts of love and kindness.

Lissa blogs at LissaRankin.com, writes The Daily Flame (love messages from your "Inner Pilot Light") at InnerPilotLight.com, posts daily on the Lissa Rankin Facebook page, and founded several websites, including OwningPink.com, where over 40 bloggers write about how to be healthy in all aspects of life, as well as HealHeathCareNow.com, where those passionate about healing health care unite. She is a regular speaker and her TEDx talks have been viewed over 2.5 million times. She has also appeared at Hay House I Can Do It conferences, the Uplift Festivals in Australia and India, the Chopra Center alongside Deepak Chopra, the Institute of Integrative Nutrition conference at the Lincoln Center, and numerous other health and spirituality conferences. Lissa is also the founder of the Whole Health Medicine Institute, where she and a team of luminary faculty like Rachel Naomi Remen, Bernie Siegel, Christiane Northrup, Larry Dossey, and Martha Beck train physicians and other health care providers about the Mind Over Medicine approach to Whole Health, healing, and Sacred Medicine.

Lissa is also a devoted spiritual seeker, professional artist, ecstatic dancer, amateur ski bum, avid hiker, practitioner of meditation, singer, "raw vegan omnivore" chef, mystic, therapy junkie, relationship explorer, recovering overachiever, and ever-evolving and often imperfect soul. She lives in Marin County, California with her Waldorf-educated daughter Siena.